Belle Out of Order

BELLE OUT

Belle Livingstone

PREFACE BY CLEVELAND AMORY

Henry Holt and Company, New York

Published, July, 1959
Second Printing, August, 1959

Library of Congress Catalog Card Number: 59–9856

85282–0119
Printed in the United States of America

Contents

Preface

Once upon a time this writer had occasion to work on her
so-called memoirs with a lady who shall be nameless. Even
before taking on the job, however, from knowing the lady we
entertained the suspicion that the difference between biography and autobiography was not wholly clear in her mind.
Accordingly one day we asked her, albeit rather gently, to
tell us her idea of the difference. "A biography," she said
firmly, "is about a living person. An autobiography is about a
dead person."

Well, in the case of *Belle Out of Order* the lady would
seem to have a point. For this is the autobiography of another
lady, Belle Livingstone by name, and yet we have in our
hands an obituary from no less a source than the New York
Times which states that on February 7, 1957, in New York
City, Belle Livingstone died. Surely this, to begin with, is
intriguing enough, and yet, strangely, it is easily explainable.
In her latter days Belle Livingstone's memoirs were, as everyone who knew her knew, the central interest of her life. Indeed, as far back as the 1930's she had already published a
short memoir entitled *Belle of Bohemia,* had written a serial-
ized account of her life for *Cosmopolitan,* and had even, in
her desk, an unpublished manuscript of her Prohibition exploits. Then, in 1944, with the able editorial assistance of Bos-
tonian Myra Chipman, she had begun work on this memoir.
Four years later, by 1948, not only was this memoir wholly
completed, but it was already in the hands of her agents. Then,
for nine years, for one reason or another, or sometimes for no

reason at all, Belle began changing her mind. At one time she withdrew the manuscript from one agent and offered it to another, at another time she withdrew it altogether, and on still a third she wanted to change the beginning and the end. Only the middle, it seemed, satisfied her.

Here let us pause for a moment to say that just why Belle was so critical of her work is not so easily explainable. For, as a writer who is on record as having said some pretty harsh words about some pretty bad autobiographies, this one is not only far from bad, it is (though about, by some standards, a "bad" woman) surprisingly good. In the first place it is a genuine memoir and not just a "me-more," or, for that matter, a platform to pay off old sores and scores. In the second place it is frank but by no means so frank as to be tasteless. ("I am writing," said Belle, "for sophisticates.") And in the third place it is about someone who was "found," not born; whose "coming-out" party celebrated her coming out of jail; whose first (of four) marriages was to a total stranger, whom she asked to marry her to be allowed to escape her foster parents and go on the stage; who once dined with four kings; and who also went around the world, on a five-pound note, for a bet of five thousand pounds, on condition she could not tell of her bet, could not either borrow or earn money, and had to be accompanied at all times by a companion who had to share her room.

Actually, the person who knows the story about the delay in publication best, Miss Chipman herself, feels that there is no real mystery about it. "At the time I entertained a variety of theories and conjectures," she says, "but now I am inclined to think that perhaps Belle was merely exhibiting a typical case of indecision sometimes manifested by very old people."

Here then let it rest, for Belle was indeed old when she died—eighty-two in fact. Nonetheless, it is surely one of the great ironies of literary history that Belle Livingstone, of all people, should have had a posthumous autobiography. For the woman who wished her tombstone marked "This is the only stone I have left unturned" lived, as Nina Wilcox Putnam once put it, "distinguishedly, luxuriously, extravagantly," but surely not posthumously. "To me," Belle herself says in her epilogue in this manuscript, "the writing of memoirs has always seemed almost as final as the writing of a will—something you do just before."

Now Belle, it seems, has done it just after—and this too, strangely, is in more ways than one entirely fitting. We have, for example, besides the *Times* obituary, in our hands a small black book in which Belle kept, in her own scrawly disorderly way and in her own handwriting, the names and addresses of all the regular patrons of her famous "Country Club" on 58th Street. We have seen nothing which either better or any more dramatically illustrates the Decline and Fall of the Social Empire. For in her book there is an extraordinary roster not only of Café Society names but also of so-called Old Guard Society names—indeed both this little black book and *Belle Out of Order* not only come under the head of, shall we say, basic research for our own forthcoming book, *Who Killed Society?*, but also indicate that Belle herself may be one of our leading suspects. More important than this, however, from the standpoint of Belle's own book, we have always believed that both biographies and autobiographies should come out when, and only when, one's life is, to all intents and purposes—particularly self-advertising purposes—over. Such books may of course come, and indeed have often come, late in their subject's life. But for Belle's to come when her life was literally over is the most fitting of all. For Belle's eras are also literally over, and this book is one of the last inside records we will get—of the Edwardian Era, all the way from the playing fields of India to the Cercle Privée at Monte Carlo; of the Prohibition Era, all the way from Mrs. Astor's Horse to Texas Guinan and the Whoopee World of the speakeasy; and, finally, of the Courtesan Era, all the way from Nell

Gwynn, Madame DuBarry, and Lola Montez, to Belle herself.

Last but by no means least in the book's favor it is written, in contrast to so many "I" and "I told you so" books, with not only a reasonably lower case "I" but also with extraordinary good humor. Indeed humor was, to the end of her days, one of Belle's longest suits. "No matter how many weddings a woman may have," she says in one place, "I suppose there can never be more than one ideal honeymoon." In another place, asked by Lord Kitchener if she had ever been in love, she replies, "No, but I have had some glorious friendships." And, in still another, answering certain slings and arrows which came her way, she declares, "Women who have been married only once give themselves almost virginal airs over the woman who has been married more than once." Let all critics, particularly those singly married, beware.

—Cleveland Amory

Part One
LIVE EASY

1 *The Sunflower Path*

Standing at the top of the broad stairs in my Park Avenue house one winter night in the Prohibition Thirties, I watched my guests of the evening, some four hundred of them, run past me down the stairs, hastily throwing on their wraps as they ran, and disappear through the open front door. It was a smartly dressed guest list, and it included celebrities and near-celebrities, social registerites and financial barons. Inside, the house swarmed with less famous persons—guests I had not invited—agents of Uncle Sam who had made a surprise appearance in my swank speakeasy, taken possession of my bar and all its liquid gold, and having made their landing with clocklike precision could now be said, like the proverbial Marines, to have the situation well in hand.

As the last of my publicity-fleeing guests melted out of sight, I felt one of the agents touch me on the arm.

"All right, Belle, we're ready."

The words were casual, but the meaning was ominous. A Federal officer took his place on either side of me and the three of us solemnly descended the stairs.

As we neared the front door, I became conscious that a considerable number of curiosity-seekers had gathered in front of the house—in New York at the slightest provocation a crowd seems able to spring up spontaneously through the asphalt itself. This was a noisy crowd, increasing rapidly, and somewhat unruly. It pushed and surged against the lines of stalwart blue-coated policemen who were resolutely holding open a path for me from my brilliantly lighted doorway into the gloom of the waiting Black Maria.

At sight of me a shout went up: "There she is!" and the crowd swelled forward excitedly in an effort to surround me. As news photographers' cameras began flashing right and left, the onlookers began to sing out typical sidewalk wisecracks. In my anxiety to reach the shelter of the police van, I paid little attention to their raucous remarks, however, until as I was climbing in, I heard one female voice shrill lustily: "Looks like the Sunflower Girl's kinda gone to seed!"

At this witticism the crowd roared appreciatively. The next moment the van door was slammed shut, gongs and sirens took over, and the van sped off on its way to the jail.

The Sunflower Girl! Huddled in my corner of the "wagon," I felt a sudden sense of shock. This was a name I had long ago given myself; a name I had all my life laughingly used to epitomize my foundling origin and the tall, showy, unbeautiful flower associated with it. As a speakeasy operator in New York, I had even built up the name as a sort of trademark for myself, and newspapers had sometimes kiddingly called me by it. Now, hearing it used unexpectedly as a taunt, I experienced a rude jolt. My mind flew back to the days of my fine carriage and horses in London, and my costly cars in Paris—it would have been impossible to believe then that I should ever be in a police van in New York.

For the first time in my life, I realized what a long road I had traveled.

Like Moses, I wasn't born. I was found.

Out on the edge of the Kansas plain, in the summer of 1875, stood a little frame house set off from the prairie by a rail fence. In the corner of the fence grew a clump of towering, golden sunflowers. One moonlight night in August a man came whistling merrily toward the house and rounded the fence corner. Suddenly his whistling stopped. From under the sunflowers came something that sounded like the cry of a baby. Jumping lightly over the fence, the man dropped to his knees and peered into the shadows. There was something there all right, squalling and squirming.

John Ramsay Graham was too good a newspaperman not to know that this story would interest every reader of his Emporia *News*. Next day's edition carried all the details. The story concluded with the statement that the abandoned child was a girl about six months old, in good health, and would be adopted by "ye editor" and his wife. She would be named Isabel.

In 1875 the West was big and raw. The Civil War was not long over and sectional differences still flamed. Newspapering was a rugged job, and there on the outposts of America my foster father was making his journalistic mark. He had grown up in Rochester, New York, and got his education the hard way; and from the day he became a printer's devil, like a bloodhound he had put his nose on the trail of news. After he had followed the usual path of typesetter and reporter, he became war correspondent for the Boston *Transcript*. He received his editorial baptism when he took charge of the Erie *Gazette*.

It was in Erie that he married my Canadian-born mother. I don't know whether it was Greeley's "Go West, young man" or the fever of the times that fired my father, but almost immediately he and his pretty bride set out for the wilds of Kansas. Of course they expected children, but to their disappointment none appeared.

Naturally I spent many childhood hours in speculation over the mystery of my birth. In my mental cinema I used to picture a romantic sequence: a great prairie schooner rolling heavily over the vast sea of waving grass, its occupants dulled by the monotony of an unvarying horizon; a stop for refreshment; a tired mother giving little sister the baby to tend; little sister carelessly laying the baby to sleep in the shade of the sunflower; the baby sleeping quietly on, forgotten in the hurry of departure; the great, creaking wagon passing out of sight on its pathless way; the agonizing discovery of the baby's loss by Mother—too late.

As I grew older and my father's devotion to me became marked, another idea struck me. I wondered if I might have been really John Graham's own child whom he had introduced by the plausible ruse of the sunflower.

Of course I bedeviled my foster parents with questions. If there was a secret, they alone held the key. But they always clung to the sunflower story, and since it's a good story I may as well cling to it too.

Those two young people on a Kansas plain who dared to take into their home a waif bringing God-knew-what wild heritage had real courage. Today adoption has been reduced to a science. Then a foundling was a most terribly unknown quantity.

But it was not enough that a six-months'-old tot should suddenly be flung into their quiet, well-ordered lives. The waif must eat; a Jersey cow must be bought. The waif must be cared for; a colored nurse must be found. Through all these adjustments I screamed lustily, I disorganized everything and everybody, but I flourished.

Dear old Aunty Gilmore, bless her prolific soul, had had fourteen children of her own, but she loved her white child as fervently as any of her black brood. She had been sold into slavery as a baby, had been set free only a few years before she came to us, and could neither read nor write. But curiously enough, this simple old woman was rearing, all unknowing, two children—one white, one black—who were to stand before kings. Her son Buddy Gilmore, his fingers vibrating with jazz, became known as the King of Drummers and frequently entertained the playboy Prince of Wales who became Edward VII. Years later, when I heard Buddy in England and watched the admiring crowds listening intently to his fascinating rhythms, I used to think how proud of him his old slave mother would have been.

To the end of her long life Aunty Gilmore loved to tell how her white child "got stole away by de Injuns." Those were the days when the redskins were moving southward through Emporia, driven out of their own lands by the encroaching whites, to territory that had been newly allotted them. Though Mother had had long experience with Indians, she always feared their stealthy ways. She could never get used to looking up and finding a copper-colored face with glittering black eyes staring at her through the windowpane. But she never dared be other than friendly, for it was rumored that sharp-tongued women got their wells poisoned. She would always buy a pair of beaded moccasins or a willow basket, and she would let the wanderers rest in the yard. At least the braves rested, sprawling on the ground and smoking their pipes, while the horses munched the dried grass along the fence. The squaws drew the water, sold their wares, and worked ceaselessly at their weaving.

One afternoon my mother put me to sleep in the shade of the house while she sat inside, sewing by a nearby window. So stealthily did the Indians creep up, lift me from my cot and vanish that for hours my mother knew nothing either of their appearance or my disappearance. When Father returned from his office and they went to fetch me in, there was only a hollow in the pillow.

In true frontier fashion the whole town threw itself on horseback and galloped off to my rescue. The search went on unsuccessfully for days. Then I was given up for lost.

About a month later some soldiers, patrolling the southern border, came across a solitary papoose tied to the branch of a tree and rocking happily in the breeze. On cutting off the wrappings, they found me strapped to the papoose board. The migrating Indians had apparently got wind of the approaching troops and, as their campfires showed, had left hastily. The experience had done me no harm.

The city of Emporia today, with its Chamber of Commerce, its movie houses and gas stations, is a far cry from the simple little wooden town of my childhood. Lying at night in my corn-husk bed, I used to look out on a spangled sky within the frame of my dormer window and breathe the odor of the lilac bush just underneath. I could hear the disdainful whistle of the Santa Fe train as it flashed past our dark, sleeping huddle of houses. It was a long, lonely sound.

Mother had prettied up the yard with lilac and syringa, and rosebushes brought from the East when she was a bride. A moonflower vine shaded the porch, and every spring its rank and rapid growth reminded me of the beanstalk in *Jack the Giantkiller*. Lying in its shade on a hot, still afternoon, I could hear the chickens ruffling their wings in the dust out by the whitewashed coop and the ponies whinnying and stamping in the barn.

In the back yard an unruly melon vine clambered and mixed with a morning-glory over the stoop, and a grapevine twined lovingly about the fence. Two giant cottonwoods, whose leaves were never quiet, glistened and rustled in the summer winds and wafted bits of their cotton fluff through the air for me to chase. And always there was a clump of stately sunflowers growing in the same fence corner.

One of my earliest recollections is that of seeing my father in his Sunday black passing the collection plate in church. I knew that Father ran a land office and owned the newspaper. But these activities were vague and distant and belonged to the world of grownups, and I could not take the same intimate pride in them that I could in watching him pass the plate, into which I always dropped one of those old big pennies. My father was a more prominent man in the town than I realized then. His integrity and likability even got him elected mayor. I have to smile when I record that his first mayoral act was to close every saloon in Emporia.

Though the Middle West of those days had passed its garishly adventurous frontier period, life to a child was fresh and fascinating. Summers brought the thrills of snake-hunting—but not out on the prairie; oh, no; right in the house! Every night, as regularly as we put out the cat, Father would take a lantern and look in every corner and under every bed and chair. I used to tiptoe behind him, bursting with bloodthirstiness, and praying that some night we'd find something really dangerous, like an adder or a rattler. Then one night it happened. On our prowl the lantern light showed two yellow eyes rising from the horsehair sofa. I turned tail and fled shrieking, and Father was left to do the St. George act alone with the dragon. The snake outwitted him in the end by slithering its long body out the front door, but not before Father had knocked over the whatnot and spilled all the doodads and sulphured the air with true deacon's profanity.

Prairie fires were another source of excitement during the summers. All Emporia children used to shock their elders by the delirious joy they displayed when a great wall of grass fire was seen far off rolling toward our frame buildings, especially at night with the sparks shooting up into the black sky. Everybody fought. The children scurried around for buckets, filled them, and passed them to the older men, who formed the bucket chain. The actual fire brigade was made up of the youngest and strongest men stripped to the waist, each armed with a horse blanket to beat the burning grass. Empty buckets were passed back by a chain of women to the happy young fry at the water base who pulled the slimy well ropes or worked the creaky handles of the cistern pumps.

Going home dog-tired after such colorful and terribly real adventure, we would have the novel experience of seeing our house as the first rays of the sun gilded it through an atmosphere still heavy with smoke. For days the acrid smell would hover over the town.

Best of all, I used to love the cyclones. Whenever I saw trees bending as flat as the long grasses under them and the great, green, funnel-shaped monster advancing across the prairie, I was fit to be tied with excitement. The family would fly about to close windows and doors, rescue the pets, and race for the cyclone cellar. Sometimes it all happened so quickly that the trap door would barely be closed before the fury would break over our heads.

One day after the tumult had died and Father had allowed us out again, we found that our barn had disappeared. Where the barn had once been, there stood a surprised-looking cow, who recognized us no more than we recognized her. We always hoped that it was a fair exchange and that the owner of the cow got our barn, but we had our doubts.

One summer there was a locust plague. I had read all about locusts in the Bible, and the Bible did not exaggerate. The locusts came in such clouds that in a few minutes trees and shrubs became as bare and naked of leaves as in midwinter. Our clothesline, as big as a log with them, sagged under their loathsome weight. Indoors we lived in a suffocating blackout, their bodies packed on doors and window screens. Even that crack Santa Fe train had to cancel its run. The great wheels of the engine slipped helplessly on the piles of locusts heaped on the tracks.

Came winter, when water froze in the pump and the mercury fell clear out of the thermometer, and the Grahams moved into what Father called "winter quarters." This simply meant crowding into one room where a stove could be kept red-hot constantly, but even then thin sheets of ice sometimes formed on the buckets of water. Red flannel drawers, ear mufflers, and "arctics" were as nothing against the frightful northers that swept bleakly down. While Father sat happily writing his next day's story about the latest Kansas blizzard and Mother sewed, I would be crocheting monstrosities to be starched and stretched on receptacles that I called collar boxes, or making paper flowers, or tracing water lilies with a toothpick on plush tidies.

On New Year's Day the sporting element of Emporia used to hire the town's band wagon and hang it with green; then in stovepipe hats they would ride forth, tooting horns, to pay New Year's calls. When the crowd landed at our front door, Father always had eggnog ready, and little cubes of Mother's fruitcake, ripened with age.

One winter was livened by the presence in our midst of Moody and Sankey, the great evangelists. In spite of the icy temperature of the revival hall, I nevertheless began to imagine so clearly the flames of the hell awaiting me that I plunged headlong into my first religious conversion. For at least a month I was a glutton in the practice of the Golden Rule, doing so much good unto others that it would have taken them their lifetimes to do it back to me. I was to have one other sharp attack of religious fever during adolescence, but from both I made record recoveries.

I was always a big girl for my age, and by the time I was fifteen must have seemed as mature, if not as ravishing, as Juliet. So Mother was early faced with the problem of my morals. She intended that I should be decent, or else!

To the young set of today, the rigid barriers of decorum in the Nineties seem almost unbelievable. Then a respectable girl could not eat a meal with a man in a public place. If a woman put up her hair in kid curlers, she was thought fast. A smooch of powder was the devil's own mark, so of course my nose was always a high light. I had it instilled into me by my mother that if my face didn't shine some bold man would try to do something dreadful to me. After a wife had borne her husband ten children, she still called him "Mister" and wouldn't for the world have let him see her bare feet showing under her long, bishop-sleeved nightgown.

Mother's choice of admirer for me was a Professor Dudley who taught history in the normal school. Mother thought the professor was an alabaster angel and always maneuvered so that I was in the parlor whenever he called. He used to take me to chorals. But it was Mother's heart that fluttered, not mine, over these attentions. To me, at that age, he was just another teacher. Still, when the professor invited me to a fancy-dress ball, I was glad for once to go with him.

For weeks I worked on my costume. I conceived the idea of appearing in headlines—literally. Using an old set of hoops for a frame, I sewed a skirt made entirely of my father's newspaper, yards and yards of ruffles in the striking black-and-white print. I was so completely self-satisfied and self-dramatized in it that I must have been disgusting. The professor eyed my flimsy costume a little askance, but I was strong in my conviction that I was a knockout.

I attracted attention all right. Before the grand march struck up, all the boys gathered around to read me. By the time the quadrille was over and the professor and I were rollicking through the Virginia reel, the hoopskirt had been caught in a few jams and bits of paper ruffle were beginning to litter the floor. Soon my legs in their cambric drawers were clearly exposed to view, and the professor and I made a dash for the outside—and darkness.

I had another admirer whom Mother did not approve of so highly but whose company I enjoyed more. He was a boy named Marion Green, whose father ran the livery stable and would occasionally let him have a nag to take me driving out to Neosha River. This was a day's trip, and since of course a girl couldn't go alone on such an expedition, another couple would have to go along for decency's sake. The four of us would pack into a buckboard behind some old crowbait of a horse and, in the name of recreation, subject our bottoms to the jolting of a springless wagon for the long journey out and back. Sometimes our wheels were hub deep in gumbo mud. Sometimes we sweltered under a blistering sun. Sometimes we were drenched by sudden downpours. The boys, as lords of creation, sat in the seat and we girls sat facing them, our backs against the dashboard, and we all ate pawpaws. Nothing ever happened. We girls never had to walk back.

As I grew older, Mother undertook to train me to be the perfect housewife. Poor Mother! If she had ever suspected my Bohemian future, she would have hidden in one of those cyclone cellars, never again to show her face. Instead she believed happily that she was preparing her daughter to marry some good neighbor's son, and she wanted me to have, besides babies, a full six cents' worth out of every nickel.

In spite of Father always having a new hen on in business, we were always poor, so the family keynote was "Thrift." Mother was so clever that she could finagle three yards of cloth on the dining-room table until she could cut out a pattern that called for four yards. Her family, the Liklys, manufacturers of Likly's luggage, were very well-to-do, both the

Cleveland and the Rochester branches, and Mother was always pleased when a big box of hand-me-downs arrived to be remade, but I resented what I considered condescension. As I cut off buttons and turned cloth, I would mutter to myself:

"If I have to marry a chimpanzee, I'll have clothes of my own some day!"

Grandma Graham, for a time a member of our household, was a beautifully educated woman who spoke French and Italian, and she had been presented at court. For some reason it seemed important to her that I should learn all she knew of court deportment, and she and Mother used to give me lessons out in the yard: make believe the lilac bush is the Queen and the cottonwood tree the King; learn to keep the back straight and the head high; manage the rest of the body gracefully and graciously. They used to put a broom handle behind my shoulders, a cup of water on my head, and make me curtsy to the royal couple over and over again until I could come through dry. An erect carriage thus became second nature, and I have always believed these lessons must have been partly responsible for the confidence I felt later on when I addressed real royalty.

Father contributed an important share to my education. Every newspaperman is a cosmopolite, and looking at the world through Father's eyes I escaped provincial narrowness. He passed on to me his cultivated taste in books. During long winter evenings I listened to him read aloud— Thackeray, Scott, Dante. My father had a well-stored mind; he spoke, as he wrote, from a rich background. He was a phrase-maker; there was zest and color to his conversation. I have no doubt that I learned more by close association in my formative years with a man of his wide interests, bookish tastes, and flair for picturesque idiom than I ever did by sitting on a hard bench in a dreary schoolroom, wishing the clock around.

I have said that we were always poor. Father never could learn to take a fool's money and call it his own. Yet he was tantalized by the knowledge that although Kansas was on the make and great fortunes were being grabbed off all around him, he was not showing enough imagination to dream up a profitable project of his own. Strictly against Mother's wishes, he began to dabble in wildcat schemes which, without exception, proved disastrous. But some of them were so fantastic that for entertainment value they were almost worth what they cost.

Not the gold mine in Colorado. To pay for that Father had to sell the *News* and the land office. Everything blithely risked on one game of pitch and toss, and lost. Then it was start at the beginning again—not too easy in a frontier town for a newspaperman without a newspaper.

The only thing to do was to scrape together enough backing to found a rival sheet, which he did, and named the rival the *Gazette*. My mother thought he had now been burned deep enough to dread the fire and she needn't worry about him any more. But this was too much to hope in a day when every second man in a plaid vest was selling land. Father decided to found a town.

Settlers were streaming in from the East and land speculators were opening up new territory for them, building homes and setting up the newcomers in business. Father's new bubble required not the sale of everything we owned, only liens on most of it. For a time it looked as if Father really had something. On the tract of land he had bought in western Kansas he succeeded in building a store, a church, and a sugar factory (this was to be a center of beet-raising)— even a spur railroad down from the nearest junction. Then he tacked up *Montezuma* on the station and came home to report that he was all ready to clean up when the next batch of pioneers arrived.

Unfortunately he neglected to organize a police force to

guard his city. In those days it didn't do to leave towns lying around loose on the Kansas prairie. When Father took his first prospects down to look over the town, it was embarrassing to find that the town had disappeared. Swiped—lock, stock and barrel—by a rival town founder. Even Mother had to laugh.

So there was Father back at his desk, a penitent man, burning the midnight oil again, a green shade over his eyes and his pen in hand. But not for long. One day I accidentally discovered in the barn a curious contrivance hidden under a barrel. When I started to ask Father about it, he laid a finger on his lips, jerked his head toward Mother and winked. I thought it was some surprise he was planning and said no more. It was a surprise all right.

Father had turned from speculation to invention. He had devised a headrest to be fastened to the back of a train seat. It was a simple, collapsible affair that a traveler could easily pack with his clean shirt. Why spend money on Pullmans? For a trifling investment one could get big returns in comfort with this gadget. No home could afford to be without one.

Every spare hour Father worked to perfect his model and finally succeeded in manufacturing and selling a few of the nickel-and-red-plush contraptions. Fast and furiously he would figure on the back of an envelope—so many travelers, so many coaches, so many days, so many headrests. An orgy of dollar signs and a never-ending procession of ciphers.

One night a traveler who had leaned trustingly on the headrest fell asleep never to awaken. The train jerked—too sharply. He never knew what happened. As neat as a lynching, the sheriff said.

The widow of the victim sued for two thousand dollars' damage. This was really kicking Father while he was down. This time it was the *Gazette* that had to be put up for sale, and Father considered himself very lucky when he found a purchaser, an ambitious young man by the name of William Allen White.

By good rights the family ironing board should have been included in this deal. I suppose the only sharp practice my father ever indulged in was his habit of dealing with obituaries. Our ironing board, I must explain, was unusually large and was used all over Emporia for laying out the dead. First sign of death was the Graham ironing board leaning up against someone's back door. Then you watched for the bow of purple ribbon on the front door. Whenever one of the neighbors who had illness in the family came over to borrow Mother's ironing board, Father sat right down and wrote an obituary and a eulogy of the sick person. In this way he was usually able to scoop the rival sheet. How I hated to see the sinister thing return to its accustomed place in our kitchen and, worse still, to have to iron on it my rickrack-trimmed ginghams and my thick, voluminous petticoats. Always I seemed to be pressing my hot iron into the face of a dead neighbor.

The sale of the *Gazette* completed and all his obligations honorably discharged, Father made plans to set off, with Mother and me, for a new life in a new job. He had secured a position on the Chicago *Dispatch*. It could not have been easy for my parents to uproot themselves from the soil of Kansas. Every association of their married life clung around the friendly little town of Emporia. After the house had been sold—moonflower, sunflower, cottonwoods, and all— and the furniture crated, one morning Mr. Green's musty livery-stable hack, with its motheaten, green-black cushions and iron tires, drew up at our door, and a few minutes later the Grahams, loaded down with satchels, carryalls, and a stack of shoe boxes crammed with eatables for the trip, were rattling away to the "deepo." Suddenly, with a sharp thrust of pain, I realized then that the word "home" would henceforth and forever call to mind an image of a little house beside the glistening cottonwoods.

All the old settlers and friends had gathered to see us off. The fireman gave many extra pulls to the bell rope as the engine started chuffing, and Father and Mother stood on the rear platform waving and waving until the faces of their friends were lost to sight.

As the train swung over the moon-splashed country that night, I sat with my forehead pressed against the car window watching the prairie fly past. I could hardly wait to get to that great, wicked city of Chicago.

In the morning there we were, caught up in a mob of people wearing linen dusters and carrying suitcases and grips and all trying to get through a small gate at the same time. Then we were being crammed into an elevated train and whisked off through the air. How shocked I was to find myself gazing in at a panorama of back doors and windows, all open or uncurtained and all revealing unappetizing details in the drama of life—a tousled head rising from a washbasin, two brats hammering each other with saucepans, a man vomiting.

In our flat on Indiana Avenue there was a porcelain bath with steaming hot water to replace the tin tub we had left behind in Emporia, and an icebox to keep things cool instead of a cistern. But it wasn't long before such novelties had lost charm, and I was clamoring to run about in Chicago as untrammeled as I had been on the prairie. When I discovered that I had lost, not gained, freedom, I became very rebellious and hard to get on with.

Mother must have been at her wits' end with me, for one day she and Father announced that I was to be sent away for further education. The school they had selected was the Convent of St. Francis de Sales, hidden away among the hills in the little village of Oldenburg, Indiana.

Perspective has softened in my memory the outlines of those first months under convent discipline. In fact, in later years as I looked back on my school days from across an ocean, I even came to know a nostalgic longing to find myself back within those brick walls and to experience again the serene regularity of study and devotion. But that is the sort of trick time plays on the mind.

Actually the cloistered life appealed to me at first about as much as a rider to a bucking broncho. Freedom dwindled to the vanishing point. Bells, bells, bells. Bells for morning prayers, bells for early Mass, bells for church history, bells for the watery stew that passed for lunch while one of the Sisters read from *Lives of the Saints and Martyrs*.

The most hateful bell of all was the rising bell. I thought Sister Villanova put viciousness in every stroke. The Sisters artfully combined piety with discipline, and to make certain we were fully awake made us sit up in our beds and shout with all our might: "Jesus, Mary, and Joseph, I give you my heart, my soul, and my life." God knows I would often have given all three for just ten more minutes of sleep. The Sisters all said my besetting sin was laziness.

But I loved Sister Veronica and Sister Patricia, and I enjoyed the companionship of the girls. I began to take the bells in my stride, and then little by little fell under the spell of the Church as I had earlier fallen under the spell of Moody and Sankey. For the second and last time in my life I became concerned with my soul and suffered an attack of religious ardor during which the thought of praying my life away seemed to me the height of earthly bliss. One day my parents were astounded to receive a letter from me announcing that I had decided to take the veil.

By return mail came the following reply:

Dear Belle:

Neither your mother nor I can see how your new ambition will change your prospects. Poverty is still our lot; there is no question of your chastity; and we have never had reason to complain about your obedience. So, dear child, come home at once and begin your novitiate with us.

Your loving Father

I returned to Chicago in a spirit of martyrdom which must have been very trying to my parents, and it probably was to get my mind off the convent idea that Father began taking me with him that winter to the concerts and recitals that he covered for the paper.

Chicago in those days was rich, roaring, and roisterous. I remember tales of the Palmer House, where the bar was paved with silver dollars. During those lush early Nineties Mrs. Potter Palmer was brightening the social scene, and among her activities during the season of 1892 were the morning concerts that my father, despite the fact that he was tone deaf, attended and reviewed. He was much admired by Mrs. Palmer for his comments. It amazed me that my tone-deaf father should be able to write such discerning articles. I have since learned that newspapermen often develop a sixth sense that borders on the psychic.

That winter two things happened that made me see that the world, the flesh, and the devil were going to be more powerful influences in my life after all than the chapel bell. First, I tasted champagne; second, the theater.

Father's boss, Mr. Wigly, owner of the *Dispatch*, was a wealthy man who lived on the North Side, and one day we found ourselves invited to his house for a formal dinner. How thrilled I was over the prospect of seeing actual butlers and footmen! Mother saw to it that the family wore the right clothes; even lengthened my dress to the floor for the occasion. I had careful coaching on table etiquette, and it was arranged that if Mother should catch me doing anything gauche, she would flag me by pressing her foot against mine, if we were seated together, or by lifting her handkerchief if we were at a distance.

I was placed between Mother and a young man, and as soon as we sat down I felt Mother's foot steal over beside mine to be in readiness. At my plate stood a glass of yellow water which tasted surprisingly good. I drained it off, Mother pedaling frantically. From the savagery of her assault I knew I should have much to answer for later, but decided it would be worth it. For the rest of the dinner Mother's heel gouged fiercely every time my hand strayed in the direction of the yellow water. Toward the end she resorted to pinching my arm. Between the gouging and the pinching I was kept sober, but a thirst had been aroused which would never be quenched.

I discovered the theater the day I went with my father to see *Robin Hood*. No Presley-mad teenager ever experienced greater ecstasy than I, sitting there entranced while Jessie Bartlett Davis sang "Oh, Promise Me." As the star took her six curtain calls, in my imagination I was taking the applause and hugging the great bouquets to my bosom.

"I'm going to be an actress!" I whispered to Father.

I had no idea how. The distance across the footlights was greater yesterday than the distance between planets today. But I would be an actress! As we were leaving, we met W. J. Davis, owner of the theater and husband of the star. When Father laughingly told him of my palpitations over Miss Davis, he generously took me backstage to meet the adored one in her dressing room. At home that night I sat on a hassock at my father's feet and let the tides of glory rise and rise.

"How do you get on the stage?" I demanded.

"You don't," said my mother. "The stage is a terrible place. All the women are loose."

Mother's stubborn attitude toward stage people infuriated me, and I used to steal off secretly to visit my idol. But even Jessie Davis discouraged me.

"I get hundreds of letters from stage-struck girls," she

would tell me. "You're all crazy. Be a nurse. Be a school-teacher. Get married. But keep away from the theater. It's a hard life."

But I was so entranced by the melodious voice that I paid no attention to the warning words and went right on doing pirouettes before the mirror. I found out that traveling companies were formed in Chicago and surreptitiously I began to make the rounds of actors' agencies. There were no talent scouts in the Nineties. In fact, I had no special talents to offer. I could neither sing nor dance, nor was I a beauty. Yet with the soaring self-confidence of seventeen I knew no qualms. Give me a part, give me a costume, and I had not the slightest doubt that I could hold an audience in the hollow of my hand.

A part—there was the rub. Many a green schoolgirl has lain awake nights over that problem. Since Mother was so firmly opposed to a stage career for me, Father took his cue from her. No daughter of theirs should leave home until she left it with a husband. I had never acted counter to my parents' wishes before, but now I felt myself taking the bit in my teeth. I was not in the least interested in a husband, and I would run away from home before I would give up my glittering dream of the stage.

After weeks of the usual discouragements and rebuffs, I finally found a manager willing to take a chance on me. A road company of *Wang* was to open in Saginaw, Michigan, and I was offered a place in the chorus and fifteen dollars a week. Torn between elation and sorrow, I signed the contract. I feared my act would mean a break with my parents, but nothing in the world would have induced me to pass up such an opportunity. I left them a contrite note and slipped off to Saginaw.

Saginaw may seem to some an unromantic port of entry into Bohemia, but to me, alighting from the train that snowy morning before Christmas, the town was bathed in glamour.

A sound of sleigh bells was in the air. People, laden with parcels, were hurrying through the streets. I registered at the hotel, feeling already very much a woman of the world.

I had had only a few hours in my cold little room, barely time to get thoroughly chilled and a touch homesick, when there was a knock on the door. I opened, to find my father standing in the hall. I was thunderstruck—it had never entered my mind that he might follow on the next train. He was very angry.

"Look here, Belle, your mother and I have had about enough of your nonsense. As long as we are your guardians, you're going to do as we say. Now you pack your things and get ready to come back to Chicago with me on the evening train."

I had never seen my father so stern. I could tell he was in no mood for argument.

"I'll meet you downstairs at six o'clock. And don't be late." And with this ultimatum Father marched off.

With a heavy heart I packed and then, there being nothing better to do, took my paper bag of lunch down in the lobby to eat and think things over. As I dropped into a chair, I noticed that a gentleman in a sealskin-collared coat sitting nearby was watching me. He was in his late thirties, very Babbitt, with heavy jowls. When our eyes met, he smiled.

"Will you have an orange?" I offered, quite innocent of the long and dishonorable history of the orange in serving as bait for flirtation. The gentleman looked pleased and accepted.

From then on it was easy to fall into conversation. The stranger's name, I learned, was Richard Wherry, he was a bachelor, a paint salesman, and he lived in Chicago. He was in Saginaw on business but was returning on the evening train. We talked on and on. In fact, the more we talked the more Mr. Wherry seemed to want to continue talking. The time flew by, and we were becoming faster friends by the minute.

Suddenly an idea flashed into my head and without stopping to consider what I was doing I blurted out: "Mr. Wherry! Would you do me a very great favor?"

"Why, sure, if I can."

"I wish we could get married this afternoon!"

Mr. Wherry looked like a man who had just had a cannon ball explode in his middle.

"I don't mean really," I hastened to explain. "Just a ceremony——"

And then, the words tumbling out, I told him my whole story—how positive I was that I could become a star in the theater if I could only get started—that I even had a part in the *Wang* company already—that Father was determined to take me out of it because he and Mother had the silly idea that a girl couldn't leave home until she was married and so I simply had to have a husband—any husband would do—that I'd never ask a single thing of him—in fact, I'd let him get a divorce as soon as he possibly could. I'd promise anything if he'd just marry me so I could stay with the show.

During this long outburst Mr. Wherry's face was a study. After I had finished he sat for some minutes looking first at me and then out the window. My heart began to sink. Finally he spoke.

"Are you sure you know what you're doing?" he said. "Are you sure you mean this?"

"Oh, do I!"

He looked at his watch. "It's pretty late," he said. "I don't know whether we can still get a license, but come on."

How vividly I remember that wedding, the first of my four. In the little Church of St. Paul's a band of willing workers were putting the finishing touches on the Christmas decorations and a sweet, woodsy odor filled the edifice. Beside the altar a giant pine tree laden with tinsel towered up into the shadowed ceiling. As Richard Wherry and I stood before the rector, Dr. Gallagher—himself as ruddy and genial as Saint Nick—the last rays of the setting sun pricked through the stained-glass window and focused on a glittering angel high up on the tree.

"I, Isabel, take thee, Richard——" I heard myself saying.

What happens if this man goes back on his word, I was thinking. Suppose he doesn't let me go either?

By the time the short ceremony was over, the interior had already become quite dim, and someone lighted a smoky lamp so that we could see to sign the register. A young couple laid down a garland of evergreen and, their hands sticky with pitch, came forward to write their names as witnesses. A moment later two rash gamblers in matrimony heard themselves being congratulated as Mr. and Mrs. Wherry and the next moment found themselves standing outside in the snowy twilight, man and wife.

On the way back to the hotel my bridegroom and I were both unaccountably embarrassed, and conversation, which had hitherto flowed so easily, dried up completely.

In the hotel lobby Father was pacing impatiently. My new husband tactfully waited outside while I went in.

"I'm sorry, Father," I said. "I'm staying with the company. Here—" and I handed him my brand-new marriage certificate—"take this home to Mother. Tell her I'm a married woman now and she doesn't have to worry any more."

2 *My Poetic Legs*

After I had slammed the hack door shut on my father and Richard Wherry and waved them a hurried farewell, I turned back into my dingy hotel, feeling, to my surprise, like anything but a "married woman." As a young girl, listening to my mother's version of the facts of life, I had always imagined myself delicately wooed, trembling in indecision, finally capitulating to violets, soft vows, and a solitaire. Then would follow a decorous period of engagement culminating in white satin and an organ wheezing *Lohengrin.*

The bonds of matrimony as I actually experienced them rested so lightly on my shoulders that as time went on I began to wonder if I hadn't dreamed the little episode in Saginaw. I didn't even trouble to write to my husband-in-name-only, and it was many months before our paths crossed again.

Like the lady who told Carlyle she had decided to accept
the universe ("Egad, ma'am, you'd better!"), my mother
decided to accept my marriage. She was determined, however, that the name of Graham should never figure in lights,
even supposing I might be able to put it there. My bargain
with Richard Wherry had not included the use of his name,
only his mythical protection. But I had to be called something.

What's in a name? A great deal, especially a stage name.
It was my father's suggestion that I take for cover to my
questionable exploits the name of Dr. Livingstone, the ex-
plorer, at one time lost in darkest Africa, who had always
been a favorite family hero. I liked the idea because the
name connoted to me a daring spirit, and I had already re-
solved that I should live daringly. So Belle Livingstone I
became forthwith.

The comic opera *Wang* had recently been popularized by
DeWolf Hopper and Della Fox, but in the Number Two
Company, in which I adorned the chorus, Al Hart and beautiful Georgia Caine were playing the leads. Nightly from the
wings I used to watch and adore Miss Caine.

Our barnstorming itinerary swung a wide circle, all
through the Southern states. As I look back, it seems to me
that for months I was either on a stage, or on a train, or trying to catch up lost sleep in some unspeakably dingy bedroom. Nights were frequently spent squeezed two by two
into the soiled plush seats of a day coach, fighting to catch
forty winks, but being stepped on instead by messy children
who incessantly trooped up and down the aisles to the stove
or the convenience at either end of the car and who insisted
on trying to carry back full watercups to squalling baby
brother but succeeded only in dumping the contents in our
laps. At least once during the night a fist fight could be depended on to break out. If anyone should be lucky enough
to grab the first of those forty winks, there was always the

train newsboy hawking popcorn and peanuts to head off the other thirty-nine. At stops, when brakemen flung open doors and bawled stations, dopey mothers and their orange-smelling offspring would stumble and lurch against every seat between them and the exit. Anyone who had been brought only semiconscious by this performance would be awakened completely next time the brakeman went through the car, swinging his lantern and hitting any part of the human form that might be bulging over into the aisle.

Finally, when the name of our town would be yelled, thirty tired bodies would stretch and grope for thirty dusty grips. Engine bell ringing and brakes squealing, our thirty tired bodies and thirty dusty grips would swing off at Mudville, where invariably some ragged urchin would be on hand to yell, "The troupe's here!" Then we would scurry to the theater, where old-timers who knew all the short cuts would always have captured the only mirror in the common dressing room and newcomers like myself would arrive to find every chair and hook labeled in top-line lettering. Being tall, I hardly ever had a full look at myself in the dressing-room mirror, and if I ever had a hook for my clothes it was because no one else wanted it.

After a while there would be a free hour when we could search for a cheap restaurant and bolt a greasy meal. Then it would be time to crowd back into the stuffy dressing room, filled with clouds of powder and the heavy odor of cosmetics and candle grease and perspiration.

When the overture was called, there would ensue the most frightful scramble. No scrimmage on any football field ever equaled the crush and confusion of that M-moment. Out of the shuffle someone always issued with a torn pair of tights that didn't belong to her, and not a needle in sight. A wig would catch fire and somebody's only petticoat be used to put out the blaze. Or in the corner of the room some sloppy

Josie had emptied a basin of water into a brand-new pair of satin slippers.

"Curtain!" and a rush for the stairs, pinning and buttoning and hooking on the way. All chorus dressing rooms were either in the lofts or in the bowels of the theater. I used to think I spent half my life dashing up and down stairs. As the curtain crawled slowly up, discovering a stage full of happy girlies swinging and singing hand in hand, our audiences little suspected that only a second before the darlings had been engaged in practically hand-to-hand combat.

Final curtain at eleven, and at eleven-fifteen the hoarse cry: "All trunks ready!"

As some burly baggage man was hauling out the last trunk, our feet would be clattering down the stairs for the last time. Out into the night we would tumble and by fast walking catch a midnight train.

But I loved it. I loved the gypsy feel of the wheels rolling and the fever to see what lay beyond the bend of the road. I didn't even mind the soft-coal smoke, and the always being a little sleepy, and the lumpy beds and tin wash basins of those cockroachy hotels. And how I reveled on stage in the laughter and applause out of the darkness beyond the foots! I took to trouping like a duck to water. Never a homesick moment; never, I am bound to admit, a shred of regret for my wilfulness toward my parents or for my outrageous marriage.

Besides the hard life, I had to take a few hard knocks. The rigid bearing my mother and my grandmother had taught me before the cottonwood was not the director's idea of seductive grace. I had to be pushed on and pulled off the stage much like a piece of scenery. Never did the merry, merry chorus make its exit that the infuriated director wasn't waiting in the wings to tell me how especially putrid I had been in that performance. I know a lot of people will expect to find me immediately toying with caviar, with the manager ogling me over champagne. But that sort of thing didn't happen to me in *Wang*. I took the bumps, and presently I began to learn my way around.

The chorus, I found, was divided into two classes, the wise virgins and the foolish ones. There were those who always had cold cream and safety pins and those who hadn't; those who had combs with teeth and rabbit paws with fur and those who hadn't. The foolish virgins, of course, just helped themselves from the stores of the wise ones.

To my surprise, it was the foolish virgins who taught me the most. My mother would have told me that the wise ones would fare best in the end—that those sterling souls who always had a clean handkerchief would attract the greatest admiration and the most flattering offers of marriage. But as I learned life, it was the foolish ones—who may have neglected to wash their necks or mend their stockings—who married the rich men. One of the foolish *Wang* maidens grabbed herself a sewing-machine tycoon. Another foolish but very gay one, Clarisse Agnew, captured wealthy Dan Reed and took astrakhan-caped coachmen and liveried footmen in her stride.

One steaming night in Atlanta, as we were trying to yank ourselves into our sticky corsets, I began to understand the showgirl slant on matrimony.

"My God," said one of the crowd as she wiped her hot cheeks, "why shouldn't Lillian Russell take up with Jesse Lewisohn? What if he is as ugly as a baboon? I bet he looks handsome to her across a lobster thermidor. Do *we* eat lobster thermidor tonight? No!"

The *Wang* company finished up its trek in a blaze of glory in Philadelphia. Several weeks before the tour came to an end, you could notice the swelling undercurrent of anxiety among the girls. What next? was the unspoken question in everyone's mind. It is not the hardships of an engagement that an actress fears, but the hardship of having no engagement. Knowing how long and heartbreaking the waiting might be for me, I was prepared to fast for an indefinite period.

But my beginner's luck still held. Young's Theater in Atlantic City was opening a season of opera that summer, and right away I landed a job in the chorus. I was in a patch of clover. A chance to unpack and hang up my clothes! Atlantic City, next door to Broadway!

If I thought the road had been tough, I soon discovered that trouping was child's play compared with two-a-day and a new show every week. Life settled down to a treadmill of rehearsal and performance, rehearsal and performance. But I was completely happy. I was no longer the raw recruit, being pushed and pulled around; I knew that at last I was beginning to exhibit professional style and snap.

Still no lobster suppers, in spite of the fact that I did have a beau. An elderly banker scraped an introduction one night and took me for a turn in the moonlight on the Boardwalk. The next night he showed up again, and the next, and so on. This went on for ten nights, and then he presented me with a pair of kid gloves.

"You can't do this!" I sobbed.

I thought I was being seduced. I had not yet learned that men are often glad enough to give to the girl who simply makes them laugh, and that many handsome presents are offered in the parlor as well as in the boudoir. Today I think my admirer got off pretty cheap for his ten nights in the moonlight with a jolly young thing from the front row.

Suddenly came my chance to step from moonlight to spotlight. When *Falka* was cast, I was given the part of the Captain of the Guard. Musical comedy in those days was very pure in line and situation. But the Nineties were the leg era, and in order to add a little fillip for the bald-headed row a male role of this sort was frequently played by a woman. Odd how the erotic appeal has swung away from legs; today a smart girl takes her legs for granted and gets herself a good sweater.

My purloined name on a program at last! The part had two hazards, however. It called for a few lines solo—and tights. I don't know which felt more naked, my legs or my voice, but I know which got the compliments.

One night during the engagement a note was sent around to me backstage. It was signed "Dick Stael," a name that I recognized as one of Charles Hoyt's musical directors. Would I call on the writer at Hoyt's Madison Square Theater in New York as soon as my present contract expired?

Would a cat lap cream!

To play New York under the swanky banner of a Hoyt show was in those days practically a passport to success. Hoyt was Broadway's white-headed boy. He had written and produced a long parade of hits and was in the big money. His *Trip to Chinatown*, just closed, had had a run of almost two years, up to that time a record in the United States. To get aboard the Hoyt band wagon was the dream of every ambitious showgirl.

Even to get an interview with a Hoyt representative was not easy, and to be invited for an interview——! My head began to swell. I began to believe that I must have a voice as well as legs. From this it can be seen that I was still very, very green. But worse, I was naïve about my clothes. My wardrobe was far from chic. At the end of the summer I arrived in New York wearing a zany pancake hat that I had made myself, a dress with leg-of-mutton sleeves, and an oversized chatelaine bag.

Very well satisfied with the way I was turned out, I presented myself at Hoyt's theater. The doorman knew my name, and this fact threw a little swagger into my gait. When I went in, Dick Stael was drumming softly at the piano during an intermission in rehearsal.

"Well, I'm here!" I announced brightly.

Stael glanced up, and his hands paused on the keyboard. I could see that he recognized me. He looked me up and down, and through and through.

"Isn't that just dandy?" he finally said. "Now we can ring up."

Furious and embarrassed, I turned away to hide my burning cheeks in the darkness of the auditorium.

As I started to leave, Mr. Stael, apparently repenting of his sarcasm, called me back. He had cast me, he said briskly, in Hoyt's new show, *A Milk White Flag*, as Leader of the Drum Corps—my legs again!—and if I would go to the office the next day I would find my contract. My vanity all in ashes, I didn't dare even to ask the terms.

I thought I was dreaming next morning when Frank McKee, Hoyt's partner, offered me fifty a week. Six weeks of rehearsals to begin at once. Fifty a week those days was a fortune. But to finance six weeks of rehearsals I had exactly thirty dollars—all I had been able to save during my summer at Atlantic City. How to live on five a week?

I began by tramping the streets until I found a room, complete with rickety iron bed and threadbare carpet, at four dollars. This left one dollar a week for meals and incidentals. I knew I should be fighting a losing battle with starvation, but remembering Elijah and the ravens, I laid my head on my sour pillow that night in the sweetest sleep I had ever known. I had made Broadway and a fabulous Hoyt contract in less than two years' time!

Next morning I awoke with my usual horse's appetite only to recall that I was on a strict diet. I decided that my restaurant would be Childs, and my menus a five-cent order of fish cakes for dinner and a five-cent order of griddle cakes for breakfast, with an occasional banana for emergency. After my five-cents' worth of breakfast I went on to rehearsal. Julian Mitchell, who was staging the show, was a martinet who drove himself as hard as he drove his company. As I listened to his barking commands, I wondered how long I would be able to deliver the pep he demanded on a dime a day.

A *Milk White Flag* was good farce fooling, with plenty of lively songs. After a forenoon of hard work the cast was ready for a substantial luncheon. While they ate, I sat in Madison Square watching the squirrels and wishing I had some nuts. It was September, and the clear, bracing air alone would have made one hungry.

A long afternoon of drill under Mitchell's sharp tongue, followed by my dinner of two fish cakes, and then I went to see Georgia Caine, who was also in New York. Georgie had been drawing a star's salary in *Wang*, so I was amazed when she confided that she was nearly broke. When she said that, in fact, she was living on chipped beef and crackers, I began to laugh and told her about my fish cakes. We decided to weather the storm together.

Somehow it wasn't so hard to be hungry after that. When Georgie and I were laughing, we could forget food. Fortunately my temperament has always been resilient enough not to become seriously depressed for long. Whenever my young spirits became crumpled, I could always shake them out, brush them off like the fluffy feather boa I wore around my throat, and come smiling through. Besides, I loved the actors in the company and in spite of my terror of Mitchell tried valiantly to "give" with the rest of them. Apparently I was succeeding.

Then one day, just as the rehearsal was about to begin, a buzz ran through the company like wildfire. Hoyt was out front! The orchestra became all attention, and even the electricians and scene shifters took a new lease on life. The actors, particularly the newcomers, began to quake. Hoyt had a reputation for his uncanny sense in discerning human weakness, and his caustic wit spared no one.

Filled with curiosity and dread, I watched the ogre stride in and sit down.

"All ready, Mr. Mitchell," I heard him twang in his strident Yankee voice.

"Sorry, Mr. Hoyt, the young lady who opens the scene hasn't come in yet."

Hoyt's face darkened, but before he could reply the door flew open and the girl herself ran in, breathless and apologetic. She was about one minute late. Hoyt turned on her.

"Wal, Miss Whatever-your-name-is, dew you think you're on the stage or on the street? I expect my actresses not to let their night life interfere with their getting to rehearsals on time. Is that unreasonable?"

The girl flushed and her eyes flooded. She started to reply stormily.

"All right, all right, never mind. Let's get on with the show."

With this auspicious opening the company proceeded with a very apprehensive rehearsal. At my cue for entrance, in I stepped leading the drum corps with what seemed to me my last ounce of verve but more likely was a grim expression of do-or-die. After my long fast I was probably pale and tense. I was still wearing the funny little hat and the big sleeves. I must have looked like a comic valentine. Hoyt snapped his fingers and the orchestra stopped. He came down front and peered at me through his pince-nez. There was a dead silence.

Finally: "My God! If I had known there was anything as funny as this in New York, I'd have written the whole comedy around her."

When the boss cracks wise, underlings have to play up. As the titter of laughter rose, I stood there and died a thousand deaths. Then Mitchell snapped us back into line and the routine proceeded. But Hoyt seemed fascinated by me and kept making jibes.

"How her parents must have loved her to let her grow up!" was his parting shot.

I fled weeping from the theater to Georgie Caine for comfort.

"It's all because I'm so hungry!" I wailed. "That man will have me thrown out, I know he will!"

"Nonsense," said Georgie. "Go home and curl your hair and get a good night's sleep."

"Sleep be hanged!" I retorted. "I'm getting a good meal. And so are you. Come on."

I had had a flash of inspiration. The last time I was in distress I had asked a total stranger to help me out. That was the solution—find another Richard Wherry.

"We're going to the Hoffman House," I announced. "And I'm going to ask the first sporty-looking man who gets out of a cab to buy us a dinner."

"Hold on," said Georgie. "The doorman doesn't let that sort of thing happen at the Hoffman!"

"You're going to be asking the doorman what time it is."

"He'll think we are streetwalkers!"

"And so I may be," I returned grimly, "if Hoyt puts me on the sidewalk."

At the Hoffman House I had not long to wait for my prey. Soon a hansom cab discharged a tall man, elegantly dressed, and I walked up to him as if I were addressing the cottonwood.

"I beg your pardon. I'm very hungry and I have to ask someone for a meal. I'm an actress, and I'm too weak to go on rehearsing unless I can get something to eat. I'm not asking for a quarter, you know, for a cup of coffee and some beans. I've got to have a steak. Do you mind giving me a real dinner?"

During this speech the gentleman's expression had shaded from annoyance to incredulity, then to amused interest. When I finished, he inclined his head politely.

"Why, no, my dear, of course not. Go inside to the dining room and order what you want. I'll sign for it." He turned to go.

"But——but——" I restrained him. "I forgot to say there are two of us!"

The gentleman looked a little pained, but only for a moment. "All right, your friend too."

Before I could bring Georgie he had disappeared. Little we cared. We tore into the dining room and ordered the biggest porterhouse on the hotel menu. It was like something out of Arabian Nights to find ourselves at a table gleaming with linen and crystal instead of the usual greasy porcelain top.

I often wondered afterwards who our benefactor was, and eventually the long arm of coincidence pointed him out to me. Many years later I was dining at the Carlton in London with a party that included Tom Johnson, mayor of Cleveland. At a table close by I recognized Eddie Kinsella and with him my porterhouse philanthropist. Shortly, Eddie came over to say that his friend would like to be presented. I told Eddie I was surprised that the gentleman did not remember me, since he had once bought me one of the best meals of my life. This message, when relayed, was of course highly mystifying and somewhat embarrassing. But all was explained and forgiven when Eddie and his friend joined our party for coffee. Then I learned that my benefactor was none other than Mr. Kilduff, well-known angel of many a Broadway play. When I recalled myself to him, he expressed delight.

"I've always been sorry," he said, "for not having taken you to dinner in person. Who was the other girl—the one I didn't wait to see?"

"Georgie Caine."

"Not really! Why, I starred Georgie in *The Girl from Gay Paree*, which ran for months on Broadway! Incidentally, fell in love with her as well. But she never told me anything about this!"

Then I related to Mr. Kilduff the sequel to the dinner—how his steak had gone right into my strut and I had not been fired after all.

Next day at rehearsal the young lady whom Hoyt had bawled out so severely was waiting for him, her face very set and hostile. She was holding a piece of paper in her hand.

"Mr. Hoyt," she said defiantly, and loudly enough for all the company to hear, "you insulted me yesterday when you talked about my being on the street. I think you should apologize, and here's my proof that you should."

She handed him the paper. Hoyt looked at it blankly.

"*Virgo intacta*—what's all this about?"

"That, Mr. Hoyt, is a certificate from my doctor that I am *virgo intacta*."

Hoyt looked at her sharply, then studied the paper again.

"Hell," he snapped. "You've got a nerve. What good is this thing? This is dated yesterday."

And so the rehearsals went, Hoyt hurling sarcasm in every direction, especially mine. When dress rehearsal came, Hoyt saw me for the first time sans flat-top and leg-of-muttons. His face changed when I stepped out in my tights and skin-tight jacket, a Philip Morris type cap perched on my boyish wig. At that moment I learned the importance of contour. As soon as the rehearsal was over, Hoyt sent for me and put a twenty-dollar bill in my hand.

"Do me the favor," he whispered, "of getting yourself a decent hat. And say, will you burn the other—you know, the flat-top?"

Hoyt was ultrafastidious about the appearance of his actors and paid excellent salaries in order that every player in his companies might be always dressed in the height of fashion. "I expect every one of my actresses, by God, to wear a fur coat that she hasn't earned on her back!" So, much as I should have liked to regard the new hat as a tribute to my charm, or at least a peace offering, I had to realize that it was meant only to maintain the Hoyt prestige.

However, our friendship dated from that day. Hoyt left off his barbed thrusts at me and began to boast about my improvement under his direction. Then I noticed he was making opportunities for conversation, and next I knew inviting me out to dinner. To his surprise he found me amusing, and he began to flatter me by saying that I stimulated his mind. Hoyt was a handsome man in his thirties, the glass of fashion with his handle-bar mustache and ascot tie. His Cal Coolidge accent was new and fascinating to my Kansas ears, and his unfailingly sulphurous vocabulary I found very picturesque. Sometimes it was hard to realize that I was on familiar footing with the man I had once so feared. Hoyt's conversion taught me that I must think more about my appearance.

Under make-up and lights, with a fresh girlish charm deriving from high spirits, I have no doubt I was passable on the stage. But I was troubled by the fact that I was built on Junoesque lines and I often wished I possessed the ravishing features of a Georgie Caine. Of course there were the Legs. These were prominently displayed on the stage in my capacity as Leader of the Drum Corps, and in the theater lobby the publicity agent had put up a life-sized poster of me in which the Legs were featured. But I would gladly have traded the pair of them for great, lustrous eyes and petite, cuddly curves.

As I was standing in the lobby one day, I noticed a man studying my picture intently, admiration stamped on his face. Finally he drew a five-dollar bill out of his pocket and walked over to the ticket window.

"Front row, please."

The ticket seller looked pleased.

"Say, you must like this show. How many times have I sold you a ticket?"

"Fifteen, mister. I go just to see that showgirl——" nodding in the direction of the poster. "Boy, is she a stepper!"

The ticket seller dropped his head and began to whisper. I knew he was telling the man that the original of the picture was standing in the lobby. The man turned, gave me one look, and his countenance altered so dramatically that I didn't know whether to laugh or to cry.

"My God!" was all he could say, as he grabbed back his five-dollar bill and fled.

This yelp of disappointment made me do some real thinking. Here was a man spending his money just to look at me across the footlights. Think what he might have spent for nourishing steaks and chops if only I had lived up to his expectations in real life. Obviously I should have to provide some off-stage substitute attraction for the Legs, which the dress of the Nineties of course did not display. Other girls, I began to realize, were padding over shaggy rugs in softly lighted restaurants, getting a run for their teeth on terrapin to the strains of "Tales from the Vienna Woods" while I was boiling a cup of tea on a gas plate. At that moment I had never had a cocktail or a regret. I decided to try both.

As soon as I got my next salary check, I went to Joseph, one of New York's top importers and *couturiers*.

"I know I'll never be beautiful—look at this pug nose and red hair! But I want dash, splash, flash. I want to look like Paris. Can you make me over completely? Do whatever you like—I won't even look in the mirror."

Joseph went to work. He made capital of the only thing I had, my curvaceous figure, and poured me into princess gowns with clinging, seductive lines. He topped me off with an assortment of provocative hats, and I barged out with new courage for my share of the velvet carpets and the soft music.

My investment in glamour paid immediate dividends. Delighted compliments from Hoyt, who promptly introduced me to a Mr. "Laffy" Gleason, one of the Republican big shots who had been practically everything but president. But when Mr. Gleason invited me to Delmonico's for luncheon, I was interested in him strictly as a prospective provider of terrapin. The luncheon party included Senator Grant and a few other notables. I must have contributed some lilt to the affair, for when it was over Mr. Gleason drove me in one of his University Club hansoms up to Dunlap's exclusive hat shop on Fifth Avenue and bought me the most expensive hat he could find.

A Milk White Flag was a hit, of course, and money poured into the Hoyt box office. Hoyt, always generous, rewarded his players with larger salaries; my fifty-dollar stipend was doubled. I had definitely struck oil. By that time I was sick to death of the odor of moldy lodging houses and I considered it high time to give myself a proper background.

There is probably no thrill in life to compare with that of turning the key in one's first house or apartment. My "first" was a tiny flat in Thirty-third Street just off Fifth Avenue. Viewing it in retrospect, I can see that the furniture was both hideous and scanty. But at that time I was living in such a golden mist behind the footlights and to the accompaniment of so much song and laughter after every show that I could accept without a qualm the Grand Rapids installment-plan chairs, the cheap, bright rugs, and the imitation-mahogany tables. I woke each morning in a glittering brass bed to a glittering new day.

One morning I awoke in the brass bed to find myself famous. The artist Charles Dana Gibson, whose Gibson Girls were the pin-up models of the Nineties, had been for some time popularizing the full-bosomed type of feminine beauty. The Gibson Girl rage may or may not have been responsible for what happened, but one day the New York *World* published a full-page picture devoted to the measurements of the ideal feminine figure. Hoyt's enterprising publicity agent immediately phoned the *World* that my own measurements corresponded to a T to their specifications. As a result every Sunday newspaper carried stories and pictures of the "ideal woman"—me. The form I had thought a liability because of its goddess-like proportions was now the envy of all my showgirl friends. My photographs increased in numbers and revelation: I was The Body.

Poor Mother! Whenever publicity pictures were made of me in various roles, I had always made it a point to send one to her, thinking that even if she disapproved my calling she would at least have a natural curiosity to know how her duckling was succeeding. But not in tights! Father wrote that Mother always scrupulously cut off my legs before she allowed one of those pictures to be shown to her friends. Now the murder was out. Reproductions of my "ideal" shape were blazoned country-wide, and one New York feature writer coined a phrase with power to change the whole course of my affairs: he referred almost reverently to my Poetic Legs.

Immediately things happened. Even Hollywood could not have asked for more. I began to get top billing, and the show played every night to SRO. Other managers began to bid for me, even to borrow me. When Ed Price produced *Jack and the Beanstalk*, Hoyt made a lend-lease arrangement to allow me to lead the beauty march. I knew well enough I was no beauty, but I had learned how to make the most of my buxom figure. It began to dawn on me that I could go further and faster on proportions, personality, and publicity than on a picture face.

P. T. Barnum, then on the crest of his wave, wired me an

offer of a thousand dollars a week just to display the poetic anatomy as one of his circus features. I declined, but I couldn't resist sending his offer on to Mother.

The legend of the Poetic Legs died hard. For many years it was constantly rising to haunt me. One night in a little Bohemian *café* in Paris I was having coffee with some very correct English friends who knew nothing of my lurid leg career. Suddenly I noted that a shabby old man in a frayed coat at a nearby table was watching me excitedly. He looked vaguely familiar but I could not place him. At last he could restrain himself no longer and came over to my table.

"You don't remember me, Miss Livingstone!" he quavered. "I was the electrician in *A Milk White Flag*— I turned the light on your Legs!" Then turning to my startled English guests: "Did you ever see them Legs? Oh, them Poetic Legs!"

Whereupon, to my confusion, the old fellow launched into interminable reminiscences of the triumphs of the Legs.

Perhaps the strangest quarry flushed by all the hue and cry over the Legs was my long-forgotten husband. I never knew whether he was motivated by a desire to claim the poetic treasure he had never even suspected he possessed or to rid himself of a possible embarrassment to his middle-class respectability. Or perhaps it was sheer curiosity that prompted him to wait for me outside the stage door of Hoyt's theater one cold winter night. At any rate, there I found him, standing in the circle of the gaslight, hands thrust in pockets and the snow sifting gently down on his hat brim. My heart jumped as I recognized this unwelcome ghost from the past. I could think of several reasons for discomfiture if I suddenly had to introduce a husband.

We greeted each other with a strained politeness, my mind racing madly in an effort to think up some method of disposing of him painlessly. But Richard Wherry was waiting merely to ask me to luncheon, and after we had made the engagement he courteously put me in a hansom and bowed good night.

We met next day at the quietest and dullest hotel dining room in New York and partook of our first and only meal together. I could see that, though he wanted to be friendly, he had no thought of forcing his attentions. Under other circumstances we might have become really friends, but the consciousness of our strange relationship served as a barrier rather than a tie. I did my best to sparkle without champagne, but in the funereal hush of so much decorum, surrounded only by silent, gloomy married couples, my gayety was forced.

Recalling that we had been married at Christmas, my husband inquired what I would like for an anniversary present.

"Give me something nobody else can give me—a divorce."

His face went blank, but after a moment he rallied.

"All right—if that's what you want."

Richard Wherry was as good as his word. Though the actual decree did not come until later, a box arrived at my flat on Christmas Eve containing a huge bunch of Parma violets and a card which read: "Your former husband. With all my regrets."

What a load off my mind! My ideas about husbands had undergone some pretty radical changes in the short time I had been behind the footlights, and certainly a stodgy salesman, who would expect me to sit around waiting for him to get home from his dull trips just to have a couple of pork chops ready for him, was not any part of my plan for the future. Let the wise virgins take over jobs like this; the foolish ones were looking farther afield.

This was the day of the great invasion of England by America, not by shock troops but by shocking little troupers

—hordes of showgirls, each one intent on making a wealthy and, if possible also, titled marriage. I had stood on the docks waving good-by to one after another of my friends as they set off to London, frankly on the make for an earl or a duke. As the months went by, I had read their letters, stuck as full of glittering names as a cushion of pins, and had tacked on the walls of my bedroom their highly-colored picture postcards from Paris, Nice, the Riviera, and the idea had begun to germinate in my little noodle that, as far as a husband was concerned, maybe I too might look further and fare worse than to pick up a nice title for myself some day.

True, by that time there were plenty of men spending money on me in New York, but they were all matrimonial ineligibles. The love-honor-and-obey kind were mighty scarce. In those days New York showgirls were given a big rush from midnight to dawn in Sherry's but overlooked next afternoon in Central Park. Reports trickling in from the foreign missions, however, indicated that prospects for a legal contract were definitely brighter abroad and that a little senility could easily be as much an asset as a liability.

The winter of 1896-97 was a record-breaker in New York. Lower and lower dropped the mercury, and white blizzards swept up and down Broadway. I was thankful for my fur coat as I snuggled into my collar on the way back and forth to the theater. Drifts were so high on Fifth Avenue that snowplows worked night and day. Fires kept breaking out in all parts of the city, and firemen were living icicles as they fought the flames. Trains were blocked, horsecars foundered. One night the wind that howled down from the North even blew shut the doors of the theater.

On that night, as I sat basking in the warmth of the open fire in my flat, came a peal at my bell. I opened the door to find six half-frozen men from the University Club, including Laffy Gleason. Gleason explained that he and the boys had found it impossible to fight their way back to the Club through the storm and that they could not even find a restaurant open. Might they warm themselves until the worst of the blizzard was over, perhaps even have a cup of coffee? As Gleason brought the men into my tiny parlor, one of them was introduced to me as Theodore Roosevelt.

My microscopic kitchen contained only three china plates, but Mr. Roosevelt, who was used to camping, insisted that he preferred tin plates anyway. But what could I serve? The training I had received in a Kansas kitchen saw me through. I made stack after stack of hot, golden pancakes and pot after pot of steaming coffee. At last, warm and filled and overflowing with sociability, the men gathered around my fire and started spinning yarns. Soon Roosevelt, a quick, nervous talker, was pouring out tales of his hunting days in the Rockies while the rest of us listened spellbound.

It was nearly morning when the snow abated enough to permit my flock of storm birds to take flight. Reluctantly we parted; it had been one of those perfect occasions when friendship springs spontaneously into full being.

This pleasant little evening had an important result—the arrival at my flat of a huge crate. When I pried open the cover, I discovered in the bed of excelsior a complete dinner service of Haviland china, accompanied by a card from Mr. Roosevelt expressing his undying thanks for my rescue to the perishing. Sitting in the middle of my imitation Oriental rug, I counted dizzily the stacks and stacks of plates and cups and saucers and contemplated their beautiful design and heavy gilt edges. I hadn't even a suitable table for such dishes. I decided I must have a proper table—and a proper room in which to put the table.

To acquire such elegance I knew that I would need an Aladdin's lamp, for I had already discovered that I was profligate in temperament. Hoyt, who by then had become a very good friend indeed, used to ask me to come along with him on some of his journeys to visit his road companies in

Philadelphia, Washington, or Boston, just to keep him cheerful. He was already beginning to show signs of the mental strain under which he was working and from which he was to die after only a few more years. On these long journeys in the private cars there was always a group of wealthy playboys who would invite me to sit in on their poker games, and from them, at a high cost, I learned the gentle art of holding the cards close to the vest. Often I would gamble away my whole pay envelope and receive at the end of the week only a statement. Still it was flattering to be a protégé of Charlie Hoyt, and I rationalized my growing taste for gambling by telling myself that it was better to rely on Mr. Hoyt's favor for future jobs than to risk his disfavor by a tight-fisted prudence.

We had good times on these trips. Often Clarisse Agnew would go along, and some of the actors and executives of the companies. Occasionally Mrs. Hoyt would come, but not often. Hoyt made no bones about letting it be known that he and his wife were not congenial. One night when the steward was serving the champagne, Hoyt set down his glass in distaste.

"George, damn you, you know this champagne is not cold."

"Sorry, boss, ain't nuff ice, dat's what."

Hoyt solemnly picked up the bottle. "Take it home to my wife, George. Tell her to hold it in her lap."

Charlie Hoyt became a legend on Broadway even before his death. Comparatively little has been written about him, except the bare outlines of his life, perhaps because so many of the best anecdotes are unprintable.

The days and nights in kaleidoscopic succession melted one into another. During all this time my friendship with Laffy Gleason continued, and through him I met Harry Gillig and Harry Strong. Diamond Jim Brady was then in the spotlight, setting up all his favorites in business in co-

quettish little millinery shops. Of course the brainless ones
promptly went broke, whereupon canny Jim would buy back
the shops, one after another, for a song and pass them on to
his next cutie crop.

With all the publicity I had been receiving it was natural
that he should invite me to his famous beauty suppers. The
real beauties never objected; perhaps they thought my pug
nose a good foil for their classic ones. But none of them out-
ranked me in high spirits. The opulence of those affairs
stimulated me as much as the golden bubbles in the stem of
the glass. More and more I was reveling in the Bohemia of
stage life, especially that section of Bohemia which a kind
Providence had stocked with sweetbreads and pierced
peach in brandy.

On those rollicking nights of the Nineties the idea of fun
was not to go out on a twosome. Showgirls liked to see and
be seen by as many as possible, and parties rolled up like
snowballs. Jack Wilson often acted as moving spirit and
general introducer. It was he who introduced me to the tobacco magnates Pierre Lorillard and James B. Duke. Mr.
Duke, who looked sedate enough, nevertheless enjoyed letting himself go at those impromptu gatherings at Delmonico's for lobster and Bass's ale.

One day a large, legal-looking envelope was delivered to
me, postmarked Chicago, bringing to mind immediately
thoughts of my ex-husband. I was scared—maybe the divorce was phony. I tore open the envelope. The message it
contained was written not by Richard Wherry but by his
lawyers. The poor fellow, I read, was dead and had left me
a legacy. This astounding news I had to read several times
before I could believe it. The amount was one hundred and
fifty thousand dollars. The firm enclosed a small pink slip
with the six figures clearly written on it.

I was floored. Why hadn't Richard Wherry told me he

had money? I had always supposed he earned only a salesman's slender salary. Where had this fortune come from?
Later inquiry revealed that two well-to-do uncles had unexpectedly bequeathed their all to him, and he, ever thoughtful, had passed along a large share to me.

Immediately I was filled with the wildest elation. My
mind flew to Europe—happy playground of the witty, the
cultured, the elegant. Now I too could crash the great
capitals—free and rich. The lessons under the cottonwood
had years ago taught me to long for London and glimpses of
royalty, even before all those letters from my showgirl
friends who were galloping over Europe under the protection of a title. How soon could I sail? To the steamship
office to make inquiries—yes, there was a stateroom on the
St. Louis.

I raced to the theater to make my adieus. I could see that
Hoyt was genuinely sorry to lose me, and when it came to
saying good-by to the company I all but dissolved. Dear
gruff old Mat Snyder, Charlie Stanley, the leading man, vi-
vacious Clarisse Agnew—we had all been so gay together.
Last of all a telephone call to Diamond Jim.

"Oh, Lord," groaned Jim. "You too? Well, if you must go,
let's kill a fatted calf for the departing prodigal."

The party Jim gave for me at Sherry's was one of his most
sumptuous. The middle of the table was a blue sea of
forget-me-nots, and as if really floating on its waves was a
replica of the *St. Louis* that was waiting to take me abroad.
All the candles were wharf lights. For the first time I saw
pheasants served in their beautiful feathers, their necks
garlanded with flowers. From the champagne that flowed
that night you would not have guessed that Jim himself
never drank a drop. My present from Jim was a diamond-
studded vanity case.

As I stepped into my cab, James Duke ran up and slipped

into my hand a square envelope. Though I little realized it then, this thoughtful attention was destined to be worth infinitely more to me on the other side of the ocean than legacies or jewels.

3 *To Marry or to Tarry*

The Englishmen on board the *St. Louis*, all of whom were betting on the outcome of the Derby, came near to letting themselves get excited when it was learned that we should land on Derby Day itself. As our ship entered Southampton waters, we were met by a tug.

"What's won the Derby?" the captain megaphoned.

"Flying Fox," a small voice floated back, and thus I chalked up on my memory board the day of my first arrival in England.

A porter to a bag at Waterloo Station, I discovered, and you mustn't even carry your own umbrella if you wanted to be classed as a lady. The musty old four-wheeler—or "growler," as Londoners called it—into which I was bundled, looked to me more like a hearse than a cab. As we crawled through London's dense traffic, I began for the first time to have a few qualms over my rash journey. All that I had heard about the snobbery of the English came back to awe me. London, I suddenly realized, was impenetrably rich, deep-rooted, sophisticated, not likely to be interested in a Kansas nobody with nothing to recommend her except a small fortune and a pair of publicized legs. I began to feel pretty much of an upstart, and thankful I had at least a letter of introduction—the envelope from Mr. Duke—in my purse.

The rattletrap old growler stopped off Cavendish Square before an unimpressive structure later to be known as the Dysart Hotel. I entered with disappointment, and a certain amount of disdain. The house was run by three little old maids and reeked of respectability. Just to raise my eyes to the framed picture of Victoria above the hotel desk gave me a feeling of watch-and-ward surveillance. My rooms were heated by grates on which a slavey spent her life polishing the brasses, and the bath was one of those deep pie-plate affairs in which one stood up like a bird and threw a handful of water on one's shivering chest. It was all true then about English hotels.

Still, here I was, and I had to make a start somewhere. After I had unpacked, my first move was to ask one of the manageresses if I might receive a caller—a gentleman.

"Certainly," she said primly. "I will chaperone you."

The name written on my letter of introduction was that of Mr. Thomas Asten, head of the American Tobacco Company in England. In due time Mr. Asten arrived, wearing all the English insignia of success—ascot tie, top hat, cutaway, gold-knobbed cane. I was taken aback, for Americans dressed up like that only for a funeral or a wedding. When Mr. Asten was ushered into the stiff little sitting room where my chaperone sat protecting my innocence, he seemed surprised on his part to meet so young a traveler. I gathered he had expected something more full-blown, and with all the fervor of my tender years I resented the uncle-ish benignancy that overspread his face. Conversation got off to a very slow start. I simpered sweetly and "yes-ed" and "really-ed" him until even my watch-and-warder looked bored.

Finally Mr. Asten, apparently tired of perching on a stiff chair, asked if he might take me to Earl's Court for dinner. The name sounded to me like something pretty sumptuous, but the place itself turned out to be nothing more than a very second-rate Coney Island with the usual fancy stucco build-ings, colored lights, and scent of popcorn. Band players dressed gaily in those days, and I remember the scarlet-and-gold trappings of the musicians who filled the air with strains of "The Blue Danube." Mr. Asten had selected the spot, I could see, because he thought my adolescent mind would be intrigued by the wonders of the waxworks, and the thrills of the water shoot, the switchback, and the roundabout, not to mention the tricks of the Performing Fleas advertised by the couplet:

Great fleas have little fleas upon their backs to bite 'em,
And little fleas have lesser fleas—and so ad infinitum.

For an hour we threaded in and out of the crowds, Mr. Asten at my elbow respectfully giving neat little informative comments on the attractions. When at last he inquired if I wouldn't like a nice cool drink, I breathed a sigh of relief. I could think of nothing more appealing to my juvenile tastes than a nice cool drink of champagne.

In the grounds there was a very large and expensive dining room labeled the Welcome Club, rather fancifully it seemed to me, for obviously none but the filthy rich would be wel-comed under its canopied entrance and permitted to sit be-neath its shaded candlelight. In this exclusive restaurant Mr. Asten carefully selected the least conspicuous table. This was carrying English conservatism a bit too far, I thought, but the evening was young.

"Will you have a ginger beer?" asked my host.

"Mr. Asten," I said softly, "take another look. Do you really think I look like ginger beer?"

Mr. Asten's whoop of laughter attracted the attention of two of his cronies dining nearby, one of them Harry Smart, the other Harry Hobson, who later became a general during World War I. It was Hobson who came over and insisted that we all take a table in the center of the room. This was more to my liking. I followed my usual habit of ordering the highest-priced items, having learned in New York that a girl who orders cheap things is never appreciated—a man thinks she hasn't been accustomed to anything better. The meal progressed merrily and soon the only ice that was left was in the champagne buckets where it belonged.

I was kept busy trying to handle my knife and fork à l'anglaise and at the same time keep up my end of the conversation. The first thing I learned of special interest and significance to me was that American women, particularly women of the stage, were really as popular in London as all my girl friends' postcards had claimed. The Prince of Wales, it seems, had visited the States as a youth and had not seen a single red Indian. Instead he had danced enthusiastically with any number of beautiful and charming girls and had brought back with him a sincere admiration for everything unaffected and democratic and American, with the result that English society, for the first time in history, had opened its doors to Americans other than diplomatic officials.

I asked what type of women the Prince preferred and was told that, not to put too fine a point on it, His Royal Highness enjoyed the reputation of being a man who flirted with every petticoat he met. That is, if she were amusing; he preferred a witty nobody to a titled crone. Yes—with a touch of pride —the Marlborough House set was pretty fast, a very mixed society of lively young bloods and frivolous women welcoming with open arms whoever was clever or chic, from what-

ever country and whatever rung of the social ladder. A great
many people, from peerage to pub, considered this set a
menace to English life and morals. Look at the gambling,
they said—like to become the national vice, and all because
the Prince was so fond of horse racing and cards. Edward was
turf-crazy; he kept his own stud, and his horses frequently
won the Derby, and at Ascot, Sandown, and Goodwood.
Whatever the Prince did the smart set did; and whatever
they did the middle classes aped. Moralists groaned over the
princely failings. In public appearances with his beautiful
Danish wife, Princess Alexandra, the Prince seemed like a
pattern of a husband, but—those quick trips to Paris! those
adventures incognito!

Edward liked the stage too, especially its lighter side. He
had been seen at music hall as well as at opera and was said
to enjoy the cancan with its saucy little flip of the ruffled
undies even more than the ballet. Tom Asten laughingly
prophesied that all England would soon be less interested in
the freedom of the seas than the freedom of the knees. Edward had broken practically all of the sacred conventions.
He had turned his back on traditionally dreary social rig-
maroles; he dared to choose his friends without regard to
Debrett—and he liked Americans.

All these comments I drank down as thirstily as I did the
champagne, and before the evening was over, knowing that
many of my Broadway friends were playing in *The Belle of
New York*, a piece that had cracked London wide open, I arranged a luncheon party at Prince's where my hosts might
meet the stars—Edna May, Helen Dupont, and Edna Powers.

Mr. Asten, by the time he took me home, had dropped his
earlier air of visiting the schoolroom, and a few months later
was the first man in Europe to propose to me. I refused him,
though I was very fond of him. Tom remained throughout
my life a good enough friend to serve as best man at one of

my weddings and godfather to one of my children, though he must have privately thanked his lucky stars later that I had not had his fortune to squander away.

The next scene of the Edwardian pageant opened for me at a tea given by Edna May at her lovely little house in Regent's Park. Tom Asten and his friends had spoken truly when they had said that La May was a reigning favorite. The smart set was stampeding her. The phenomenon of finding an actress visited openly by bluebloods delighted me. In New York, though gay sparks were plentiful enough, they usually waited until nightfall to be seen with showgirls. But in London, as I discovered at once, where the old Shaftesbury's walls were bursting with blond, monocled Johnnies—hair parted in the middle, tails halfway down their calves, who came again and again to see *The Belle of New York*—showgirls were taken out in the daytime ostentatiously. Pretty girls were part of the wealthy Englishman's life, and a gentleman never thought of apologizing for his stage friends. In fact, he often took them into beautiful ancestral homes.

The first English house where I went to dine was Lord Kinnoull's. As the heavy carved doors swung open to me, revealing the centuries-old interior, so carefully guarded, a curious thought flashed through my mind: Am I really going up in the world, or are these people coming down?

After dinner Lord Kinnoull asked me to sing a little ragtime. The Prince was mad over colored minstrel songs, and Londoners, trotting behind him like sheep, declared they were all mad over them too. The Prince never got tired of listening to "She's My Baby," "The Bully," or "Push Dem Clouds Away," so it was easy to be a hit at a party simply by sitting down at the piano and ragging some of his favorites.

To have been invited by Edna May brought me to the attention of other smart Bohemian hostesses and I promptly received a flock of invitations. The Duchess of Manchester was very kind to me, as she was to all stage folk. Mrs. Reginald Ronalds I would describe as the Elsa Maxwell of the Edwardian days. She would never bother with anyone who didn't matter. In her house in Cadogan Square I met Sir Arthur Sullivan and Nellie Melba, as well as many who mattered in professions other than the entertainment world. At first I was a trifle awed by the great names, but when I discovered that many of those to the manner born had the same tastes and zest for living as I, I began to meet them on an equal footing.

After two months I sat down and made a list of my London acquaintances and found that my new friends included —besides the theater crowd—peers and peeresses, celebrities, and big financiers. Obviously it was time to graduate from my first little hotel, with its cheap lace curtains and its pervading atmosphere of cabbage and chastity. In the Hotel Walsingham, where the Ritz now stands, I moved into ideal rooms, and within their beautiful old oak-paneled walls I began to entertain gayly and informally. Immediately my circle of friends widened still more.

It is probably as true today as it ever was that if a girl can demonstrate that she honestly does not need the money she is much more likely to be offered a job than some poor shivering thing clutching a thin dime. So it proved for me. No sooner was I smartly established with a flat of my own in the Walsingham, jewels and furs, a maid and a saddle horse than I was offered the position of understudy to Helen Dupont in *The Belle of New York* company. This was a connection that suited me perfectly—a minimum of work with a maximum of time to devote to my own highly interesting affairs.

By this time I was bringing in the sheaves from my English beaus in a harvest that made New York beaus look like pikers. Never before nor since have I seen such magnificent gestures of generosity. Those were the days when a box of Parma violets might contain—and often did—a diamond bracelet.

Or presents might take the form of gowns and hats. I remember a party given by David Sassoon, a disgracefully wealthy Parsi, in the fall of 1897. Mr. Sassoon, who rather fancied himself as a judge of women's clothes, exploded when he saw the gown I was wearing—a black *point d'esprit* over which swirled huge velvet autumn leaves.

"Good Lord, Belle, where did you get that dress? I can just see old Queen Vic herself down on her knees cutting it out!"

Next day Mr. Sassoon rushed me over to Paris for an outfit nearer to his tastes, though the costly chinchilla he selected might just as well have been a gray tabby, so little did I know of furs at that time.

Enchanting froufrous of the Nineties! When I look at the man-tailored female form of the Fifties, I wonder why women were so silly as to give up their flounces. What contradictions we must have seemed to men!—lacing in our waists with those ironclad corsets, but letting out our original sin in foamy frills and furbelows.

For sharp dressing the men were not far behind, with their monocles and their mustaches, and their carnation boutonnieres and collars so tall that their chins were always held high in air. The slim-waisted Life Guards especially, those gorgeous scarlet-and-brass creatures on whose helmets and breastplates the sun shone or the fog settled while they were on duty, were the sartorially impeccable ones on whom the night light glittered when they were off duty. Being squired to the Savoy or the Carlton by these well-mannered, well-spoken men was one of the new intoxications of my first year in London.

I am a child of the night, I love the night; yet London was a town that I could also enjoy by day. A smart canter on a crisp autumn morning gave me as much pleasure as wining and dining. Fortunately I was at home on a horse. When I was only a very young child, my father used to take me for long rides with him across the Kansas prairies. So in London, as soon as I had provided myself with a decent animal and a habit that did justice to my figure, I confidently joined the smart set as they trotted briskly on their gleaming mounts through Rotten Row. Many a flirtation begun on horseback culminated in ortolans and orchids.

With so much fun and so many exciting presents to be had without benefit of clergy, I kept postponing in my mind the idea of tying myself to one man. There would be time for that later on, I argued with my usual optimism. Some of the *Belle of New York* girls, however, held opposite views, and as soon as they could grab an earl's ermine with one hand they rang the wedding bell with the other. These were days for marrying, not for tarrying, they said. Dangerous gamble to wait—a bird in the hand, remember. They referred to the law of supply and demand; every boat that docked from New York was dumping another load of fluffy fichus and picture hats down the gangplank. You could always tell when the time was getting ripe for action with one of the company— sooner or later out would come a book on etiquette. Whenever you found a show girl ready to lay aside her gold toothpick and keep her mind on the right spoon—to be a lady even if it hurt—it was time to congratulate her.

I must have been secretly a little romantic and, remembering the prosaic aspects of my first marriage, hoping for something better on my second matrimonial venture. It used to annoy me sometimes to see how all the young men flocked around the older women. One night at Covent Garden I found myself next to Lady Allister Campbell's box. Every one of the doddering old fogies in my box had lost the key to the garden of love, but there was Lady Campbell, sixty if a day, surrounded by stalwart forms.

"How do you do it?" I whispered.

She laughed. "They feel safer with me," she whispered back. "Wait till you're my age. You'll have them all then."

Since I have passed the sixty mark, I have often thought of this prediction, so ironically true.

Among the many graybeards clustered about me exhibiting their fatherly interest, one mustache, however, stood out crisp and black. It belonged to Lord Jim Athlumney and it adorned a very handsome face. During the First World War Lord Athlumney was the serious and dignified Provost Marshal of London, but at the time I knew him he was just a man-about-town taking his fun where he found it. Jim was not only young and handsome and a bachelor, but he was Irish and his brogue was most rich and delightful. There was a combination of romantic qualities! Yet Jim never proposed to me; instead, he adopted me and became my British Emily Post.

One of the things that troubled him was that I sometimes opened my own door instead of letting my maid do it. In fact, I was far too energetic in my own behalf. Good form demanded more repose. And there were many pronunciations to be corrected, and I mustn't say "sir," because only servants said that—and so on. I was terribly fond of Jim and I have blessed him many a time for the trouble he took to civilize me. Jim had a small house with only a couple of servants. His favorite way of entertaining informally was to dismiss the servants, give every girl a maid's apron, a bowl, and a spoon, and send couples into the kitchen to forage for their supper.

Shortly after I had got myself happily set up in my new world, I received a letter from the Shire brothers—the Shuberts of their day—asking me if I would take one of their actresses under my wing and give her a friendly steer in getting started in London. The girl was Marian Winchester, and she danced ragtime on her toes.

After she had been in London a month or so, Marian called on me. She walked into my drawing room—or should I say rattled in?—the most bedecked female I had ever seen, more

jeweled than a Swiss watch. Great diamond hatpins weighed
down one side of her hat. A diamond dog-collar had a stran-
gle hold on her throat; diamond stars and butterflies twinkled down to her waist where an immense diamond buckle
held her jeweled belt together. Hanging from the belt was a
diamond-set chatelaine, and in one beringed hand she carried a jeweled parasol.

I'm giving no lessons here, I thought, with a touch of sour
grapes. I'm taking them. If this girl is just starting now, by
the time she gets under way the rest of us will have to go out
of business.

But Marian turned out to be very likable, and a few years
later when she was living in Paris, adored by George I of
Greece, she and I became good friends and met frequently.

I have said that England, following the lead of Edward,
was gambling-mad. The really big gambling sport of the day,
however, was not racing or games but speculation in stocks,
and it was played not on the turf or on green baize but in
hotel rooms and restaurants and around directors' tables.
Wildcat schemes of every sort were being promoted glibly,
and there seemed to be no end of suckers. Money was dirt
cheap. The favorite get-rich-quick plan was to invest in
mines. Mining engineers from all over the world were flock-
ing to London. You could take your choice of silver in South
America, gold in Australia, emeralds in India, or diamonds
in South Africa.

The Hotel Cecil on the Strand was the hangout of American promoters, some of whom were selling mines by the
layer, one above the other. Every one of these experts had
his own little package of clay which, if you could believe
him, was proof of a fortune kicking around loose somewhere.
Promoters stood the treats—and what treats!—for prospective investors, and each new prospect was an excuse for a
lavish affair. Their usual stunt was to call on their American
showgirl friends to help entertain the suckers, and we girls of

the *Belle of New York* company attended innumerable elaborate luncheon and supper parties. When one of the ventures panned out, we would be handed suitable remembrances—a valuable block of stock, or sometimes an envelope with a thousand pounds enclosed—and there was always the opportunity to "get in on the ground floor."

If only I had acted on some of the tips I picked up during that winter I might have become very wealthy indeed. At first I was not particularly interested; possibly my Wherry inheritance still seemed large enough. Later, when my gambling instincts warmed up, I took a few flyers, two of which turned out very favorably. On the advice of Lawrence Goldstone, one of my engineer friends, I bought some Boulder Main Reefs stock on which I realized a quick and painless profit of forty thousand dollars; on another block of mining shares I made fifteen thousand. Then I really plunged, as all London was doing. I invested half of my whole fortune, seventy-five thousand dollars, in the Great Fingal Mines. But of that later.

One day in the fall of 1898 I received an invitation to a dinner at Willis's Rooms, signed by ten of London's biggest financiers and mining experts. These men—I called them my "syndicate"—were all close friends of mine, and many of the big deals they handled were discussed and settled in my little apartment in the Walsingham.

This apartment was very conveniently arranged. It was on the ground floor and had three entrances. It could be reached directly from the street, and also by the Piccadilly and Arlington Street entrances to the hotel. In those boom times financiers knew that a great many people were watching their movements. Often it was enough for two or three speculators to be observed in conversation to cause important rises or falls in stocks in which they were concerned, so an apartment like mine, offering easy entrance and quick exit, was an ideal haven of safety for quiet talks. There no word even of a meeting would leak out.

One of the "syndicate" was John Hays Hammond, always the ladies' man. Hammond was then making London his headquarters in connection with the Consolidated Goldfields of South Africa, and his influence was enormous both in prestige and in money. Another was that tragic figure, Whitaker Wright, who had promoted the London tubes, a Titan of finance. The big West Australian gold boom was on then, and Wright shortly afterwards became entangled in an undertaking of questionable repute. When he was brought to court in connection with the alleged fraud, he refused to give evidence that would implicate any one of his friends. He escaped his own jail sentence only by committing suicide as he left the dock—by means of prussic acid in the end of his cigar.

Yerkes, a partner of Wright in building the tubes, was one of the group; another was Frank Gardner, charming and retiring. Gardner's photograph had just been published as that of one of the seven richest men in the world.

Then there was plump, genial Horatio Bottomley, looking like John Bull himself, the picture of rock-ribbed honesty. At that time he was staggering the imagination of the whole British Empire with his promotion of West Australia enterprises, but unfortunately he eventually promoted himself into penal servitude. Big, breezy Dick Dickerson from New Zealand and the Australian Rudolph Henning, both very wealthy owners of Australian mines, were associated with Bottomley.

At the dinner to which these financiers invited me I received another evidence of the generosity I have mentioned. One of my hosts rose and with a very charming presentation speech put into my hand a small box. I opened the box to discover a gift from the entire syndicate—a string of pearls.

But that night at Willis's is memorable for something far

more valuable to me even than a string of pearls, for it was on that night that my lifelong friendship with Lord Kitchener began. Kitchener, the fighter of dervishes, was at that time Sirdar of the Egyptian Army. He had just finished his great campaign against Omdurman and was the idol of every English heart. Everywhere I had heard the most incredible tales of his adventures in the desert.

I remember him as he looked that night, tall, square-shouldered, and very imposing in his scarlet uniform. He wore a heavy mustache, but the dominating feature of his face was his steel-blue eyes, brilliant and piercing and authoritative.

Kitchener was a man of tremendous drive, burdened with heavy responsibilities, moving always in a glare of publicity. I think he found me a novelty, with my Kansas accent and my conviction that the world was my oyster. Chiefly, however, I suppose it was because our personalities "clicked" that this great soldier and empire-builder came so often to my little apartment that fall. We had long, long talks, for Kitchener, contrary to the impression the public had formed of him, was not taciturn but talkative, even humorous. He drew me out, and soon I was daring to express myself freely with him.

Once I even ventured to spoof him a little about his reputation for sternness. How had a man so genial, I asked, ever acquired such an habitually fierce expression? Then he told me the story. When he was a very young man on a surveying expedition in Palestine, he had noticed that subordinates jumped noticeably faster at his commands when he flashed full on them his frightening blue gaze. So he had deliberately cultivated the art of giving orders with flashing eyes. Over many years, he sighed, he feared he had not only frightened subordinates but scared away some of his equals as well. The man unquestionably had hypnotic power. Let him but look at me and I wanted to do as he wished. I think he liked it that I was never afraid of him or his great fame but treated him as simply and casually as I did all the others. He used to like to tap at my window of an evening, after finishing one of his innumerable official engagements, and come in and lounge an hour or two in complete relaxation. Slouched in his chair, his long legs sprawled out before him, he seemed to fill my small sitting room.

There was never the slightest hint of romance between Kitchener and me. The strange and wonderful friendship that developed out of our chance meeting was all the more remarkable because by popular report Kitchener was a woman-hater. I think if I had made any seductive advances he would have vanished overnight, never to be seen again. Instead he remained my friend throughout all three of my Continental marriages, even making a special trip across the Channel on one of his visits home in order to meet my last husband.

But if at one end of my scale of friends was Lord Kitchener, completely platonic, there was at the other end a sentimental youth, son of a well-known solicitor to the Bank of England, who was completely enamoured. He was determined to put me on a pedestal, and he wooed me with pink-and-white Victorian devotion. The new phrase "naughty but nice" distressed him. He wanted me always nice and never naughty. From his point of view niceness would consist of my leading a cloistered life, my only thrill the daily bouquet of lilies-of-the-valley that he brought to my apartment every morning.

One day when he discovered that I had been out with someone else the night before, he was broken-hearted and tried to exact from me a promise never to do such a cruel thing again. In sheer softness of heart I made the promise, fingers crossed, but the suspicion of my naughtiness continued to haunt him and to determine whether I was keeping my word or not he devised a most ingenious scheme.

One evening my maid Annie observed him sealing my

apartment door with a postage stamp. She knew that when I came in late from a supper at the Savoy that night the postage stamp would be torn and my duplicity exposed. So to save the boy heartache when he came next morning with my bouquet the poor girl sat up until I returned, then leaned far out the window and replaced his torn stamp with another just like it. This went on for weeks, to my amusement and Annie's continued loss of sleep.

I told Kitchener the story the last time he came to see me before he returned to Egypt. I could see that he was amused too, but nevertheless sympathetic with the puppy-love suffering of the youth. On that particular night as Kitchener left we looked to see if the pink stamp had already been affixed. Sure enough, and broken by Kitchener's exit. When Annie went to get another stamp to replace it, she found that I had none of that color.

For a moment it looked as if the game were up. But Kitchener was too good a strategist to see me lose the battle of wits. Late as it was, he took a cab to his club just to get a stamp of the right color, returned with it, and with many chuckles said another good-by and sealed me in.

It was shortly before Kitchener left that I had bought my turquoise mine. Since I had listened unmoved to so many hysterical prospectuses regarding diamonds and emeralds, it might be supposed that I had become immune to fairy-tale descriptions of heaps of glittering gems lying in some remote spot just waiting to be garnered. But while ordinary people were satisfying themselves by staking claims on lost temples in India, I must have been waiting for something really spectacular to come along. It came, in the form of the historic mines of the Pharaohs, located in Arabia, those mines from which Egyptian rulers for centuries had dug turquoises to decorate themselves and their palaces. All that was needed, I was assured, was to dynamite the desert off these extinct enterprises and turquoises could be shoveled up by the barrel. Admittedly, there was the slight matter of dynamiting; and before that, the problem of getting a concession.

My fancy was so captured by the idea of becoming the turquoise queen of all time that these problems seemed to me no more than slight formalities. I pictured myself dripping turquoises from head to foot; I wallowed in imagined profits. As to concessions and dynamiting, Kitchener I knew would be able to give me good advice.

"Dynamite the desert!" he scoffed. "Just about as profitable as plowing the ocean!"

But I had swallowed the bait and I was firmly hooked. I replied merely by asking how I might get a concession. Lord Kitchener, ever generous with his time and prestige, promised reluctantly that he would help me and he kept his word.

It was about the time this fantastic deal was simmering on the fire that I met Prince Edward. Lord William Beresford and Lord Charles Beresford, both men of middle years who were friendly with the Prince and shared Edward's passion for horse racing and betting, had begun taking me to the races at Sandown, Ascot, and Goodwood. Society of course was out in full force those hot summer afternoons, the lawns dotted with men in blue serge and white duck and women under picture hats and lacy parasols. One day at Sandown, as we were crossing the lawns, Lord Bill Beresford exclaimed: "Look, here comes the Prince!"

Sure enough, there was the famous personality coming directly toward us, accompanied by two of his intimates. One, Lord Lonsdale, known as the Dean of the Turf, florid as a butcher, was a figure not to be overlooked in his lemon coat and startling plaids. Behind him towered the Portuguese Marquis de Soveral, big-nosed, dark, and heavy-set. The Marquis was reputed to be a special favorite of Edward's because of his never-failing flow of risqué anecdotes. The Prince seemed to be in high spirits; when I came to know him better I learned that his special gift for appearing always to be enjoying himself was a large part of his magnetic charm.

"I'm going to present you," Beresford whispered.

Of course I was frightened. "What shall I do?"

"Just be yourself. He is sure to like you."

I gasped through the presentation, which included a democratic handshake, but Edward's eyes twinkled so kindly at me that I was soon "myself," as Beresford had advised. It was hard to feel too much awe in the presence of that genial smile.

Just then a majestic woman holding a lorgnette swept by.

"Looking very county as usual," Beresford remarked.

I couldn't resist inquiring what "county" meant.

"It means," said Beresford, "that her pearls are real but her hair is a mess."

At this Edward exploded loudly and then asked me how I liked the county sort.

"The few Englishwomen I've met, Your Highness, seem to keep their smiles on ice," I replied.

He laughed again. "England's not all dull," he said, "and I fancy you'll find the brighter side of it."

This was the first but not the last of my meetings with His Royal Highness. I had become acquainted with so many of Edward's friends that it was only natural that the Prince and I should encounter each other often at races, receptions, and suppers. Beauty suppers were as popular in London as in New York, probably because of the Prince's interest in the so-called professional beauty, and many of these charmers, both English and American, were also members of circles in which Edward moved. Although in public he was always very dignified with his intimates, as I met him he was usually in a frivolous mood.

He seemed to take no precautions to avoid being recognized as he went about London, although when the coachman of the royal coupé was seen without cockade it was un-

derstood that eyes were to turn the other way. There was a
report that three or four gentlemen in society were very vain
over the accidental resemblance they bore to the Prince and
took pride in dressing and walking like him, so much so that
it was not always easy at a glance to identify each one with
certainty.

The extreme freedom which Edward exercised in his personal life gave rise to many racy anecdotes regarding his
amours, real or supposed. Edward was aware of his reputation as a Don Juan and once, after I had become well acquainted with him, he made a laughing reference to the as-
tronomical numbers of his supposed illegitimate children.

"My word!" he protested. "If all the stories they tell about
me were true, I should never have been seen outside a
boudoir!"

4 *The More Abundant Life*

All around me showgirl friends were chatting as casually of
Paris and Monte Carlo as I might have talked at home about
Chicago and Philadelphia. I began to feel provincial. Within
a few months after landing in England I saw that to keep up
with my set I simply had to have a whirl at the Continent.
My earlier visit to Paris with Mr. Sassoon had introduced me
to a few smart dress shops. But I wanted to learn Paris from
the inside.

Before poor Annie knew what had happened to her, she
found herself unpacking my trunks in the Ritz while I leaned
out the window trying to swallow all of Paris in one gulp.
Down in the street a raucous voice was crying *"La Presse!"*
and for years afterwards, whenever I heard that paper
shouted, it brought back vividly my first excitement at being
on my own in Paris.

Next morning, when streams of people came knocking at my door and I couldn't tell what they were trying to sell me, I knew I had been born in the wrong country. No getting away from it—if I wanted my share of fun in the most fun-loving city on earth, I'd have to learn French.

The few verbs and nouns left over from convent days barely served to buy me a couple of grammars. With *French While You Wait* and *French Made Easy* spread before me I plunged in head first. I find it hard to be polite to people who pretend they had no difficulty in learning French. I found it excruciatingly difficult. Twenty times a day I would ask Annie if she had seen the umbrella of my aunt and assure her that I was going well, but I still couldn't order a meal or buy a hat.

Finally I engaged two Frenchwomen and made them talk to me constantly, in two-hour relays. I got a flat off the Champs Élysées and settled down to boning. For weeks I hunched my back over those hellish conjugations. Then I located a good tutor and he pulled me through the more hellish subjunctive. My accent, I could tell, was pure Fiji. But finally I was able to read *La Vie Parisienne,* and when I found myself swearing at an impertinent coachman I knew I was over the hump.

I loved Paris; it was such a fervent city. After the clipped correctness of British speech, the lilt in French voices charmed me. Paris seized me for her own.

London beaus dropped in whenever they made trips across. All the time I was getting acquainted with the language, they were getting me acquainted with the famous restaurants and show places.

Café society glittered with royalty, and with the exquisitely dressed and jeweled women who accompanied royalty. In those days kings were not, as today, rare as baby pandas. That winter eight crowned heads, or heirs apparent, were amusing themselves in Paris.

King Leopold II of Belgium, a very likable old fellow, was seen everywhere with Cléo de Mérode, *première danseuse* of the Opera, at whose feet he was laying fortunes mulcted from the enslavement of the Congo. Cléo wore her glossy black hair parted in the middle and drawn tightly over her ears into a knot at the nape of her neck. She did it that way because she had ugly ears which stood out from her head. An old nurse had neglected to tie them down when she was in her crib, and this oversight became responsible for a fashion which circled the globe. Women everywhere—whether their features were long and peaked or round and puckcheeked, whether their eyes were bug or shrunken—began to stare out from a frame of hair pulled tightly over perfectly good ears.

The young King of Portugal was winding larger and larger pearls around Gaby de Lys' small throat. (It was his brother who later married the beautiful charmer Nevada Hays.) Edward of England, when bent on strictly private business, used the name of the Duke of Lancaster, but he was easily enough recognized. His brother-in-law, George, King of Greece, was often with him. The Kings of Spain and Sweden were in town, and the Khedive of Egypt, and the little King of Siam, Prajadhipok, with his Eastern retinue. With a sprinkling of Indian princes and a liberal measure of Russian grand dukes added, the café social pie was pretty high flavored.

Rich Americans were plentiful. They nudged into the spotlight by the free way they were spending fortunes made in railroads, steel, oil. They had no sense of inferiority. As a matter of fact, many were extremely civilized and sophisticated. Harry K. Thaw was there that winter with his pretty bride, Evelyn Nesbit. I first saw them sitting in the Café de Paris, Evelyn wearing a becoming bonnet tied under her chin with a large bow at one side.

Billy Leeds, Sr., the tinplate king, amused himself by distributing huge diamond hearts profusely among the heartless ladies. One day when I was lunching with Billy at the Ritz I found a small package by my plate. I hated to open it, for I knew the satin case contained one of those vulgar lumps that almost every woman of my acquaintance was wearing. After lunch Billy took me to Tiffany's to buy a chain. A relative of my family, Will Sleater, who worked at Tiffany's, helped us select it and then stood by smiling while Billy hung the garish thing about my neck—he knew Billy bought hearts wholesale. I felt as if I were sporting a locomotive headlight.

I was with Billy the day he met the woman he afterwards married and widowed, Nonnie May Stewart. Nonnie, one of the many strikingly lovely American women who decorated the European playground in the Nineties, was originally a barefooted country miss from Zanesville, Ohio, a hoyden who wore her hair in pigtails and climbed trees with boys. (Strangely enough, one of the boys who used to carry her books to school was destined to become my third husband.) That afternoon at Armenonville, where he was taking a crowd of us to tea—the French had not yet learned to cocktail—Billy fell hard for this charmer. Her social climbing proved to be as good as her tree-climbing, for eventually she landed in the topmost branches as wife of Prince Christopher of Greece, where she was henceforth known under the impressive title of Princess Anastasia!

In spite of the fact that so many European courtesans have been American-born, the genus courtesan has never flourished on this side of the Atlantic. It was on the other side that I discovered them as a class, those brilliant women who wielded such influence in the Edwardian scene.

Noah Webster defines a courtesan as "a loose woman"; Larousse states that she is a woman distinguished by her "elegance and wit." From the flicker of kerosene to the glare of neon, I have had the honor—or dishonor, according to the point of view—of knowing intimately many of my famous courtesan contemporaries. I have witnessed their conquests of the hearts of famous men; the brilliant marriages of many; the fortunes in money and jewels acquired by most; the luxurious lives lived by all.

If I express admiration for the drama these witty and elegant women afforded and describe the extent to which I shared their fortunes, let not the aspiring hordes of amateur Circes in every town in America—potential recipients of a pair of nylon stockings and a three-dollar dinner—conclude with some wishful thinking that they are the stuff courtesans are made of. The courtesan, alas, is gone, extinct as the American buffalo.

Most of these enchantresses of kings and statesmen had risen from humble origin, even poverty, to lives of regal magnificence—a pattern that has been evident through the ages. Thaïs, Phryne, Theodora, Nell Gwynn, Madame DuBarry, Lola Montez—all rose from obscurity.

To bait and catch the male has always been woman's first and most natural interest in life. But to be outstandingly lovely and beguiling, to inspire more than passing desire, to win and hold men's minds as their hearts, requires technique. With the siren it becomes an art.

All the courtesans I knew in Europe captivated by their art of graciousness even more than by their beauty. Even after one had left a room, you could still feel the touch of her irresistible personality.

They lived by the art of daring. Imaginative and adventuresome, they had the vision to play for big stakes and the mettle to publicize themselves by showy splendor. No columnist or press agent wrote the story or beat the drum of the famous courtesan. She dramatized her own life, created her own role. Her original, recherché clothes, her bearing, her manners—even her eccentricities—she magnified to fullest advantage.

In Paris I found a distinction drawn between the demimondaine, a product of her glands, and the courtesan, an expression of personality. A courtesan and a mistress are types as far apart as the poles. Anyone can become a mistress; one has to be born a courtesan. Ladies of the half-world, whom George Moore called the *"haute cocotterie,"* might live in great luxury, but their protectors were usually wealthy vulgarians who required no mental stimulation or subtlety— only possession.

The courtesan never became a personal possession. She knew that her sponsor was an escapist, weary of the unsophisticate. She took him out of the temperate regions in which he lived into a torrid zone of voluptuousness. But all the formalities were punctiliously observed; the lover was guest rather than master of her house. It takes a very big man to stay in the background of his own show.

Courtesans were often scintillating in conversation. Quick as a whip in repartee, with a wit as effervescent as champagne, they nevertheless could be serious when occasion demanded, or even silent when men talked of things that mattered. Frequently they were confidantes of the men they attracted. In their salons, from five to ten, would be found diplomats, writers, distinguished foreigners, fashionable women. Their gift for harmonizing different interests was what made sovereigns relax with them and lesser nobles sigh for them. It was tantamount to a certificate of good standing to be found in the drawing room of the reigning royal favorite, whose health was always the toast after the king's at all smart gatherings.

The famous beauty of those days held a position that no longer exists. When she appeared in public she was almost mobbed. The most conservative people stood on chairs or tables to catch a glimpse of her; respectable families waited long hours just to see her carriage rumble through the streets.

Nothing in my memory is more thrilling than the remembrance of Paris in June, with the horse chestnuts in flower,

and those world-famous beauties on parade. Up the Champs
Élysées in their shining victorias, enveloped in feathers and
laces, trailing clouds of perfume, whirled those truly glamorous women. They were a dying race, though none would
then have believed it.

Following in their scented wake, I heaped myself with just
as much lace and just as many feathers. It was the day of the
grande toilette. Gowns offered a lot for the money. Every
dress had its lining, with embroidered-in whalebones. Designers thought nothing of loading on one evening dress gold
lace and bangles, and masses of tiny ruffles on the inside of
the skirt and the long train.

The *Grande Semaine* was the fashion show of the social
year, and then the rush on Paris dressmakers was fierce. Exclusive designers worked for months in advance. Such sophisticated, cosmopolitan, richly and meticulously dressed
crowds Paris has never seen since. During the Big Week
there was racing every day in the vicinity of Paris, and every
night both winners and losers celebrated.

The racing crowd I knew in London came over for the
week—Lord Lonsdale, the Marquis de Soveral, Sir Philip
Sassoon, Sir Donald Stewart, Lord Athlumney, and Freddy
Guest; and six Guardsmen, including Sir George Prescott,
Spender Clay, and Gerald Paget—all young, all tall and
slender and blue-eyed, the Guardsman type.

John Drew invited me to one of his jolly supper parties
where the guests included royalty, courtesans, and stage
stars. Actors and actresses then were at their highest point
of prestige and a halo shone around everything theatrical.
Lucien Guitry was there, looking like a prosperous businessman, and I met Réjane for the first time, fiery and spanky
as a bobtailed pony.

The high light of the week was "The Drags," the coaching
party specially gotten up for women of fashion. I had been
invited by a wealthy Belgian admirer, Florent Lambert,

who kept a fancy string of horses and with whom I often went driving. On Drags Day the topflight sportsmen would assemble their own four-horse coaches in the Place de la Concorde. There the four-in-hands, with a dozen or more guests loaded on each coach, would form into a procession and take the road to Longchamps—bands playing, post horns blaring, banners fluttering.

The night before my first Drags, I dined with all six of my big blond Guardsmen. When the boys learned that immediately after dinner I was due at Beer's for a final fitting on the gown I was to wear next day, they insisted I take them along.

Miss Barton, head saleswoman at Beer's, was more like a schoolmistress than an exponent of fashion, dressed always in British tweeds with stiff collar and cravat, and well used to the client who came for fittings accompanied by the checkbook in person. She had a wonderful insight into bank accounts and saw to it that her customers ordered right to the limit. She ought to do a good job on six checkbooks, I thought.

But that night it was Beer himself who came in to superintend my final fitting. Beer was one of those couturiers who considered that the designer who creates a woman's dress is as much an artist as the portrait painter who reproduces it. He took one look at the outfit they put on me and wrung his graceful hands.

"Ah, *non, non!* This dress is not for Madame. Take it off, someone—take it off!"

"But M. Beer," I protested, "I must have a dress for tomorrow!"

"No matter—I cannot permit Madame to wear this one! I will create another. Quick—bring me some materials!"

The offending costume was hurriedly stripped off me, and the dozen or so women and girls who danced attendance on M. Beer's every waking moment scurried away for more materials. Soon they were back, staggering under bolts and bolts of silks and laces. One after another these fabrics were draped over my torso, while M. Beer bit his nails and frowned and shook his head. The pile of rejected materials grew higher and higher and the excited seamstresses' hands began to tremble. Somebody opened the door to ask a question. Beer clutched his side as if he had been wounded by a spearthrust.

"*Nom de Dieu!* Do you not see that I am composing?" he screamed. "Ah, Madame, these stupid creatures!—Go on, go on! *Non, non,* that is not right. Go on, go on—ah, wait! Let me see that again! *Oui, oui—ça y est! Ça y est!*" and M. Beers clasped his hands rapturously.

At this moment one of the fitters had the misfortune to drop her shears. Beer took his face in his hands.

"It is too much! She knows the one thing I cannot stand when I am creating is the clashing of shears! Take her away!"

This scene of course had provided my Guards with such superlative amusement that they refused to leave until the work of "creation" was completed. While the whole shop was turned loose on my finery, the boys and I had a late supper at the Café de Paris and then returned for my next fitting. This time the boys, knowing that the women and girls in the shop were going to have to make a night of it, arranged a little fun on the side. On their heels followed waiters bringing mountains of cakes and baskets of champagne, and then ensued what was probably the maddest night in the history of M. Beer's establishment.

Little French seamstresses, who had probably never tasted anything more exciting than *vin ordinaire* found their spirits suddenly soaring. Instead of considering it a hardship to work all night, they pinned and stitched with a zeal and an inspiration they had never known before. Machines whirred and corks popped and jokes and laughter crackled all over the shop. It was as much of an adventure to the Guards as it was to the girls. When the final fitting came, the boys peeled me down to my richly embroidered lingerie, M. Beer hooked me into the new gown, and the whole staff—by then much exhilarated—cheered wildly.

The dress turned out to be a guipure-lace over flesh-colored silk, inset with hand-painted orchids. Someone had even found time to hand-decorate a parasol to match. The hat was pink tulle, gold-threaded, and ornamented with tiny black ostrich plumes.

I am afraid some of the girls came out of the affair with headaches. I came out with one of Beer's choicest, the boys with a sense of winning for the old school, don't you know, but it was Beer who really came out on top. His saleswoman had not lost sight of the fact that this was the psychological moment to turn an honest franc, and while the boys had been plying her with champagne, Miss Barton had been plying the boys with suggestions for suitable accessories. As a result, I departed in a cab filled to the roof with hats, parasols, handkerchiefs, perfumes, scarfs, and what-have-you.

Toward the end of the *Grande Semaine* it was the fashion to relax by taking long drives through the Bois behind fast, high-stepping horses. As I was cooling off one evening behind a lively pair of roans, I heard a sepulchral voice beside my carriage: "Tonight at twelve at Cubat's!"

I turned, startled, and recognized a tall figure on horseback. It was Harry Thaw. When he saw that I understood his message, he laughed and galloped on to the next carriage and the next, repeating the announcement in the same doleful chant. Soon all up and down the Avenue des Acacias acquaintances were waving to each other and bandying the password: "Tonight at twelve at Cubat's! Be sure you're there!"

Everyone was intrigued by the manner of giving the invitation. Thaw was known to be an eccentric, but to a playboy with his millions many eccentricities could be forgiven. Cubat's was then one of the smartest restaurants, operated by an ex-chef of the Czar's, in a house originally built for the famous courtesan Païva. The alabaster staircase and gold-carved balustrade were sensational.

I attended with the Duc de Morny, Fanny Ward, and Fanny's husband Joe Lewis. We arrived promptly at midnight to find that tables had been laid in the garden for a very large party. In the moonlight the scene was enchantingly beautiful. The meal progressed in jollity until cigars, coffee, and liqueurs were passed.

Suddenly our host rose from his place, his face like a thundercloud. "The party is finished. Get out!" he roared.

Everyone sat for a moment, stunned.

"It's all over! Go home!" he bellowed again.

The whole company rose without a word. As we filed out quietly, the Duc de Morny whispered that Thaw, seeing one of his guests help himself to a handful of cigars, had been seized with one of his uncontrollable black rages.

While I had been kicking up my heels in Paris, I had nevertheless not forgotten my grandiose scheme to become the turquoise queen of all time. When the word finally came from Kitchener that my concession had been secured, I immediately notified the great London mining firm of Bewick, Moreing & Company, who had the matter of my mine in charge, that I would like an expedition arranged to begin operations and that I would accompany the expedition in person. Strenuous objections were promptly raised to the practicability of a woman, even an owner, accompanying a crew of young engineers into the Arabian desert. I was adamant, however, and went ahead with elaborate preparations for the trip, including plans for a stopover in Cairo.

5 *Fleshpots of Egypt*

Cairo in the Nineties was a garrison town, where a crack British regiment was stationed. Often when the horses had been too slow or the cards too swift, young officers were glad to be transferred to Cairo where they could retrench on expenses and catch up with their bills. In spite of the fact that these wayward sons of good families had a reputation for being always broke, what was known as the "fishing fleet"—shiploads of English girls, chaperoned by hopeful mammas—used to set out for Egypt every winter for a season of husband-fishing. In the spring, when the fleet sailed home, all the eligibles who had escaped the dragnet used to toast their delivery in champagne.

I could imagine the homegrown entertainment the English colony would go in for—polo and tennis, tea drinking and gossiping. I wanted none of that. Besides, what good were the men if they were penniless? Egyptian aristocrats were known to be very rich. I preferred finding out what Egyptian men were like. I wanted the Cairo that was not in the guidebooks.

Before I left London, when I was talking one day to Mr. Preston, secretary to Prince Hussein of Egypt, I told him of my approaching visit.

"Do I have to see Cairo like a visiting schoolmarm from the windows of a hotel? Isn't there some way I can see Egyptian life from the inside?"

In answer to this plea Preston gave me a letter of introduction to famous "Daddy" Longworth and—this was beyond all my dreams of good luck—also arranged for me to occupy one of Prince Hussein's villas.

It was my habit in those days to carry with me yards and yards of lace, satin bed covers, and even satin floor pillows in colors to match any decorator's scheme. These I scattered in profusion through my hotel rooms or apartments. To dress in the midst of such showy luxuries gave me the feeling that I was a picture in a gilded frame; it bolstered my ego. In Prince Hussein's villa, however, I had no need of such accessories for an exotic background. When I stepped into my bath, I thought I was stepping into Cleopatra's own—the mosaic floor, the great peacock spreading its tail over a velvet couch, and everywhere the smoking bowls of incense.

The rooms of the villa were large and lofty, kept in perfect order and mosquelike silence by Arab servants who padded noiselessly about over the marble floors. I never quite got used to all their embarrassing attentions, especially to their habit of thrusting a tiny cup of thick Turkish coffee at me every few minutes. It seemed to make no difference to them that I never drank the stuff.

I was much impressed when I learned that Prince Hussein had given me not only beautiful horses to ride behind but

also a handsome *sais*—a youth with bare brown legs who
ran leaping and shouting ahead of the carriage to command
the crowds to make way. You needed a *sais* in Cairo. The
streets were jammed—camels, donkeys, dogs; victorias, bi-
cycles; water-sellers with dangling cups; vendors of rugs,
scarabs, brass, all yelling their wares; patriarchal sheiks,
Nubians, veiled women, smart English officers; and everywhere—darting in and out of the traffic, under the very
hoofs of the horses—the beggars, the cripples, the children,
with their eternal "gimme" cry of *"Baksheesh!"* At night my
sais carried a torch, and under its wild, flickering light a
ride was mysteriously thrilling.

If London had been a comforting gin and bitters, and
Paris a heady champagne, Cairo was like a legendary nectar,
at once exciting and subtle.

When I first looked on the yellow-blue waters of the historic Nile, I thought of the bulrushes and wondered if a
tourist guide would be able to show me where the world's
most celebrated foundling was fished out. Then I fell to
picturing to myself the gilded barge in which the greatest
courtesan of all time had long ago floated down these same
jeweled waters, under this same golden sunshine. Barges
still floated on the Nile, only the Egyptians called them
dahabeahs. The dahabeah seemed to me the most enticing
thing ever devised, something like a houseboat, with peaked,
slanting sails; luxurious, loafy, and soul-inviting. Never once
did it enter my head that my own barge would one day
follow in Cleo's royal ripples.

David Garrick Longworth, to whom I presented my letter
of introduction from Mr. Preston, was known lovingly
around the world as "Daddy." The day I first met him I felt
his immense personal charm. Circus-born Daddy was a
showman par excellence, a world-traveled Bohemian who
had settled in Egypt. When Theodore Roosevelt went into
Africa on his big-game expedition, it was Daddy who was

selected to make all arrangements for the trip. Preston had said that he could show me behind the scenes better than anyone in Cairo. Sure enough, Daddy obligingly trotted out all the Egyptians he knew—and a few others—and I began to get around.

Racing in Cairo was even more fascinating than in England or in Paris. Under the tropical skies, among the stately palms, Mussulmans in fiery red tarbooshes mingled with English officers in smart white uniforms. Women trailed their long lace skirts over the lawns, while the gentle breeze off the Nile played among the plumes on their large hats. Their gem-studded collars, belts, and parasols glittering in the African sun outshone the trotting harnesses of the horses. Fortunately my own trappings were dazzling enough to assure me many a jingling entrance into these colorful race-track gatherings.

There's a sexy atmosphere in Cairo. All around you are sighs and passionate glances. Latticed harem windows suggest the countless sex intrigues going on behind those bars, within those dim interiors. You get sex from the flattery of the Egyptian men, who are anything but goody-goody. Perhaps it's partly in the climate, or in the old, old civilization. Anyway, it's there, and very soon you feel yourself falling under the spell. Even a grandmother would long for a lover in Cairo.

Lovers are not hard to come by; Egyptian gentlemen are very impressionable. Their ritual of flirtation is the simplest in the world. They begin by much hand-kissing. Then they load you with incredibly silly compliments. Their small talk is the smallest I have ever heard. They love to say nothings and laugh at nothings, like very young children. Not a sensible word could I ever get from any of them. If I asked an Egyptian what he was laughing at, he would say he didn't know. So then I would laugh too, and say I didn't know. We had wonderful times.

There is so much witchery in the air of Cairo that almost any man passes for a romantic figure. Later on, when I was back in London or Paris and one of these romantics would show up for a visit, it was often a great shock to me to see what an awful person he really was in frock coat and top hat, fat and greasy and silly-looking, with a vulgar, heavy gold watch chain festooned across a pudgy belly.

One day I told Daddy that I had had all the tent-peggings and love-makings I wanted, and wasn't there something really sensational he could suggest. He thought a moment and then said he guessed Ibrahim Bey Cherif, one of the richest noblemen in Cairo, was my man.

Next morning a tarbooshed Egyptian aristocrat was bowing over my hand and kissing it and begging in choicest Oxford English for my company on a ride to the Pyramids.

The Bey called for me with a six-in-hand instead of a four. This was outdoing the Drags. I was dressed up to the occasion with Beer's most startling coaching outfit. It was fawn-colored, with red velvet collar and cuffs, gold-embroidered, a red hat and red shoes. Knowing Egyptian men's tastes, I didn't forget even on such a sporting occasion to drench myself in strong perfume.

As a charioteer, Ben Hur was just a Ding-dong Daddy on a Toonerville trolley compared to Ibrahim Cherif. From the moment we lunged off to the moment we hauled to a stop before the Sphinx, the Bey kept the foaming horses at a dead gallop. Camel trains scattered before us like chickens before a Cadillac. I had only two concerns—to hang on to the seat and my smile at the same time. Across the Nile Bridge, down the road Ismail built overnight to please the caprice of a favorite concubine, the hoofs clattered, the whip cracked, the horns blared. I wondered Old Lady Sphinx didn't raise her paws in consternation at this disrespectful approach to her inscrutability.

The drive back was just as fast, but this time I settled myself to watch my seat and never mind the smile. All Egyptians are speed-mad. They never seem to think of horses as flesh and blood, but always lash the poor beasts into a breakneck pace.

Next night the Bey arranged a dinner party in his palace. The dining room had an almost religious atmosphere, with its Moorish arches supported by slender columns and its churchlike lamps hanging from the ceiling. The dinner was a strictly Egyptian affair—in those days the British and the Egyptians did not mix socially—and, except for myself, strictly masculine. I was the only woman among twenty red-fezzed Moslems. In Egypt the men apparently speak the first language that comes into their heads. Remembering my awful struggle with French, it maddened me to hear these men glide so easily from Arabic and Turkish into Italian or German or French.

After dinner my host asked if I would like to visit his harem. Would I! With a stepped-up heartbeat I crossed the bridge of sighs that leads from the real world into that half-world of the oriental woman. The strapping eunuch who guarded the entrance rolled his eyes slightly as I passed. I wondered if he might clap the door on me.

Inside, in the soft light and the haze of cigarette smoke and incense, I had to wait a moment until my eyes could take in the scene. Everything was too something. The carpet was too gaudy, the walls too gold; the wives too fat and sluggish, their dresses too voluminous, their hands and arms too weighted with barbaric filigree; the atmosphere too thick.

The Bey's ladies were disenchantingly taking their ease on bright-colored couches. Most of them were stuffing themselves with sweets, or drinking the caffein concentrate they call coffee, or smoking. Only one of them, probably Number One Girl, sat up and offered me a cup of coffee and a cigarette. Either the others were too indolent to more than glance at me, or perhaps it was not their prerogative to offer hospitality. The Bey introduced me to an interpreter, then abandoned me.

Conversation was difficult. The women were not interested in anything I said. The only things they enjoyed about me were my dress and my jewels. I was wearing a gown of gold cloth over which floated a silver gauze. They fingered the long train, and the ribbons, and the rhinestone studdings, and the sequins. (At that time I was given to wearing as much jewelry as a snake charmer—I smile now when I look at my photographs of the period.) The childlike creatures caressed and examined minutely my bracelets and the pearl necklace my syndicate had given me, and Billy Leeds' diamond heart, and my big rings. They even lifted my skirts and squealed over my trailing lace-trimmed petticoats.

While I was letting myself be pawed over as Exhibit A, I was examining the examiners with equal curiosity. There are doubtless harems and harems, just as there are homes and homes, but looking at Ibrahim Cherif's collection of wives and concubines, I couldn't help feeling the Bey hadn't done too well for himself. All my illusions of the beauty and seductiveness hidden in the Eastern seraglio took flight out the latticed window. My first disillusionment was to discover that the *yazmak*—the gauze veil the Egyptian woman wore over her mouth—was a glamour necessity. If a few modern dentists could ever be turned loose in those Eastern countries, they would make fortunes. Not an upper set in the lot. And what fat! Even in the day of the bounteous bosom and swelling hip, these women were oversized. They were a startling object lesson of what luxury and laziness can do to the female form.

It was a relief to find myself out in the night air again. My host and I recrossed the bridge and joined the other guests in a balcony overlooking the courtyard of the palace. The Bey had promised a "feast for the howling dervishes"

as the evening's entertainment, and the banquet was about
to begin. Down in the yard about a hundred dervishes had
been swaying and moaning in self-hypnotic frenzy for the
past eight hours; the light of flickering torches played over
their rhythmic naked bodies. The Bey explained that these
men were deeply religious and were putting themselves
into a trancelike state to prove that man can be exalted to
a point beyond good and evil.

Soon after we were all seated, a servant entered the yard
carrying a large basket. This he placed on the ground,
gingerly opened the top, and then scuttled. From the
basket hundreds of small snakes quickly uncoiled themselves and started darting about among the swaying figures.
Immediately each exalted soul reached for a snake, lifted it
high in the air, and bit off its head. The courtyard became
a welter of headless snakes writhing in contortions of death,
while the dervishes with dripping jaws calmly chewed up
and swallowed their bloody tidbits.

Ibrahim Cherif chortled with delight at the evident effect
the entertainment was having on his American sensation-
seeker.

"But wait!" he cried. "These are only the hors d'oeuvres.
The next course is better."

Servants were bringing in a huge red-hot brazier which
they placed in the middle of the crowd. Extending from
the fire were the handles of a dozen or more swords, and as
the dervishes pulled the swords from the fire I could see the
red-hot blades gleaming like live coals. The first man passed
a blade through his cheeks; I could smell the odor of cooking flesh. Others licked the blades with their tongues. I
began to pass out. The Bey, seeing that I had gone livid,
clapped his hands to order the removal of the brazier and
the swords.

"You do not care for the grilled meat, Mademoiselle? I
will toss them some vegetables!"

At this, one of the innumerable attendants ran down into the yard to a group of cactuses growing in a corner. With a large knife he cut off portions of the spiked growth and tossed fragments among the crowd. The dervishes caught them in mid-air and with complete nonchalance began to munch them like dainties and swallow them, thorns and all.

The Bey laughed again. "Now for an ice dessert, eh?"

Dessert turned out to be thick glass tumblers. Each man took his glass and bit into it with relish. Quite irrelevantly, I couldn't help noting the fact that a hundred madmen chewing glass make a softly musical sound.

"Is there anything further you would suggest?" the Bey inquired politely.

"A glass of brandy for me," I gasped. "And I hope Allah appreciates all this."

One day I received an invitation to dinner at Matariyeh from the beautiful Clara Ward whom I had known in Paris. Clara was just a girl from Detroit who had married a handsome prince with a fairybook name: the Prince of Caraman-Chimay. But Clara had fallen hard for the gypsy violinist Rigo, and to escape husband and society the two had come to Egypt where they were living in romantic seclusion. All for love and the world well lost, except that in this case Clara had been able to carry a fair-sized chunk of the world's goods with her. They were famous lovers of the day, as much talked of then as the Duke and Duchess of Windsor some decades later.

My first glimpse of their Moorish palace was by moonlight. The huge pile was so white and ghostly that it looked almost like a mammoth sepulcher looming up on the edge of the desert. Around it scattered date palms stood silhouetted against the night sky.

Through a large gateway I entered a courtyard where a fountain played and pillared galleries made sharp shadows

under the brilliant African moon. At the far end of the courtyard was a statue of Hathor, Egyptian goddess of love and
beauty, which the two lovers worshipped.

The dinner party was large and polyglot. But I thought
the Princess was especially glad to see one of her country-
women, for she spent much of her time with me. After dinner she slipped her arm through mine and suggested a stroll
in the gardens. She seemed to want to leave her glamorous
present and relive her schooldays in Detroit. We talked
of old-fashioned Middle West cooking—gingerbread and
strawberry shortcake. I promised to return and teach her
chef how to make a lemon pie.

A wit once said that twenty years of romance will make a
woman look like a ruin, but twenty years of married life will
make one look like a public building. Clara had not reached
the ruin stage. That night as I sat on the terrace and sipped
my coffee, I watched and admired her beauty and daring.
To me Clara's affair epitomized the search for romance that
defies conventionality. *The Garden of Allah* had not then
been written, but here before me was a real story of pagan
love in the desert.

Swarthy-skinned Rigo was a Rudolph Valentino type. In
the course of the evening he brought out his violin and
played, ostensibly for his guests but in reality for his Princess. I shall never forget how he poured out his music over
the moonlit garden while his eyes never once left his mistress' face. After he had finished, and while we all sat silent
in the thrall of the moment, Rigo clicked his heels and bent
over Clara's hand with exaggerated devotion.

I went to another and very different dinner party given by
Prince Hassan at Shubra Palace. Hassan, blond as an Englishman, was cousin of the Khedive. He was later married to
a beautiful American actress, Ola Humphrey, whom he deserted almost at the altar. Shubra Palace, with its wide-
flung verandas, stood high on a bank overlooking the Nile.

It reminded me of a decayed Southern plantation, except that the servants were impassive Egyptians instead of smiling, lovable American Negroes. At dinner was another royal guest, Mohammed Ali, the Khedive's brother.

Prince Hassan was served separately from his guests. I supposed this formality might be merely his way of taking precaution against poisoning until I began to notice the size of his helpings. When the meats were served, a whole lamb was brought in and laid down before his plate. In horrified fascination I lost my own appetite as I watched him tackle the creature. Evidently my face told my story, for the Prince laughed heartily.

"I always feed well," he said. "When I was at the Fifth Avenue Hotel in New York, my first luncheon was three dozen bluepoint oysters, two broiled lobsters, and a porterhouse."

All this time two Paris-designed cowboy-type suits—my own and my maid's—had been hanging in my closet, ready for the journey to my turquoise mine in Arabia as soon as the engineers from the firm should arrive from London. Eventually they came.

Like a dream that is very convincing by night but very silly by day, my vision of dynamiting the Pharaoh jewel box, which had seemed so possible in London, had begun to lose point as I got nearer the time and scene of operations. Still I was committed to make the attempt; to save face I had to go ahead. Lord Kitchener had taken considerable pains to indulge my mad scheme, even to arranging with the director of the Suez Canal to put a small yacht at my disposal. So one night my party and I boarded it, and we crossed during the cool darkness to the shores of Arabia.

Fashionable gowns and satin pillows were left behind in Cairo. For comfort I had only yards of mosquito netting to protect me from the fierce Arabian sun; for service only one badly frightened Frenchwoman; for glamour only a large bottle of perfume which I had been warned I would need to use liberally for my own olfactory relief.

At dawn we sighted a flat beach that looked like the rim of complete nothingness. As we neared and were set ashore, I saw that this desolate spot contained for population a dozen camel boys, all sprawled lazily in the sand beside their beasts—my Arabian expeditionary force. Through an interpreter I expressed the wish to be off and away to the mine at once. Nothing doing. The camel drivers all shook their heads vehemently and pointed to the sun. It was certainly hot. My feet began to feel as if I were standing on the proverbial burning deck itself, and soon we Europeans were obliged to crawl for refuge into the few inches of shade offered by a crumbling, roofless hut a few yards away. There we waited through the long sizzling day for the shades of night.

At midday the Arab camel boys, thoroughly at home in the inferno, unconcernedly began to cook their dinner in the sand. Suddenly my nose and stomach were assailed ad nauseam by the strong Eastern odor from their stewpot. To relieve my distress one of the men sent out a call for water, and in a wink up came a smiling boy with a goatskin. The goatskin sounds delightfully picturesque, but as a container for drinking water I do not recommend it to a delicate stomach. I watched the boy open the ragged neck of the dead beast, pour out a cup of water, then tie up the neck again with a filthy piece of gut—and that was enough. I blacked out.

The sun dropped with the suddenness of the tropics, and when a wave of coolness began to spread like water over the desert it was time to mount the camels and be off. The amateur camel rider is not usually a happy person. The saddle is no saddle at all, but a queer wooden contraption. After much difficulty I was hooked around mine and the kneeling beast was exhorted to rise. Reluctantly his front part heaved upward, while I clung like a sailor to a tossing mast; then the back lumbered up while I went into reverse. When the long legs were finally unfolded and camel and I were under way, the sense of elevation and speed of travel was enormously thrilling.

Through the long, starry night, single file, over the sea of sand our camels swung rhythmically. The silence of the desert was so intense that all chattiness was smothered. There was only the crunching sound of the camels' soft, broad feet, broken occasionally by an Arab guttural.

By early morning we had reached the mine. It didn't look like any mine I had ever seen or heard of. I had pictured a shaft drilled into the ground, but I found only a large shed roof under which was a bowl-like excavation. Arab miners worked on the surface of the ground, using small hose and baskets as their only implements. Squatting on their haunches, these men would hack up small patches of the earth and patiently sift the soil through their fingers as they searched for the infrequent turquoise matrix My smart engineers had figured out that a blast of dynamite would bring the turquoise vein to the surface, thus saving years of time and labor and greatly increasing the output.

Before actual dynamiting could be done, however, certain political formalities had to be rigorously observed. The mine was located in an area over which an old and powerful Bedouin sheik held sway. Dynamite speaks a strong language, and it would hardly do to anger a neighboring potentate by unexplained explosions which might be taken as evidence of unfriendliness. In the East, time schedules exist only in the imaginations of occidentals, so our little troop settled down in the midst of primitive discomforts to await as stoically as we could the coming of the local poobah.

Much has been written about the beauty, the stillness, the terror of the desert but little about its flies. The flies were legion, and insatiable. Perhaps it was the scent I had brought that attracted them to me. At any rate, I evidently delighted them, because they passed over my maid and the engineers, the Arabs and their rich-smelling camels, to feast on me. Flies swarmed about me in such dense clouds that I could barely see through them; my hair was full of flies; I couldn't get a bite of bread into my mouth without swallowing flies; by day and night I listened to their fiendish buzzing.

Our long-awaited dignitary appeared one day as a fast-approaching cloud of amber dust. In those days desert chieftains were not regarded primarily as wolves in sheiks' clothing. My sheik turned out to be simply a fine old Bedouin patriarch. He was accompanied by his four sons, and as the party galloped up on their black Arab horses, their dazzling white burnooses streaming out behind them, I envied the grace with which they rode. To watch their swift, powerful movements, to see how perfectly they were adapted to the desert, was to realize how little we outsiders belonged there.

The visitors pitched their tent, enjoyed a meal, and rested; then it was time for the ambassadorial flubdub to begin. The patriarch paid a dignified visit to my chief engineer. After a seemly interval the visit was returned with equal ceremony. When we were sure the sheik would not feel offended, a formal proposal to allow us to use a charge of dynamite was laid before him. After due consideration, the proposal was agreed to. Nothing then remained but to touch off the fuse.

Even with all the explanations that had been made about the character of dynamite, the poor old man was totally unprepared for what happened. At the earth-shaking roar of the explosion he fell flat on his face in terror, with every known Moslem supplication to Allah. The blast jarred all the flies loose from my person, blew a goat we were reserving for

the sheik's banquet sky high—well studded no doubt with
my turquoises!—demolished the shed, churned the sand in
the bowl-like excavation over and over, and that was all.
Kitchener was right. Dynamiting the desert was like plowing the ocean.

The fiasco couldn't have been more complete.

Back in Cairo I found a letter awaiting me. Helen Dupont,
of the *Belle of New York* company, who was then cruising
the Mediterranean in her yacht, wanted my company
aboard. This I knew would be a lively change of scene.
Helen's set of friends were made up with complete disregard
for conventions. Their married or moral status did not interest Helen; only their ability to amuse. The yacht was on
its way home and would drop me off at Monte Carlo. Delighted, I wired prompt acceptance. At that point I was glad
enough to shake the sands of the desert from my feet.

My maid, twittering with joy to be Franceward bound,
packed my eighty-five hats overnight, and I said quick
good-bys to Daddy Longworth and my Egyptian admirers
and put a farewell gift of fifty pounds into the hands of my
Greek-god *sais*.

At Port Said, as my tender came alongside Helen's yacht,
faces leaning over the rail called loud greetings; whistles
blew; flags dipped in welcome. Best of all, I heard the strains
of an honest-to-God ragtime band. After months of nothing
more cheerful than the mournful flute, I felt that a little
percussion was just what I needed.

6 *High Stakes and High Jinks*

There is a feel of money in the very atmosphere of Monte Carlo. Aboard Helen Dupont's yacht, as it lazed gently in the harbor, I took my first look at the world-famous casino, blinding white in the gilded noon sunshine. Against the hilly coast of Monaco, orange and mimosa trees splashed patches of gold and yellow.

When I dropped my own anchor at the Hermitage, I told my maid to drag out the yellow satin cushions. Color of gold was all I wanted to see. For my first public appearance I chose yellow tulle, the skirt embroidered with gold baskets out of which bright flowers tumbled. The cape consisted of layer upon layer of tulle, each thickly embroidered with golden butterflies. I must have looked as if I were walking in a swarm of something.

As I was leaving for the casino, a visitor was announced —M. Lewis, my Paris milliner, who had already made a small fortune out of me by supplying me with more hats than I could possibly wear. I reminded him of the eighty-five I already had, but in Monte Carlo, he pointed out, I would be up against terrific competition and he cajoled me into ordering a dozen more.

Poring over the application blank at the casino, I recalled the warnings I had received not to stab out any fancy auto-biography with the fancy pen they give you, for their card index system was perfection. Dun and Bradstreet are ama-teurs compared with the financial intelligence department of Monte Carlo, where the last farthing in your bank bal-ance was known to the smooth gaming overlords. A com-plete record was kept not only of the money won and lost, but also of each gambler's habits and idiosyncracies.

The first room to which my card admitted me was dubbed in slang the "Kitchen." Here, during the height of the season, dense crowds played around some fourteen tables. Those who would pay a supplementary fee might pass on into the *Cercle Privée*. The Private Circle rooms were very much like the public ones except that they boasted carpets and vaulted ceilings and their windows admitted air and daylight. There the beautiful sea was on view for any who cared to look up from the game, and there Joseph the barman concocted perfect cocktails for jubilant and sorrowing alike. Still further along was the Sporting Club, which kept open all night. If you belonged to a smart club in your own country or could afford a thumping en-trance fee, you might enter here to hobnob with the elite.

The rooms were crowded with Europe's notables. Many I recognized from my acquaintance in Paris and London. Never in its history had the little city of leisure known such boom times as in those Naughty-naught years when every train was bringing its load of nobility, smart cosmopolites, wealthy Americans, adventuresses, courtesans, famous beauties.

All social bars were down. At the gaming table the woman of pleasure could sit between two duchesses and outshine them both in the richness of her *grande toilette;* in fact, it was the *haute cocotte* who dictated fashion.

While some of the women were gambling for a livelihood, many were there for the excitement of being seen—of showing their dresses and their jewels and their money, of being the momentary center of attraction before a sea of eyes. Actually no actress or prima donna ever had a finer stage or a more elegant audience than the casino provided. There were other kinds of excitement, too, such as rubbing out old scores. Seeing a hated rival blinking before a diminishing pile, a woman enjoys walking up and carelessly flinging down her own handful of large notes. Flashy types got their thrills by playing to the galleries, going from table to table, exchanging pleasantries with the croupiers, throwing their last and all on the green cloth with feigned nonchalance. The guarded type preferred to prolong their performance, to spend many days and nights losing their money. They got their pleasure out of pushing it slowly out and taking a very little slowly back again, knowing their audience would be staggered that anyone's resources could stand the strain so long. As I passed one table, I saw a woman pushing out her money with an arm covered in bracelets from wrist to shoulder. At another, the chic wife of a Chilean diplomat held admirers spellbound while she risked five hundred thousand francs on the turn of a card.

The first acquaintance I bumped into was James Gordon Bennett, owner of the New York *Herald,* whom I had known at parties in New York. It was a joke between us that he had been the man to send Stanley into Africa to find the original Livingstone. Bennett, in his late fifties, was a distinguished figure, with graying temples and the walk of a successful man. Though he had spent many years abroad, he was still the American type. With him was Pierre Lorillard, American tobacco king, whom I had also known in New York, gracious and polished and wearing his own aura of security.

"What the devil are you doing here?" was Bennett's unceremonious salutation.

"Learning a new set of ropes," I replied.

"Here's where you hang yourself then," he retorted. "Nobody but a fool would ever try to beat this place. You just put your money down and they grab it."

With the two men I walked through the hushed quiet of the rooms where only the mechanical voices of the croupiers broke the silence: *"Faites vos jeux, messieurs."*

The marvel of Monte Carlo is the croupier. Without appearing so, he is on the alert for everything. He must rule out the inadmissible play; watch and count the money; balk the stake-snatcher who sneaks the money left by anyone more interested in his surroundings than in his *mise;* and forever watch the faces. Hard faces with narrowed eyes; cruel faces with thin, drawn lips; rapacious faces gloating over a win—all listening intently for the sepulchral voice to announce without exultation or excitement the result of each play. I have often wondered that croupiers' minds don't snap under the tedium of having to repeat over and over the same phrases and to look forever at the same gambling faces.

Once that winter a long-suffering croupier did give way. It was in the Kitchen about noontime. A croupier who was dealing *trente et quarante* accidentally let fall a card. The faces groaned. He glared at them for an instant, then before anyone could stop him he picked up the rest of the cards and threw them over his head; then all the money and dashed that in the air too. Such a scramble followed as had never before been seen in Monte Carlo. Despite the rigid rule that only an attendant may stoop to pick up money that falls under a table, dignified socialites fell on the spoils like greedy street gamins and clutching hands were everywhere.

But this was known to have happened only once. In the training school under the gambling rooms, where croupiers were disciplined in pacification, precision, and powers of deduction, any man who showed a tendency to go loco would never have qualified.

One might think that a croupier off duty would start running and never stop until he had reached a country without a gaming table in it. Instead, by way of recreation, croupiers often went downstairs and gambled among themselves. Every soul in the principality was imbued with the spirit of gambling. Even tradespeople and employees, who were allowed to visit the casino only one day a year, never tired of telling of their triumphs on that one day.

I had heard a good deal about systems, pro and con, and I asked the men what advice they could offer a greenhorn.

Pierre Lorillard told me that he had been going to Monte Carlo for years and that his winnings had always averaged a hundred and fifty dollars a day. His only system was to play in the mornings. Then the rooms were freshly aired and he could think clearly. He believed it was overwrought nerves, caused by feverish stuffiness of the late nights, that made gamblers plunge so wildly and disastrously. W. K. Vanderbilt, who played only roulette, never sat down to one wheel. He would walk back and forth among the tables, playing several at a time, always in small amounts.

I soon learned, however, that the real system-player is the exception rather than the rule, because a system requires concentration. Also that all system hounds are a delight to casinos, who figuratively hold out their arms and say: "Come right in, dope, and have your money took."

I have seen croupiers exchange glances when a woman approached, armed with a roll of money, a bundle of sharp pencils, and a great scroll covered with hieroglyphics. Wizards in far-off lands may closet themselves secretly and while their roulette wheels whirr merrily fill pages with mystic signs. But as certainly as the system comes before the real wheels of Monte Carlo—which are leveled each day by experts before independent witnesses—the masterminds are confounded. Of course, the woman system-player always thinks she would have lasted if it hadn't been for the ghastly heat; or the offensive perfume on the woman next her; or the offish way the croupier sent the ball spinning, or the man who would knock her hat about when reaching over her to play. Perhaps the women who play only to show off are the smartest after all.

My hands were itching to get at the money in my purse. I wanted to learn *trente et quarante* at once. But Bennett seized my arm roughly and launched into a regular harangue against the deteriorating effect of the gambling mania, all the while dragging me in the direction of the bar.

As we passed a croupier, I had just time to slip two gold louis' in the man's hands and whisper: "Put them on black."

At the bar, meeting Victor Bethel, young brother of Lord Westbury, we settled down for several drinks. I noted that a good many who had run short of money after banking hours made frequent visits to the bar as an excuse for looking up a moneylender. Moneylenders were in their element at Monte Carlo, where they could demand such exorbitant interest as a louis on every thousand francs for each twenty-four hours. You could see them strolling among the tables, spotting possible borrowers.

It was some time before Bennett and I started back through the overheated rooms. As we neared the table where I had surreptitiously dropped my money, we saw that a big crowd had gathered and we pushed into the mob to see what had happened. At sight of me a wild yell went up: *"La voilà! La voilà!"*

On the board was a heap of gold as big as a prize Kansas pumpkin. Finally I got it through my excited head that during my absence there had been a run on black and that my two louis' had doubled progressively from my initial toss, worth approximately eight dollars, until my winnings had skyrocketed to about twenty thousand. (Today such a thing could not happen, as the rules regarding unclaimed winnings have subsequently been changed.)

Bennett was so furious that he immediately left me. After he had been at such pains to explain the odds against me, my good luck must have been annoying.

The Chef de Jeu offered to exchange my gold pieces for banknotes, but I refused. I had never seen so much gold in my life before and I was fascinated by it. I carried a basket of gold back with me to my hotel room and emptied it on my dressing table.

Next morning when my maid drew the curtains, she nearly fainted at the sight that greeted her eyes. Gold, gold, gold—piled against the mirror, spilling over on the chair, and scattered like daffodils on the carpet. I was in ecstasy. I knew I should put the stuff in the bank, but it was so beautiful I couldn't bear to part with it.

Bennett sent me yellow roses that morning with a characteristically savage note enclosed: "You will find as many thorns in your gold as in your roses. You are now an incurable gambler."

This gloomy prediction was quickly realized. I began to play for higher and higher stakes, and in no time the twenty thousand and much more had slipped through my fingers. Worse still, an appetite for play, from which I have never since been free, seized me. I soon learned to my cost that the only lady who can beat the cold, calm monster with not a nerve in its mechanism is Lady Chance, and she is so fugitive, so ephemeral, so pressed for time, that hardly does she appear than she is on the wing again. Camille Blanc, long the head of Monte Carlo, knew this so well that he once made a daring challenge: he would pay five hundred thousand francs to anyone who could play any or all of the games, high or low, and come out a winner of five francs for ninety consecutive days. Hordes tried, but no one succeeded.

Only once again did I have such spectacular luck. This was many years later, in 1913, in Enghien, a little place outside Paris where I won a hundred thousand. My real luck there was that the Enghien Casino was shut down before I had a chance to lose my jackpot back again.

My first royal flush in Monte Carlo having thus pushed me into the limelight, I began to make new acquaintances. Among them was a tall young Italian count, possessed of the euphonious name of Florentino Ghiberti Laltazzi, an attaché in the Italian diplomatic service who was on leave from his post in St. Petersburg. Count Laltazzi told me immediately on presentation that he had been trying for several days to meet me and that he was saddened beyond measure that his affairs would call him away the next morning. It was obvious that he was very much attracted to me. Before he left, he sent me a huge basket of flowers with his card enclosed: *"Pour prendre congé."* For some reason, although he was so charming, I was not particularly impressed, and as his flowers faded, so did my recollection of him. I was busy playing around with a very lively crowd.

Fanny Ward and her husband Joe Lewis were giving swank dinners at which the table decorations were elaborate beyond belief in this day of the bud vase. I remember one centerpiece made up as a water-lily pond, with flowers floating realistically among rushes and reeds. Fanny's jewels matched her dinners in ostentation. In those days every woman of our set was wearing a diamond tiara, and Fanny's was the highest of them all. I was green with envy and became obsessed with a determination to get hold of a head-piece just as fancy.

While the rivalry between Fanny and me was entirely friendly, Monte Carlo that winter was the scene of other rivalries that were anything but friendly. Two of the most brilliant courtesans of Europe, the stately Otero, famous for her collection of handsome Russians, and the fascinating Liane de Pougy, later the Princess Ghika, famous for her French noblemen, attempted to outdo each other in their display of jewels.

Otero led with her rubies; de Pougy countered with sapphires. Otero came back with her immense, lustrous pearls and white mantilla. De Pougy trumped with emeralds and dazzling satin. Otero then changed her suit to diamonds. Her dress was not noticed at all under the sunburst she presented; she was almost literally covered with diamonds. When she entered the casino, you could hear the gasps of amazement and envy. But de Pougy made the grand slam: next night she sauntered in wearing a Dolly Varden sort of gown with a rose at her waist and another in her hair, and close on her heels, following her through all the rooms, walked her little peasant maid loaded with every jewel de Pougy owned—sapphires, pearls, diamonds, emeralds.

It is hard to realize now, when so many women of the world live with as much abandon as women of the half-world, how sensational then were the lives and personalities of these bejeweled hetaerae. That season there were at least a dozen courtesan queens in Monte Carlo, their doings reported in detail and their wit quoted in all smart gatherings.

To understand the place of the elegant woman of those days it is necessary to understand the elegant man. The sporty Edwardian plutocrat, following the example of the Prince, held his wife above reproach, even though she might be dull company. But the "other woman," socially free and uninhibited, he often found a more intelligent and satisfactory companion than the one whose mind had been hermetically sealed by Victorian conventions. He considered her as much a part of his moneyed privileges as a yacht or a racing stable, and he took it for granted that he should spend huge sums of money on her.

It was precisely her expensiveness that was the cocotte's chief attraction. The same principle is true today. Ask a man for half a dollar and he calls it panhandling. Ask him for a hundred thousand and he regards it as a big deal. Often the Edwardian man of fashion would require little more of a reigning favorite than to be seen with her in public and to let it be whispered that she was living on his bounty. To be pointed out as one who supported the extravagances of a talked-of woman guaranteed a man's reputation as a wild devil. Among all the great spenders, none were more generous than the Russians, and the dream of every demimondaine was to be kept by a grand duke.

Many of these talked-of women I came to know intimately. One was the famous American actress Anna Robinson, who was visiting Monte Carlo with Rudolph Henning, an Australian mine owner, member of my "syndicate." Anna told me how she happened to go on the stage. She was a waitress in her mother's theatrical boardinghouse in Minneapolis. One day her beauty attracted the attention of a show manager, and a few months later she was offered a role. Eventually the little waitress became Lady Rosslyn, sister-in-law of the Duchess of Sutherland. But even after climbing to such heights, she slipped most tragically. Anna was a victim of narcotics, and after Lord Rosslyn divorced her she died in poverty and degradation.

Another favorite that season was Lina Cavalieri, later to marry New Yorker Bob Chanler and well-nigh drain his bottomless purse. Lina, who had begun her musical studies but had not yet sung in opera, was the center of an admiring circle of wealthy, titled Italians. How people stretched their necks to see her pass, her gowns crusted with rich decoration!

My own contribution to the overdressed scene was a little number by Beer that had won first prize in a great designers' contest in Paris. When I first saw this dress I was wild to purchase it on the spot, but Beer refused to deliver it until the end of the exhibition. It was of white satin, embroidered with rhinestones and inset with sheerest lace of the most elaborate pattern. Beneath the panels of lace glimmered gold cloth. The train, also rhinestone-studded, was almost long enough to wear at court. Six hundred dollars, and well worth it. The dress became my pet costume whenever I wanted to create a sensation.

Imagine my feelings then when one night I looked up from the gaming tables and found myself staring at a facsimile of my prize dress. The wearer was none other than Mrs. Edith Fox, an authentic favorite of Prince Edward. A few nights later whom should I see but Anna Robinson breezing through the Hôtel de Paris in another copy, and at the opera, sitting in a box, a fat lady from Peoria, Illinois, preening herself in still a fourth. I was seething over Fox and Robinson, but the lady from Peoria made me see the humor of the situation, at least from Beer's standpoint.

When I told Bennett about it, he roared with delight over the way we four women had been rooked.

"Tell you what," he said, "if you can wangle the four prize dresses together, I'll give you a prize dinner to match them."

This wasn't hard to manage. To each of my victims I sent a note expressing my admiration of her gown and asking her, as a special favor, to wear it at a little dinner party at Ciro's. I kept my fingers crossed on Mrs. Peoria, hoping she would never find out that she was the only respectable woman of the party.

Bennett had arranged with Ciro to hustle the women into the restaurant by different doors as soon as they had checked their wraps. The place was jammed, and La Robinson and Mrs. Fox, both of whom moved in a perpetual spotlight, attracted much attention as they entered. Ralph Hickox of Cleveland and the other two dinner partners were in on the conspiracy and managed to keep each woman's attention engaged until we all stood around the table. Suddenly the room rocked with laughter, as the joke burst simultaneously on everyone. My guests, who at first glance were inclined to turn stony, had to melt; the four of us locked hands in spontaneous sympathy and roared with the crowd. The lady from Peoria had a whale of a time that evening, and I trust her reputation was not permanently injured.

In January, 1901, Queen Victoria passed on to a presumably better, if possibly less exclusive, sphere than Buckingham Palace. Her legendary personality had dominated the English-speaking world for so long that it was hard to realize the British Empire had been suddenly and callously abandoned by Providence, dumped into the lap of a dancing, yachting, deerstalking, gambling, racing, flirting playboy of a Prince, who all his life had stood in popular imagination for nothing more serious than the laying of a cornerstone. Edward's character at once became the burning concern of millions of his subjects. Sermons were preached from pulpit and press.

"Come now, Your Royal Highness, sober down. No more high jinks. Serious business afoot, old boy. The Boers, you know—and your nephew Wilhelm getting so cocky—and all this balance of power to attend to. A bang-up coronation, and then—your Royal Nose to the grindstone."

The original date of the coronation was set for June, 1902, and London plunged into a hectic precoronation season. It almost seemed as if society were retorting: "Sober down, if you must, when you are King. Meantime have a last fling."

When the English set in Monte Carlo began to head back to London, it seemed the smart thing for me to do to go along too, especially since my gaming losses had been so heavy that I could hardly afford to remain where I was. I was about to become a "corpse."

It is not the grounds of Monte Carlo that are littered with corpses, in spite of the romantically gruesome belief that every man who goes broke immediately rushes out into a convenient patch of dark shrubbery and blows out his brains. This popular notion, I discovered, is not true. The average duffer who lets himself in for such embarrassment merely goes to the credit office and receives a *viatique*—a ticket home. He can even borrow back a proportion of the money he has lost. This loan of course has to be repaid before he can ever enter the gaming rooms again.

No, the corpses are not on the grounds; they are at the tables. A person is described as a corpse when frightfully bad luck pursues him. Those who frequent gaming places to win bread for the day thereof prowl around like jackals looking for a corpse. Who wants to play against a winner? If the jackals find a poor soul marked for misfortune, they stake their money against him.

When I learned that the jackals were looking for me, I thought it was time to clear out.

In London Fanny Ward found for me a charming little house in Walton Street, off Sloane Square. I gave the outside a freshly painted façade, striped awnings, and window boxes of scarlet geraniums; transformed the interior with bright chintzes and set out the cocktail shaker. To be a little out of the ordinary run of hostesses that season, I kept open house on Sundays, offering brunch made up of American dishes only. After a whirl at the cocktails, how those Englishmen tore into my fried chicken and corn pone, baked beans and brownbread, scalloped oysters and lemon pie!

The old crowd began dropping in, and a lot of new friends as well. Lord Jim Athlumney, who had cared enough for me to be my social mentor, brought around his friend Montefiore, a wealthy banker. Young Sir George Prescott dropped in often with Charlie Ansell, also young and immensely rich. Report had it that Charlie gave his wife a hundred thousand pounds a year just for her dress allowance. Sir Donald Stewart, home on leave from the Gold Coast of Africa, was very fond of American showgirls. Lord Bill Beresford was now married to a close friend of mine, Lily Hammersley, formerly Dowager Duchess of Marlborough and, before that, the American heiress, Lily Price. Edward Fitzgerald, the mountaineer, back from climbing the Andes, often climbed my steps. Bert and Louis Swift of Chicago, who were in town spending some of the money made by their pork-packing papa, were regular Sunday morning callers.

Bert, in fact, generously began to spend some of his pork fat on me by sending little nosegays with little presents in their centers—little pearls and that sort of thing. Then he began to use his imagination and send larger and more varied centers, always enclosed in larger and larger nosegays. In one bouquet I found a very handsome but much infuriated Persian pussy, trying to scratch the thorns of the roses as much as they were scratching him.

I had everything I wanted in life except a diamond tiara, and one night I confided to a very, very young peer my ambition to own such a bauble. The suggestion worked faster than any I had ever made, for on my breakfast tray the very next morning was a parcel. What a tiara! Taller than Fanny's, taller than any I had ever seen. I screamed with delight, clapped the crown on my head, and wore it all day long. I could hardly wait for someone to come in so I could display it.

At teatime Jim Athlumney called. I came running down to meet him with my head in my stars. I could see his face freeze.

"Where did you get that?"

I told him.

"Look here, you couldn't wear a thing like that except at court. And it's far too old for you. Besides, I'm ashamed of you for taking anything so costly from that boy. Promise me you'll return it."

I tried to argue that other women of my age and set wore tiaras, and that it was no business of mine how fools parted with their money.

Jim was inflexible. "If you don't return it, you and I are no longer friends."

As it happened, I had no choice about returning it. That night a note was delivered from the lawyers of the young peer's mother stating that the tiara now in my possession was the property of the Duchess of —— and that a messenger would call for it at my earliest convenience. I will not give the family name, for twelve years later the boy was one of the first to enlist in Kitchener's First Hundred Thousand and one of the first to fall, cited for bravery. No doubt he thought his mother would never miss a tiara from her immense collection of jewels, but I could hardly blame her for demanding it back.

It was a season of social extravaganzas. For one of my own parties I turned the whole interior of my house into a winter scene. Only once though, because Charlie Ansell slipped on the imitation-snow-covered stairs and nearly broke his neck. I could hardly afford to break the neck of a man worth as many millions as Charlie. So my next party was laid in Venice, minus only the Grand Canal to prevent drowning accidents.

Hector Tennant, director of the Empire Theater, gave marvelous suppers that winter, at which stage stars clowned for each other's amusement. Helen Dupont was back in town; also Elfie Fay, the very charming American comedienne who was delightful at these stage-folk shindigs. It was Elfie who introduced me to Sir Paul Chater, a Hong Kong millionaire, soon to play a more important role in my life than either of us then realized.

Lord and Lady Beresford gave a supper for the Prince to which Elfie Fay and I were invited and they served the cocktail invented by Edward himself. (Here is the recipe: a little rye, a little champagne, small square of pineapple, piece of lemon peel, a dash of Angostura bitters, a few drops of maraschino, crushed ice, and powdered sugar to taste.) Edward was in high humor that night and roared heartily at everything. Williams and Walker, the colored minstrels, sang for him "I Am a Jonah Man." Elfie Fay impersonated some of the Guardsmen, and I told stories.

"You have the real American spirit, Miss Livingstone," the Prince said.

Apparently in the mood for compliment, he let his eyes roam appreciatively over my figure and continued in the horsy vernacular he often affected with his intimates: "You wear your trotting harness very beautifully too. Another thing I like about you is that you'll never need a checkrein —you carry your head high enough without one."

Probably just the royal "line," but of course I ate it up.

At some of the more private parties the fun often became less and less decorous as the evening advanced. For example, the longer-stemmed American beauties would sometimes amuse themselves and the crowd by competing to see who could kick the highest. I remember one night when Edward held the champagne glass I surprised him by sending it flying out of his hand.

Besides entertaining the Prince himself, I was sometimes

called in on a far more difficult assignment. During the period that Mrs. George Keppel was enjoying royal favor, Jim Athlumney would often send me an SOS to liven up a dreary evening for George.

The Prince was famous for his punctilio in paying debts to women. His pocketbook had always been strictly guarded by his frugal mamma, Queen Victoria, but when he was not in funds he made generous promises to ladies who charmed him and he always made good. He once asked a woman with whom I was acquainted what kind of present she would like from him.

"A pair of bracelets, Sire," she answered.

It was several years before Edward could offer her a pair fine enough for his tastes, but when they came they blazed!

He had a long memory in other ways too. He always saw to it that his unmarried women friends made good matches. To many, this little attention was worth more than bracelets.

A decade or so earlier, long before I came to London, Lily Langtry had been his great favorite. For years Edward's adoration of her was recognized by the Marlborough House circle. Her great influence in London was sung in the popular rhyme:

The Langtry slipper and the Langtry shoe,
Langtry purple and Langtry blue,
The Langtry carriage and the Langtry cot,
And every woman's hair was in a Langtry knot.

But the Jersey Lily forfeited her standing when she offended the dignity of the state. Edward was a stickler for good form in public. He never forgot that he was royal and he never allowed anyone else to forget it. When the droll rumor started that Langtry had slipped a piece of ice down his collar at a dinner party, she suffered an eclipse of royal favor.

When Langtry came to New York, with her great reputation as an actress and a beauty, she swept everything before her as she had in London. In Manhattan she lived in a lovely old house set back from the walk on Twenty-third Street, far over on the West Side, a present from Freddie Gebhard when he was squandering his fortune on her.

Langtry came back socially in England when she married Hugo de Bathe, later Sir Hugo. I was well acquainted with both Lady de Bathe and her husband. The fascinating grace of this noted courtesan can hardly be described. She was not brilliant, but her magnetism was great. Even in a very large room full of people everyone became conscious of her presence. Yet her personality stole in, never crashed in. To the end of her days she retained her regal, seductive walk. Like Cléo de Mérode, she never changed the color or style of her hair, but always wore it in a low chignon at the back of her neck, probably to accentuate the shapeliness of her head.

I have never been able to associate anything but the natural perfume of flowers with Langtry. In her villa at Monte Carlo every vase was filled with roses, mimosa, carnations. When she appeared in the Sporting Club, she always wore a large, drooping leghorn hat on which were pinned real flowers. If any of the blossoms wilted, her maid, watching from the side lines, replaced them with fresh ones.

One night in London her husband, Hugo, called for me in his electric brougham to take me to a small dance in a house in Park Lane. When I opened the brougham door, I saw an enormous shaggy figure sitting on the seat beside Hugo. I jumped and squealed. It was a cinnamon bear, blinking his eyes in the light from the street lamp.

"Don't be afraid, Belle," said Hugo. "Brownie's a good fellow. I called up the hostess to ask if I could bring an extra. Don't you think she's going to be amused when she sees who it is?"

"If you ever brought a bear to one of my parties, I'd have you in jail," I said. "Will he bite?"

"No, no, get in," said Hugo. "Look!" And he took the bear in his arms in a big rough-and-tumble caress. "Brownie's perfectly harmless. Naturally he's had a sedative."

I got in and sat down. Brownie behaved well enough, but I have never had a ride that I relished less.

"Brownie loves to dance," said Hugo. "I thought he would enjoy a good orchestra."

Brownie was easily the sensation of the evening. Footmen paled, the hostess shrieked, and one of the women fainted. But on the whole I had to admire the way the party carried on. Brownie danced with Hugo and then did a few solos. After this, one of the men insisted that Brownie must be getting thirsty and gave him a bottle of champagne. Brownie lapped the golden bubbles down like water and then warmed up. When he began reaching for the violins, the musicians began reaching for their hats. After he had snapped all the strings and broken up most of the furniture, the guests were ready to leave too. I understand the place was a shambles by the time Brownie's keepers arrived.

In her magnificent palace loaded with treasures of art, Millicent, Duchess of Sutherland gave many beautiful parties for stage stars. She was sister of Lord Rosslyn, who later married my friend Anna Robinson. The Duchess was a Liberal, but her social position was so well assured that she could entertain alien corn and get away with it. When the Andrew Carnegies tried to crash English society and got snubbed, the Duchess of Sutherland took them up and made them socially accepted. Later, when the Duchess came to live in New York, it was Mrs. Carnegie's turn to play fairy godmother.

As the date of Edward's coronation drew near, all the British colonies sent colorfully costumed native potentates and native troops to march in the great pageant. From Buckingham to the Abbey, the entire route was lined with stands covered in scarlet. To illuminate the streets during the nights following the coronation, great crystal constellations were erected. Houses were decked out with flags and bunting.

In the midst of all these preparations a large florist van appeared at my door one morning just as I was going out, and the foreman of its crew of workmen informed me respectfully that he had come to decorate my house.

"But I have ordered no decorations!" I cried, aghast at the thought of what a vanful of flowers would cost.

"If Madame will permit, I have orders to decorate," the man insisted.

"Go as far as you like," I said, "as long as there's no bill sent to me."

The crew at once jumped into action, following a prepared plan, and I left them to their own devices. When I returned, the entire façade, from roof to basement, was hung with garlands of flowers.

The next night I went to a small supper for the Prince given by Consuelo, Duchess of Manchester. I had been invited because the Duchess had heard how well the Prince liked my stories and she wanted me to tell some more. When the evening was over, the Prince whispered to me: "I understand your house is very much *en fête* for the coronation."

"It's beautiful, Your Highness," I replied, "and I only wish I knew whom to thank."

Edward smiled broadly and gave me a very knowing wink.

7 *Global Hitchhike*

The cat that sleeps on a satin cushion and laps cream from a silver bowl may some day find the cushion pulled from under him and the cream spilled by a spiteful maid. I was having altogether too good a time in London that season of the coronation. No wonder Fate grew spiteful and not only pulled away my cushion and spilled my cream but set me out on the doorstep in the chilly dawn.

I was getting such big dividends from the Great Fingal Mine that I was in no hurry over the rich marriage I knew I should eventually have to make. But suddenly, without warning, all Great Fingal stock folded up like an accordion. It was the old story of a dishonest official and scores of victims. Many of my best friends got caught, even Lawrence Goldstone on whose advice I had invested. When the news burst over London, half the people I knew retired into their chambers, as I did, and leafed feverishly through their assets, trying to scare up enough to foot the month's bills. Some, like myself, came out from that inventory ready to adopt a disguise to escape creditors.

As I sat looking over my account books, a picture remembered from childhood crossed the pages—a man on a pony, leading a cow behind him across the Kansas prairies. He had lost everything in a cyclone except those two animals, but he was trekking out to stake a new claim. His face was etched with fatigue, yet he was whistling "White Wings." Reminiscently I hummed the words:

White wings, they never grow weary
But cheerily carry me over the sea—

My spirits began to rise. My vast wardrobe of Paris clothes ought to take me as far as any pony or cow.

The first Job's comforters to arrive were Frank Roudebush, Dick Dickerson, and Lawrence Goldstone. As soon as I heard their voices, I ran down the stairs singing "White Wings."

"Listen, Belle, you're broke—I'm broke—everybody's broke," Lawrence remonstrated. "What is there to sing about?"

"I've lived on fish cakes before," I flung back. "Why can't I do it again?"

Soon other sympathizers were ringing the bell, and still others. By the cocktail hour the house was full of those who came to mourn, but remained to drown their sorrows. I needed no cocktail to rally my spirits; I was becoming intoxicated by the thought that I was again on my wits. I had the piano shoved into the middle of the room and sat down to play and sing the Prince's favorite song, "Push Dem Clouds Away." Soon some dozen lusty male voices got behind the clouds and pushed too. My domestics, peeping and listening downstairs, must have shaken their heads over the craziness of Americans who shouted songs when they should have hung crepe.

The whole crowd then accepted Charlie Ansell's invitation to supper at the Café Royal, to discuss and decide what was to become of "poor Belle."

Frank Roudebush proposed a "whip round" to tide me over. Bill Beresford suggested acquiring the Royalty Theater and putting me behind footlights again; Jim Athlumney thought I could make a success of a hotel run on strictly American lines and offered to buy the old Dysart for me—that musty, ultrarespectable roof under which I had first slept in London. Goldstone brought forward a stockbroker friend who promised to carry me in any speculation I might want to make. Sir Donald Stewart thought he could buy for me a certain big tea room in London.—If only I had let him do this! The tea room was bought for another woman, who made her fortune out of it, not by grounds in the cups but by the sale of the site to the city for a tube station.

But I declined all these offers. Some instinct urged me not to run to cover in a hotel or a theater or a tea room. When everything seems lost is the time to take long chances.

Finally the only two bachelors at the table—a couple of broken-down baronets—proposed marriage. What a shout went up in honor of those daredevils! Everybody jumped up with a toast, and then the crowd burst into the wedding march from *Lohengrin*. But I had no intention of playing May to some old peer's December, so I waved these offers away.

"No," I said, "men are nicer to the women they don't marry. Look how grand you've all been to me. I'm ready to take my chances on getting along with or without money. My waistline is my fortune. Why, I'm so full of self-confidence this minute that I'd undertake to go around the world on a five-pound note—if I had the fiver."

The Little Girl from Kansas

*Enchanting Froufrous
of the Nineties*

*Off on the Global
Hitchhike*

With the Children in Paris

Belle in her Paris Boudoir

Most Dangerous Woman

Opposite: As Queen of her New York "Salon"

Exterior of Club   *The Entrance*

Country Club in Manhattan, 126 East 58th Street. Final Scenes of Belle's Career as Speak-easy Operator

above: This Broke the Law

left: The Indoor Golf Course

below: Mythological Décor—Leda and the Swan, Venus, Circe and her Swine

The Historic Red Pajamas

*The Striped Gingham of
Harlem Jail*

The party began to buzz like a beehive.

"Say," called Charlie Ansell, "who'll bet five thousand pounds with me on that proposition, Belle to get the stake if she makes good?"

"Nobody," answered Dickerson. "Everybody knows she could do it!"

"Then I'll put up the stake myself," Ansell countered. "I hereby offer Belle the five pounds and drafts for the five thousand, which she may carry with her in case of need. But if she comes back to London without having cashed the drafts, I'll make her a present of them."

"What if she fails?" questioned Montefiore. "There would have to be a penalty."

"Let her accept one of the proposals of marriage!" someone shouted.

"Fair enough," I agreed.

Immediately the whole party was fired with sporting enthusiasm. The wager must be shipshape, every contingency provided for. Waiters brought pencils and paper, and conditions were proposed, argued, rejected or confirmed, and finally a certain number committed to writing. The result was a unique document, made in duplicate, and signed by Charlie and me and everyone present.

For many years I cherished this contract among my most prized souvenirs, but it was eventually torn into shreds by a jealous husband. There were eight conditions, mostly prohibitions, to which I had to agree:

1. I must make the trip on five pounds and my wits.
2. I must not reveal the circumstances of the bet for the purpose of creating sympathy.
3. I must not borrow money.
4. I must not show the drafts to anyone.
5. I must not earn money by singing or playing the piano.
6. I must not appear in tights or show the "poetic legs" in *poses plastiques.*

7. I must not accept employment of any kind, except journalism.
8. A companion must accompany me and share my rooms and cabins.

Five pounds and my wits—some would have called it my gall! The first problem was to find the companion. I had recently met a woman, May Jerome, who lived in Teddington Square in a house next to Lily Langtry. May was persnickety-neat in her dress and equally neat in her mind. Never have I known anyone so predictable. Her big, dashing, wealthy husband had just divorced her, and she was frightened to death at the loss of her security. I decided to offer her a chance to drop her damp handkerchief, stop moping, and get a change of scene. May agreed to join me, and we made plans to leave within the week. The sooner the better, before my creditors lit on me.

The furniture in my pretty house was sent to auction rooms to be sold, and from the sale my solicitor was to pay off some of the debts. I was so thrilled to be on the go again that I didn't mind parting with tables and chairs; but my love for animals made it hard to part with my carriage horses and my hunter and my Persian cat, Tiddly-winks. Finally the turmoil of dismantling was over and my trunks stood packed and ready.

At Prince's Hotel a crowd of intimate friends gathered for a farewell supper. The most thoughtful going-away gift was from Edward Fitzgerald—a flexible gold purse filled with sovereigns.

"You will never be unsporting about these," he said. "But hold them against some emergency which, in your wild optimism, you may have overlooked."

On the trip to the station I took the last ride behind my chestnuts. Old Evans, spotlessly groomed, booted, and breeched, had the brougham literally shined to a fare-ye-well and he held my horses' heads higher than ever as we swung into the Mall. My conscience smote me when I remembered the many hours I had often kept the old fellow waiting for me in the fog and the rain. At the station I kissed him good-by and the horses too.

"Thank you, Evans, and be sure the horses are sold to someone as kind as you."

Overflowing with champagne and good advice, May and I were snugly tucked into our compartment aboard the London-Dover express, Paris-bound. My ticket had taken a big bite out of my five pounds. If ever I needed the "glad looks" Charlie Hoyt used to talk about, it was then. The more May sniffled, the more I would have to grin.

By the time we had reached the Gare du Nord I had thought of a way to escape cab fares.

"Hotel Terminus," I said to the porter. This was one of those hotels built to tempt patronage by being practically in the station, like the Commodore in New York.

I immediately got on the telephone, for a plan was forming dimly in my mind. Just after making the wager, I had heard that Sir Paul Chater, the lively old merchant prince from Hong Kong whom I had met at Elfie Fay's, was in Paris on his way back to the Orient. His would be a good flag to sail under; the only question was how to stow aboard.

I remembered talking with him once about Louis of the Café de Paris, at that time one of the most autocratic and omniscient of the famous *gérants*. Like all Parisian maîtres d'hôtel, Louis, apparently servant, was really tyrant, diplomat, and actor, strutting his part and cracking his whip like any ringmaster, while the fashionable world considered a glance of recognition from him an invisible decoration. From our conversation I had gleaned that Sir Paul knew Louis very well. I also knew Louis.

"Louis—Belle Livingstone speaking! Sir Paul Chater is in town. I suppose you have seen him?"

"Ah *oui*, Madame. Sir Paul is dining here tonight with Mr. Gubbay."

This was too good to be true. I was well acquainted with bulky, genial, rubicund Gubbay, another man of immense wealth and a relative of my old admirer David Sassoon.

"Have they reserved a table for two—or more?" I cannily inquired, not caring to encounter any hostile women.

"Two, Madame."

"*Merveilleux!* Give me a table for three next to theirs— it's most important, Louis!"

Next was an escort, but this was easy. In Paris some impecunious young artist can always be turned up for a good meal. In this case it was Carl Mathers, whose evening clothes would pass a more searching appraisal than his pink cows in purple landscapes. There was still the matter of the dinner check, however, which would be considerable.

Arrived at the *café*, I buttonholed Louis. Louis' ear was the confessional of all Paris, and his discretion well established. They were a special race, those Louis' of Paris in the Nineties. Only the parish priests knew as much of the inner life of the populace, and perhaps the Louis' outdid the priests in sympathy. For many years Louis remained my firm friend, knowing and remembering more about me than I could about myself. To the last day I was in Paris I was the recipient of his most thoughtful attentions.

On this night he had covered my table with pink roses and violets, and I was happily aware that I looked my best in a most provocative mantrap gown. Still it was anxious waiting. What if my two victims had been tolled off by some other schemer? I lingered lovingly over every mouthful. At last I heard the familiar booming voice of Gubbay. As soon as the two men had been seated, they noticed me.

"Well, what luck!"—putting into words exactly what I was thinking.

After introductions, the two tables became practically one conversational party, with me not only exhibiting glad looks but hauling out all my newest stories and jokes. During coffee and liqueurs it was Louis' cue to approach my table and make his little speech—for the benefit of the other table.

"If Miss Livingstone will permit, her dinner party will be the guests of the management. We should like to have the honor of making a little celebration of her birthday."

This inspired piece of deception was delivered with just the right air of deference and compliment. Messrs. Chater and Gubbay rose to the bait like a couple of king salmon to a Royal Coachman.

"A birthday? You don't say! This calls for champagne!"

After a magnum of golden water even the wiliest of millionaires are liable to let down their defenses. The next natural move was in the direction of Maxim's, at that time enjoying the reputation of being the naughtiest place in Paris. Cornuche, the proprietor, had opened it in the early Nineties with what was then a bright new idea. He reasoned that a few beautiful women sprinkled through the rooms would be sugary bait for business and accordingly had collected a choice assortment of mannequins, dancers, and *filles de joie* to lure the lonely male patron into costly libations. "Lolo, Dodo, Joujou, Cloclo, Toto, Froufrou" paid handsome dividends, and Maxim's had already become world famous and Cornuche a world figure. Later on he was to win more notoriety when, as revue producer, he was the first to put feminine nudity on the Parisian stage. That night when we entered, Cornuche bowed himself almost double as he led my merry moneybags to a choice table.

While we were watching the dancers and sipping our

champagne, Gubbay asked the question I had been waiting for.

"Look, Belle, there's nothing imperative about your going direct to Monte Carlo, is there? Why don't you and May take a little trip to Port Said with us? Paris-Rome express tomorrow night—boat from Genoa the next night. Paul and I need a little cheering up on board. We'll see that you get a steamer back to Monte Carlo from Port Said. What do you say?"

I didn't dare to look at May. I knew her jaw must have dropped and I couldn't afford to laugh. I spread my fingers reflectively on the table and studied them intently, seemingly trying to decide what to say to this kind invitation but in reality hoping that my jewels might create an impression of financial strength.

"I'm afraid not," I said finally, and May's jaw dropped wider. "I am having some dresses fitted, and besides, I have to wait here until my lawyer sends a draft to my Paris bank. He doesn't think I should carry large amounts when I am traveling."

"Pooh, if that's your only excuse," Chater interrupted, "the matter's all settled. We'll call for you at seven tomorrow evening."

"Well," I murmured, trying to sound weak, "of course I'd love it. What do you think, May?"

May gurgled and choked something that sounded like a "yes," and for the rest of the evening my gaiety was genuine. I could hardly wait to get to my hotel where I could send a wire—collect—to Charlie Ansell: "Leaving for Port Said tomorrow evening. Next address Hotel Savoy, Cairo."

I spent practically my last centime on the wire to the Savoy reserving a suite. Chater and Gubbay, I knew, would expect us to return to Monte Carlo, but I also knew we could elude them at Port Said and use the ticket money they would give us to finance the trip to Cairo. For the moment I was plenty cheered to be handed a ticket across the Mediterranean. I was so cheered that I couldn't resist rushing around next day and ordering a few more gowns and hats to be sent on to me at Cairo, my credit fortunately being still good with both Beer and Lewis.

Although the rail trip to Genoa was not particularly entertaining, I consoled myself with the thought that at least the wheels were turning. The farther my Lotharios got from Paris and Maxim's the more they reverted to type. The two of them settled down to long discussions of business. By the time we were aboard the steamer which was to land us in Port Said, they were buried in stacks of papers and May and I might have been just a couple of wives.

In the evenings, however, when Mammon let his devotees off for dinner and recreation, I threw myself to be entertaining. I was anxious that Gubbay and Sir Paul should have pleasant memories of the trip, for I had already mentally marked Hong Kong as one of my ports of call and I had every intention of digging into their pockets again in their own home town.

So I felt I had scored when Gubbay said on parting: "We wish you were going all the way. You're a circus, Belle."

"Listen for my calliope—you may hear it again, some day," I promised, with more guile than appeared on the surface.

The little purse that Mr. Gubbay slipped into my hands —"for tickets and a few flowers"—seemed satisfyingly heavy. When I peeked inside later, I found ten rolls, each one containing twenty-five sovereigns.

Immediately I began to spend like a drunken sailor, with practical-minded May cautioning me every minute not to get delusions of grandeur. May groaned over the big suite I had ordered at the Savoy. Might as well be hanged for a sheep as a lamb was my motto, and I was cocky enough to believe that somewhere in Cairo another nice old ram was waiting to be sheared.

My plans from Cairo on were rather vague. Kitchener, who had returned to Egypt after the coronation, might or might not be in town. But there was Ibrahim Bey Cherif (only no more rides with him!) and Daddy Longworth, and the great and influential Catahoi family whom I had met on my earlier visit. With two hundred and fifty pounds to jingle and a suite at the Savoy, something was bound to develop.

The hotel manager bowed low at the door to inquire if all my wants had been met. I remembered the style in which I had lived during my earlier visits.

"I want a carriage," I answered, "and a couple of *sais*, and don't forget fresh flowers every day in my drawing room. And a bottle of champagne now—extra dry."

May was practically wringing her hands. She was a girl who wanted to get around with the smart ones but lacked the nerve to swing it.

"Can't help it," I said. "If I'm going to act rich, I've got to feel rich, from the inside out."

The next night, as we started to dress for dinner, a knock came at the door. I opened to find on the threshold one of the hotel employees accompanied by a native boy.

"This boy insisted on seeing you personally, Miss Livingstone. He says he has a message for you, and he refuses to give it to anyone else."

"All right," I said. "Let's hear it."

"Tomorrow, at four o'clock, will Madame come to a point just below the new bridge and board the dahabeah flying the American flag?"

"What's this?"

The messenger repeated the invitation over and over again, parrot fashion. Even so, I had to call May as witness before I could be sure that I heard it straight. But no matter how I cross-questioned him, I couldn't discover the name of the owner of the dahabeah.

Who doesn't love a mystery? I lay awake most of the night turning over and over in my mind all kinds of solutions. An American, obviously. I finally fell asleep on the thought that it was undoubtedly one of the old crowd from New York trying to act prankish.

Next day, my two *sais* clearing the way through the wild riot and confusion of Cairo streets, I drove to the foot of the new bridge. Sure enough, there were the Stars and Stripes dipping from the stern of as charming a little dahabeah as I had ever seen. The upper deck of this kind of craft is always an enticing picture of comfort, with its striped awnings, bright rugs, and big lounging chairs. This particular houseboat gleamed from stem to stern with fresh new paint, window boxes spilled bright flowers. Yet no one seemed aboard; no laughing crowd raised glasses to me from the upper deck; I heard no music. As I left the carriage, an Arab servant who had been squatting near the rail jumped up and ran down to meet me and with obsequious gestures motioned that I was to follow him.

With all the assurance of a Steve Brody I followed him up the gangplank. As I stepped on board I was conscious of a heavy scent of roses. On the lower deck the Arab lad bowed himself out of sight, leaving me to wander about at will. I walked all about the decks, the heavy scent everywhere present, and finally pushed open a cabin door.

The door opened into a miniature of my London bedroom, where even the satin pillows had been duplicated, and the long mirrors, and here at last I found the roses. The floor was covered with them. Bewildered, I walked across to the dressing table, through a carpet of roses ankle deep, at every step smelling the perfume crushed from the petals. The bed was covered with the same beautiful flowers.

Leaves and stems had all been removed, leaving only a thick blanket of fragrant pink velvet.

It got me. I flung myself on the bed and buried my nose in the blossoms.

I must be having an attack of fever, I kept thinking.

I jumped up and looked for the bell. There it was, in the same place as at home. I rang madly, and in a moment the silent, smiling Arab lad appeared and handed me the inevitable coffee syrup. For once I was glad to see the stuff and gulped it down.

"Tell me," I chattered, "who owns this boat?"

The boy shrugged and pointed to a note lying on the tray. The note itself is now yellow and torn with age and travel, but I am copying its exact words as they appear in the faded ink:

> An old friend of yours permits himself the liberty of asking if he may dine with you tonight on your boat; and may he suggest that you wear riding kit, as it is how he best remembers you in London?

My boat!

I was fairly well used to the unexpected, but this topped everything. I had just enough sense left to put the note in my purse, for I knew very well that within half an hour after leaving the boat I should never believe my own recollections, and then ran back to my waiting carriage, the scent of roses still with me. In the carriage I sat a few minutes and looked back. The dahabeah was certainly not a mirage, for I heard my two *sais* admiring its clean-cut lines.

Something warned me not to tell May of the note, because I had found that May could be depended on to rub the bloom off any adventure. By now I was convinced there was nothing sinister in the mystery and I wasn't afraid to meet the anonymous writer. It was a little unusual, to be sure, to don riding habit at eight in the evening; but May, shut up with one of her migraines, fortunately didn't know that as I slipped out the door, I was wearing under my long cape a dark princess riding habit and hiding a tricorne hat. Very self-conscious, I hurried through the lobby of the Savoy and into the darkness of my waiting carriage.

At the bridge I saw "my" boat brilliantly lighted. I was evidently expected, for the same Arab servant was standing patiently at the foot of the gangplank. As I crossed behind his slippered feet, that odor of roses, stronger even in the moonlight than it had been in the afternoon sunshine, floated out to greet me. A familiar figure detached itself from the shadows on the deck and came forward. It was Kitchener!

"I knew you'd come, Belle," he said, giving me one of his hearty handshakes. "Tell me, is it a surprise?"

Over the eternally English warm gin and bitters I tried to describe my sensations of discovery, especially of my rose-carpeted bedroom. I could see that he was tremendously pleased at the effect of his little joke. Dinner was not exceptionally good, for in Egypt most eatables come out of tins, but we lingered over it. Finally, as Lord Kitchener lighted his cigarette, I got up courage to ask a few questions myself.

"I don't understand how you knew I was here! I came so suddenly I hadn't had time to let you know."

"You forget you have been gazetted here."

I remembered then that I had been written up in the Cairo press. There were columnists in those days too.

"But," I persisted, "these furnishings! You knew my suite at the Walsingham very well, but you were never in the house on Walton Street! How could you know my color schemes, and my fabrics?"

He laughed. "There is no mystery, really. Lady William Beresford was very kind about sending diagrams and she selected the silks."

My mind flew back to the day when Lily Hammersley

had walked through my rooms, making comments on everything. She had apparently been taking notes then. Suddenly Lord Kitchener lapsed from his laughing, casual mood into a sentimental vein that was new to me.

"Belle"—with his shy, half-smile—"you may want to know why I asked you to dinner in riding togs. I saw you one day in your riding habit standing in front of the Walsingham waiting for your horse to be brought around, and ever since I have been wanting to ride with you. Will you come out on horseback with me tonight? Look at that moon."

His figure standing by the rail was outlined sharply against the smooth, silver surface of the placid Nile.

"Nothing I would love better," I said.

"Come along then. The horses are waiting."

It was nearly midnight and the city was flooded with brilliant moonlight. We mounted and picked our way through the narrow, nearly deserted streets, heading for the outskirts. As we passed the race tracks, Kitchener drew rein.

"How about a top-off?" he proposed.

We entered the empty grounds. The track was white in the moonlight. Though I had known it well during my previous visit, I had never pictured myself as jockey on it, especially under such circumstances. We put our horses into a gallop and flew around the circle. As we came to a halt, I could see Kitchener's face clearly, his eyes lighted up by enjoyment.

"You know, I seldom succeed in evading people. This is my night. Let's go out on the desert."

We turned toward the sand-swept road leading out of the city. As we rode, a new intimacy sprang up between us. Kitchener was in a mood new to me. He talked freely and I listened. I became aware that this great man deeply hated the fierce white light in which he was obliged to live and that it was a relief to him to escape into the night and unburden his soul into a sympathetic ear. After a while we dismounted.

"Let's sit down and talk," he said.

Looking at him in the moonlight, I was conscious as never before of the power written on his face. He had a kind of magnetic force, centering around his fearless, compelling eyes. Strange that a man like this, reportedly asexual, shy and nervous, who avoided society, should find his release with a nobody like myself. I said something to that effect.

"But you are not a nobody, Belle," he replied. "People who dare, speak a common language. I believe I understand you better than most."

I thought of my mother who had known me so long and so little and nodded.

"It's not my concern that you do not choose to keep within accepted social bounds," he went on. "You have a great talent for living and for making people enjoy being with you. That ought to be your vocation. Your life will be full, as it deserves to be. I wish I were sure that I should be able to share more moments with you."

He drifted on into reminiscences of Egypt, the land of wars, intrigues, and romance. Suddenly:

"Have you ever been in love, Belle?"

"No," I said. "Not really in love. But I have had some glorious friendships."

He jumped to his feet and slapped his whip against his boot.

"Friendship—that's what I believe in! Friendship is infinitely the finer sentiment. Look at the men and women you know. It infuriates me to see the deceptions people practice on those they say they love.—I thought I loved once."

I waited.

"If she and I had remained only friends we might have

been spared much unhappiness. That's what I like about you, Belle. A man needn't be in love with you to enjoy you. You can be a friend." His voice changed. The great military organizer had disappeared, and in his place stood a man, speaking passionately from his heart. "Let's make a pact of friendship, Belle. I know that in asking for your friendship I am probably asking for more than other men who will ask for your love, but in return you can ask more of me than of those men."

He held out his hand, and I laid mine in it. Few have spoken of Kitchener's hands, most biographers having been impressed mainly by his remarkable eyes, his stern expression, and his striking figure. But I used to note his thoroughbred hands, full of purpose and determination, yet sensitive. As he held mine for a moment there in the desert night, I felt the intensity of his words and knew that what he had said he had meant with all his heart.

We rode back under the stars, just before the first glow of an Egyptian sunrise. Behind darkened latticed windows Cairo was still sleeping. We spoke little; words seemed unnecessary.

As we parted, Kitchener said: "The dahabeah is yours. Do what you please with it. I am leaving almost immediately for the Durbar at Delhi. By the way, would you like to see the Durbar?"

All the stories I had heard of the magnificence of durbars swept through my mind.

"Of course!" I cried.

"Another boat is leaving in a month. I will have a cabin held on it for you. Steamer to Bombay, then rail to Delhi. My staff will make arrangements for your accommodations. A durbar is always worth seeing.—Good-by, and remember our pact."

He kissed my hand and turned away. The fiercely ideal-

istic Irishman in the moonlight had changed back again into
the Sirdar of Egypt, bound on business of Empire.

To live in a dahabeah on the Nile is to fall incurably in
love with Egypt. As day after day I floated and dreamed
and listened to the seductive whisperings of the Nile, I was
in danger of forgetting that I was an adventuress on a
global hitchhike.

After Kitchener had left for India, I drove out on the
desert one day to find my old *sais*. With the money I
had given him when I left Cairo before, he had set up a
household, complete with wife, camel, goat, and white ox.
No longer did he have to wear out his young life running
before fashionable horses. When he saw me step out of the
carriage, his face shone with adoration. The poor fellow
even knelt and lifted the hem of my skirt to his lips with
Eastern extravagance.

"My beautiful mistress! Behold your grateful servant! See
what prosperity I now enjoy! Allah is good! I serve you until
death, my mistress!"

Looking down into his glowing eyes, so full of real grati-
tude, I believed that he actually would have done so if
I'd wanted him. He must have told the two boys who were
attending me that I was an angel from heaven, for as I
drove back to Cairo they flew like birds before my carriage
with loud shouts of something that sounded like professional praise.

In fact, my carriage became a little too swift to suit the
police. One evening when I was accompanied by one of the
influential Catahoi clan, a noted banking family, a policeman arrested me for fast driving. This disgrace crushed my
boys, whose ambition seemed to have become nothing less
than to carry me on wings. Fortunate that I was with a
Catahoi, for when Harvey Pasha, chief of the British Mili-

tary Police, recognized my companion, he let me off for a small fine.

The next time I encountered the Chief of Police was a few nights later at the opera at a performance of the inevitable *Aïda*. I sat in the Catahoi box, adjacent to one occupied by a group of British officers, including Harvey Pasha. Our box was filled with Catahois, every sister and cousin and aunt ablaze with diamonds. I had never before seen, even at Monte Carlo, so many jewels loaded on so few women. Suddenly, during intermission, I had an inspiration.

I was wearing a diamond ring that had cost six hundred pounds in London. As the lights dimmed for the opening of the last act, I quickly slipped it down inside my corsage. Then: "Oh, oh!" I screamed. "I've lost my ring!"

The effect was terrific. Every Catahoi went into immediate action. The women sizzled with sympathy; and the men got down on their knees and began searching every inch of the floor of the box. The house being in complete darkness, they had to light matches. The matches burned their fingers and nearly set fire to the wispy finery of the sisters, the cousins, and the aunts. At sight of the flickering will-o'-the-wisps of flame the audience broke into a gabble. If anyone had shouted "Fire!" there would have been a panic. Harvey Pasha, whom I had quite forgotten was sitting in the very next box, instantly appeared at our door with a couple of officers and demanded to know what had happened.

"I've stupidly lost my ring," I whispered.

"How very strange," he replied with peculiar emphasis. "I saw it during intermission on your hand."

Instantly I was frozen with fear. I had not figured on arousing official suspicion. Had this Sherlock seen me hiding the ring inside my clothes? What if he should have me searched? I hardly dared to breathe. For some minutes he watched the frenzied, fruitless search; then, apparently not wanting to risk a mistaken accusation against a Catahoi guest, he withdrew and left me to finish out my brazen act.

"It's really nothing," I declared in my most offhand manner. "Don't bother any further."

My nonchalance was a complete success, for at supper afterwards everyone was full of admiration for the calmness with which I had met my loss and I went to bed well satisfied with having pulled off a good trick. The only question was, would it work? It worked, and beyond all expectations. Next day punctilious Papa Catahoi sent around formal and tangible regrets in the shape of a solitaire worth twice the one I had presumably lost.

The days drifted on, and the time approached for our departure for India. One night as May and I were sitting at dinner at the Savoy, I saw a tall, handsome man approaching our table, wearing on his face an expression of delighted surprise. For a moment I had difficulty in remembering him; then I recognized Count Laltazzi, the charming young Italian attaché who had scraped an introduction at Monte Carlo. He clicked his heels and bent low over our hands.

Though I was outwardly friendly, secretly I felt a little annoyed. I remembered that the count had shown signs at our first brief meeting of becoming romantic, and at this point I had no time to bother with an admirer. In only a few days we would be sailing, and besides I had my hands full with other matters. The sale of my dahabeah was breaking my heart at the moment. Still I melted under his graceful compliments enough to ask him to sit down.

This proved a very unwise thing to do. Count Laltazzi, obviously in seventh heaven at having discovered me again, lost little time in trying to find out all he could about me, and finally, throwing diplomatic finesse to the winds, he came out at the end of the evening with a very blunt question. Uppermost in his mind apparently was the possibility of a husband somewhere in my background.

"Certainly I'm married," I retorted. "I have a perfectly good husband in America."

But at this May giggled, so of course he knew I was fibbing.

If I had hoped snubbing would discourage him, I had not reckoned with the Latin temperament. My indifference may even have fanned the flames of devotion, for from then on I stumbled over my handsome Italian at every corner I turned. Although I knew he was not wealthy, he showered me with small gallantries. Our hotel suite began to look and smell like a florist shop. If I had eaten half the exotic fruits he sent, I should have been ill; May gobbled his sweets. Every day boys bearing choicely worded notes lay in wait for me.

Still I remained aloof. It was very unlike me, actually, to play upstage in this manner. Ordinarily I would have reveled in good times with such a personable and distinguished man as the count. The only reason I can offer for my uncharacteristically cool attitude was that I actually was busy in preparations for departure and I didn't want anything to get in the way of that all-important wager. Besides, I attached no real significance to his attentions. Just another amorous male, I thought. Once I was aboard the lugger, I told May, he would return to his diplomatic duties in St. Petersburg and forget all about me.

"You're wrong," May kept insisting. "That man's really in love."

8 *East of Suez*

The Delhi Durbar of 1902, celebrating the accession of Edward to the throne, was the durbar of durbars in the history of India. The little city of Delhi was packed to its roofs. Besides innumerable English peers and peeresses, high-ranking officials of India, both native and British, were crowding in. If any grand mogul was not present, it must have been because he was on his deathbed.

Never was the oriental genius for ceremonial and ostentation given greater scope. India itself is intoxicating to the newcomer, but add to the ancient magnificence and greatness of the country the drama and spectacle of a durbar, and the experience becomes overwhelming. So many carloads of extravagant adjectives have already been dumped on paper by those who gazed at the Delhi Durbar and then flew to pen and inkpot that it seems unnecessary for me to haul out more superlatives. Yet as the scenes of Elgar's

Pomp and Circumstance cross my mind, I feel the tempta-
tion to write like a press agent.

As I close my eyes to recall Delhi streets, a kaleidoscopic
melee of color and movement tumbles through my mind.
Hardly a man who was not in glittering regalia, though the
gold braid and knightly orders worn by British officers were
dim in comparison with the ornamentation of the Indian
nobles. I shall never know how many maharajahs I saw in
Delhi, vying with each other in display of fabulous wealth,
in jeweled costumes and turbans.

The pageant of the procession itself is difficult to describe
without glory-shouting. Banners of rich colors shone in the
sun. Always I had been fascinated by elephants, even in
childhood days in Emporia when I used to rise before dawn
to watch a circus train unload. Here in their native element
the great beasts in their gold-and-silver howdah cloths were
truly majestic. What a regal beast the Viceroy Lord Curzon
rode!

As to his wife, lovely Chicago-born Mary Leiter, every
American present must have been enormously proud that
this democratic country had bred a woman so naturally
beautiful and queenly, the equal of any blooded aristocrat
there. After Lord Curzon had seated himself on his throne,
his consort came forward to make a low obeisance, her
diamond-crowned forehead almost touching the red velvet
carpet at her husband's feet. I shall always remember the
picture she made kneeling there, glittering in diamonds
and emeralds, in her blue gown with its extraordinarily long
train falling from her shoulders, embroidered with jewels
in a design of peacock feathers.

After all the balls and receptions were over, and the
captains and the kings had departed, it was time for a
couple of global hitchhikers to depart too. As Kitchener had
foretold, his days and nights had been so filled with official
appearances that there had been little time for personal

relationships during the two weeks in Delhi, and as soon as he was free he was obliged to return to Egypt.

I was anxious, moreover, to be on my way. My beloved dahabeah had sold for a round sum—to Mr. Isaac Emerson of Bromo Seltzer—and I knew it would be wise to invest in a ticket before the money slipped through my fingers. I had mentally marked Colombo as my next port of call, partly because I was acquainted with William Saunders, manager of the famous Grand Oriental Hotel there. Several months earlier in London I had met Mr. Saunders and his brother, who was Postmaster General of the Straits Settlement. While I was in Cairo, I had opportunely remembered Saunders' "Come and see us sometime," and had written to warn him that his general invitation was being specifically accepted. In Delhi I received his reply, a warm letter to the effect that he would expect us to stop at his hotel, the G.O.H. Another lucky break. I knew this meant there would be no hotel bill.

Other warm letters reached me in Delhi too, passionately fervid protestations of devotion from Laltazzi. The count, I discovered, wrote as brilliantly as he talked. He was obviously a man of great culture. In these letters I began to discern a new tone toward me—fewer of the elaborate compliments which are such an art with the well-bred Continental and more sincerity. May, who had long been won over by his charm, declared she could not understand my cavalier attitude toward him.

"I tell you that man is really in love with you. And what have you got against him? He's well-bred and titled. You've got to marry sometime, haven't you?"

But my one-track mind was intent on winning a wager. Nothing else seemed to matter.

Crossing the tranquil Indian Ocean, I found little to do except endure the exhausting heat. Daily I wondered how

the English who live in the tropics have the energy to keep
so immaculately laundered. The whole ship was dressed in
white—officers in smart white ducks, crew equally spotless,
and everywhere white awnings suggesting rest and relaxation. I am inclined to think it may have been the Englishman's ability to keep well-groomed in any climate, as much
as his talent for government, that was responsible for the
creation of the British Empire. No one but the English
bothered with the interminable deck games. As Coward
says, "Mad dogs and Englishmen——" In my chair I used
to close my eyes to shut out the sight of those horribly
strenuous youths and maidens bouncing about in the furnace-
like heat. The Spaniards on board shook their heads over all
this waste of energy. I was glad enough to see land ahead.

As we anchored off Colombo very early one morning,
boats from the shore began to approach our ship. I watched
them idly, trying to pick out the G.O.H. launch that May and
I expected to board. The shore of Ceylon is beautiful
enough to justify the island's claim that it is located only
forty miles from heaven. Colombo is a heart-stopping city,
scented by flowering cinnamon trees.

It was here in the harbor of Colombo that I was kidnaped
for the second time in my life, only this time with my
knowledge and consent. As the boats drew nearer the ship,
I noticed one containing a strikingly handsome man lolling
on his cushions while his natives, melting in the intense heat,
tugged on the oars. As this boat came alongside, I was surprised to hear a hail to the captain: "Is Miss Belle Livingstone aboard?"

I did not recognize either the face or the voice, but the
gentleman was so distinguished-looking that I asked no
questions and in a few minutes found myself reclining
among the many cushions beside him. The stranger introduced himself as Phil Davies and proved at once as amiable
as he was handsome.

At the dock, rickshaws were waiting to take us to the hotel, which to my further surprise proved to be not the G.O.H. but the Galle Face. We arrived just in time for breakfast, to find several of the ship's officers and fellow passengers already gathered in the dining room. There it was whispered in my ear that my escort was one of the sons of the world-famous jarrah wood king, who had made a colossal fortune in wood paving blocks, used at that time to pave the streets of nearly all the great cities of the globe. Davies *père* had headquarters in Perth, Western Australia, but his forests were scattered all over the Orient. Fortunately he had enough sons to enable him to appoint one as his viceroy in each of the world's continents. One son ruled the African continent, another South America, another Europe and Canada, and my host was lord of Asia. All very interesting, but I still could not understand why he had kidnaped me, sight unseen, from the G.O.H. to the Galle Face.

Although it was only about six in the morning, the dining room was jammed with the gayest breakfast crowd I had ever met. Women were exquisitely dressed. Hidden among flowers, a military orchestra was playing sweet, crashy music, and after breakfast everybody danced. Saunders came in, learned I had been kidnaped, and only laughed. I began to feel like Alice in Wonderland.

By nine in the morning the air was a sheet of fire. There was nothing to do but go to bed for the day. At least to one's room, to lie about inertly under the whirring fans. Such is the sacred ritual of life in Colombo; until sunset brings relief from raging heat, nobody stirs.

Although we were supposed to sleep during the daytime, I found precious little chance for naps. Between the innumerable servants sneaking up and scaring me to death— men with long black hair done up with combs in tight knots at the back of their heads, even spookier than those Arabs in Egypt—and the incessant drone of the fans, there was little peace. But it was the sacred crows that really gave me the jumps. When I first saw all the crows on my floor, I got ready to take the water cure. But they were real all right. All windows had to be open, and those hideous birds of ill omen flapped in and out constantly. Back and forth across the bare floor flocks of them stalked and croaked noisily. Lying under my netting, I would just be dozing off when—clack, clack—a shiny black devil would parade across the table at my head and—peck, peck—attack any bright trinket left exposed. Outside in the trees they wrangled and quarreled. Until these raucous pests went to roost at sunset, there was no relief from their squalling and wing-flapping.

After sunset there was no thought of sleeping, for then life in Colombo really began. While I was dressing for dinner, a servant brought me flowers from Mr. Davies and a box containing a ruby-and-diamond bracelet. A bracelet is always good news, and one should never look a gift horse in the mouth, but I decided the mystery of Mr. Davies' attentions would have to be solved. When I came down for dinner, a full band, which had come ashore from a battleship anchored in the harbor, was playing. Through the long windows floated in the odor of cinnamon. Dancing lasted all night.

There is something about the tropics that particularly enhances masculine beauty. Perhaps it is the background of the palms and the bright-colored flowers that makes the officers look so striking in their immaculate white uniforms and gold braid. At any rate I thought I had never seen such gorgeous, handsome males. Every ugly man ought to buy himself a white suit and move out to the Equator.

As soon as I could find opportunity, I asked Phil Davies, point-blank, to explain the bracelet.

"Do you remember," he said, "meeting my brother Arthur at your house in London just before you left? Well, Arthur was here in Colombo not long ago. It seems he had heard about your wager to go around the world on your wits and thought you might show up here. He took occasion to caution me about you in case you should come. He said you had the reputation for being very attractive to men, and he wanted to warn me that a fool and his money are soon parted."

"I don't see that his warning has taken effect," I replied.

"I guess it took effect in a way he didn't expect. I might have followed his advice if he hadn't offered it to me at the club in front of a lot of other fellows. That made me feel as if I wanted to capture you while you were here, just to show off maybe, to prove I wasn't afraid of a siren. I thought if I obligated you to show me attention while you were here, it would give me a reputation for being a gay dog, and incidentally I might help you win your sporting wager."

Phil was as good as his word about helping me win my way around the world. Before I left he gave me a tiara of diamonds and rubies. I hung on to this bauble for some time before I eventually had to part with it. It sold for three thousand pounds. Dear Phil—he was a lot of fun and a beautiful dancer.

Laltazzi, meantime, was still at my heels, figuratively speaking. His really beautiful letters, which continued to arrive almost daily, had begun to make an impression on me, and to my surprise I found myself even looking forward to receiving them.

After I had dreamed and danced away a couple of weeks in that lotus land, an incident occurred that, though it seemed at first like a cloud on the horizon, turned out to be the proverbial cloud with the silver lining.

In the Orient, where all whites tend to cling together, Americans easily recognize each other and gladly acknowledge kinship. I had noted an oldish gentleman, who nevertheless seemed to want to be convivial, sitting in one of the wicker chairs on the veranda. He wore a beard and, in spite of the fact that he was an American, a monocle. Upon inquiry I discovered that he was James J. Van Alen of Newport, Rhode Island, one-time ambassador to Italy and a member of New York's original Four Hundred, who had married John Jacob Astor's daughter. The combined total of his fortune and his wife's was said to be something to conjure with. The wife was dead, however, and Mr. Van Alen was not averse to cheering his lonely hours. So May and I did what we could to help out, generously overlooking his Newport airs and prissy accent.

Casting our bread thus upon the waters brought the usual reward. Came an unlucky day when the purse filled with sovereigns, which Fitzgerald had given me against the ultimate extremity, disappeared, probably stolen by the thieving crows. I was so upset that Van Alen promised to wipe away my tears by making good the loss. Furthermore, as he was headed toward Japan to collect Ming pottery, he offered to annex May and me and carry us along in his suite. Of course we accepted with enthusiasm. This was better than finding the purse.

But there was a noticeable loss of enthusiasm on our part when we learned that Van Alen proposed first to make a trip into the jungle to visit the lost and ruined city of Anarajapura. Object? Madness, in my opinion, though he called it collecting.

Van Alen engaged a train of elephants, five for provisions alone, and an army of servants, and our caravan set forth— Van Alen and his valet, May, and I. I shall never forget the slow heavy rhythm of that elephant train—pad, pad, pad— steady and determined, deeper and deeper into the Cingalese jungle. I had always imagined that the jungle lay in heavy, steaming stillness. In reality it is the noisiest place on earth. Monkeys laugh and chatter. Parrots shriek inanely. Unseen beasts roar. Only the snakes are silent.

On the way the guides told us to look at a certain spot for a well-known sociable old boa who made it his habit to watch for the passage of caravans. No one could figure out how he knew when an elephant train was expected, but he was always on hand, eager as a small boy to see a parade. Sure enough, there he was, wound around his usual tree, his inquisitive head hanging far down and weaving in and out among us. May moaned that her last hour had come. Even the natives were on guard.

On and on we pushed, a week's journey. Nights we slept fitfully in the circle of light around our great campfires. Finally, exhausted, we reached the village of Anarajapura, reputed to be the oldest city in the world—the heart of the Garden of Eden. There our caravan was to rest for a week.

Our inn was a bamboo shack raised on stilts, with an open veranda running around it, and was kept by a Hindu who served us Indian curries and tea. Even in the village, fires burned all night to keep away lions; the flickering light made our rooms bright as day. We were warned not to leave shoes on the floor lest centipedes or scorpions crawl into them. In fact, we were advised to put all wearing apparel under our mosquito netting along with ourselves and to tuck the fragile barrier under the mattress. Van Alen amused himself by making forays to pick up assorted pieces of crockery. But May and I had little to do except to gaze upon the decaying village, its streets filled with living skeletons, their faces eaten away, their hands outstretched for alms. If this, thought I, is the Garden of Eden, Eve was plenty smart when she got herself put out.

Finally, the caravan rested and Van Alen's lust for souvenirs glutted, we turned our way back over the long trail to Colombo again.

Soon after this villainous jungle detour, May and I and Papa Van Alen got under way on the next stage of our journey aboard the steamer to Hong Kong via Singapore, where I planned a stopover. In London, at one of George Edwardes' suppers, I had recently met the Sultan of Johore just after he had defied the traditions of his country by marrying an occidental—a beautiful showgirl from the Gaiety. It was the Sultan and his latest wife—he had also of course a typical Eastern harem—whom I planned to see at Singapore.

The Malay monarch's bungalow—his palace was used only on special occasions—sat on a height commanding all Singapore and the harbor. It was built of wood, the rooms light and airy and filled with touches of English comfort. An immense veranda ran around the great house, furnished with deep chairs and tables of cool drinks. The Sultan was deeply in love at the moment with his newest wife, who being an occidental was allowed to live her own life independent of the harem. Her pictures were to be seen everywhere, and the Sultan, a true Anglophile, talked of scarcely anything but his pretty English acquisition. They were a strange contrast, he so brown and stocky, she so white and dainty. He had the same childlike quality as the Egyptian princes I had met, with a habit of giggling in an almost girlish way.

He was an immensely wealthy man—part of his wealth made on English race tracks, part of it coming from taxes, rubber plantations, and his famous Gambling Farms where Chinese came in crowds to lose their money on Fan Tan and Po—and Miss Gaiety got a huge settlement when she married him.

After a rich and heavy meal, I was accorded for the second time the privilege of visiting an Eastern harem. The Sultan's was much smaller than Ibrahim Bey Cherif's, consisting of not more than nine or ten wives. Neither were the appointments as sumptuous.

Toward evening a servant informed the Sultan that a small tiger had been discovered nearby in the jungle, and a hunt was promptly organized. As I had had enough jungle to last me for the rest of my life, I begged to be excused from the chase and instead to be taken back to my ship. From the flower-bedecked veranda the happy voice of the Sultan called farewells as my rickshaw started off down the winding drive that led through tropical gardens flooded with exotic perfume.

Next morning, just before we sailed, I received a parting gift from the Sultan—the tiger's skin. Still a little bloody and sticky, to be sure, but in the Orient one learns not to be squeamish. A tiger skin is a royal present and I accepted it as such.

The expected packet of letters from Count Laltazzi before we went aboard, and then we were off to Hong Kong. May and Papa preferred not to stop there, so they went on ahead to Japan, but I did not propose to lose the chance of seeing that famous city. Besides, I banked on further hospitality from Messrs. Chater and Gubbay, from whom I had so gaily and profitably parted in Port Said.

Those two gentlemen were surprised enough to see me again, but they unrolled the red carpet and entertained me royally. One evening, after dining with Sir Paul, I was taken on a *ronde de nuit* through Hong Kong's famous "street of sinful joys." Thanks to the influence of my hosts, I was enabled to see not only the exteriors of the houses but some of the interiors. Not even in the great capitals of Europe could have been found such beautiful women of every nationality, but American, English, and Danish were preferred. As Hong Kong was headquarters for the English fleet, we naturally saw many Britishers in the narrow street. The women were so choice that many of them succeeded in making very wealthy marriages. I could name a bank president who took his bride from a house in the "street of sinful joys" and settled a magnificent palace on her; also a well-known merchant prince and a French baron.

One day during my stay at the Hong Kong Hotel—a dismal spot—as I was sitting in the Salon de Lecture I saw a familiar figure approaching. I could hardly believe my eyes. It was an old friend whom I had known well in London, Wilson Porter, whose uncle, General Horace Porter, was ambassador to France.

We greeted each other with the warmth and exuberance Americans always exhibit toward each other in the Orient. When he learned that I was catching the next boat for Nagasaki, Japan, he beamed.

"Well, this is wonderful! I'm booked on that steamer too."

Wilson, I learned, had made a Madame Butterfly sort of marriage in Japan and was returning to the home he had established in Yokohama. He and I immediately joined forces for the trip.

We dropped anchor at Nagasaki sometime during the night, and so my first glimpse of Japan was through my porthole in the morning. What I saw reminded me of an immense Japanese print with vivid colorings. The green fairly shouted from the shore, and a red plant afar shrieked out: "I am red, all red." I loved Japan from that moment and often ached from the beauty of it. The country cast a spell over my spirit.

Papa Van Alen's guide, Nakamura, was waiting to come on board and accompany me on the steamer to Kobe where Papa and May were expecting my arrival. I found Papa already deep in his Ming-collecting mania. To really know a collector one must travel with him. Papa was apparently determined to leave no piece of Ming undiscovered in Japan, and to this end he had Nakamura organize a pilgrimage that took us through highway and byway. Nakamura was a treasure. He arranged everything in scrupulous order, and with bowing politeness; his tourists were left with nothing to do but breathe. Our party traveled in seven rickshaws—Nakamura leading in one, Van Alen in the next, I following, then three rickshaws piled high with luggage and spoils, and May, looking very sick of life, bringing up the rear.

Along the way, if Van Alen thought he spied one of his blue bowls or cups inside some poor little paper house, or in some tiny kitchen, he would halt the procession while the guide explained to a bewildered family that the American gentleman would like the dish from which the little child was eating his rice. Sometimes a whole village would turn out to see what was the matter. And always I would have to look at the prize and listen to Papa's ravings.

We stayed in delightful country inns chosen by Nakamura, clean beyond words—the rooms adorned with irises, lilies, and wisteria always fresh and brilliant—and usually with a view of Fujiyama towering in the distance. After a bath in a tub sculpted out of a big tree, in hot water perfumed by pine, there was always the silent, sweet little Japanese girl waiting to rub one down. Cherry trees were just beginning to blossom, and toddling everywhere under the blooms were darling Japanese babies in gay kimonos whom I hugged and kissed indiscriminately.

Finally Papa must have decided he had licked the Ming platter clean, for our trip came to an end in Yokohama, where at the Grand Hotel I found an accumulation of letters from Laltazzi waiting for me.

By this time I was finding it necessary to do a little planning. My money was beginning to run low, and I had still two oceans and one continent to cross before getting back to the Savoy to collect from Charlie Ansell. May, as usual, was fretting. She was now advancing the preposterous theory that if I kept Papa at just the right distance I might get him, instead of the Count, to marry me. I had no intention, however, of letting myself get stuck in a glass case in Newport, of all places, alongside a horrible blue-and-white bowl.

But though I knew the time had come to hit up Papa, I also knew something about American millionaires: they're hard nuts to crack, and Papa was no exception. Papa kept the color of his money pretty well hidden inside his fist. It was hard sometimes to hold a straight face as I listened to him tell how unhappy he was in his big house in Newport and how he wished he had been born a peasant, so that he could work in the fields and really enjoy Nature.

At last one night I decided to screw my courage to the sticking point and tackle him. I racked my brains to cook up a story that would wash. If I should say my family was sick, Papa was the sort who would ask for a doctor's certificate.

Papa and I dined *à deux* that night, for I didn't want May's face around, giving me away at a crisis in my hard-luck story. The dinner was unusually good, and Papa genial and full of repartee. I hated to spoil things for him. When I sprung the news that I was out of funds, Papa called for another brandy and observed that he'd be lucky himself if he had enough to get home on. I came right back to the point. Papa got out his pencil and began to figure on the tablecloth. He had supposed that I was traveling on a letter of credit, and taking the imaginary figure I had rashly quoted him one day, he kept trying to prove by adding up my expenses that I couldn't, simply couldn't, be out of funds. Up and down, and back and forth, over that cloth he added and subtracted.

Well, figures don't lie but a liar can figure. All I could do was to enter into the game with a few figures of my own, and by the time Papa had the tablecloth completely covered I had him covered and convinced that it was up to him to see me to London. In the end there was nothing for my stubborn Yankee to do but come across, but I must say I had never before talked myself so hoarse for five thousand dollars.

Halfway around the world, and with five thousand on the credit side, I woke up pretty jubilant the next morning. In imagination I was already cashing in on Charlie Ansell. Then I heard May, who was standing at the window looking down into the Grand Hotel courtyard, give a little shriek of surprise.

"Look! Look!" she screamed.

I looked. A familiar figure was alighting from a rickshaw, tall, dark, distinguished-looking. It was Count Laltazzi. I'm afraid I shrieked too, but with joy.

In less time than it takes to tell it, he was knocking at our door. There was an air of determination about him, and he wasted few words in the formalities of greeting.

"I'm here to carry you off to a church," was almost the first thing he said, ignoring May's presence and disdaining the customary preambles. "Will you come with me?"

I looked at Count Florentino Ghiberti Laltazzi, handsome, elegant, standing there with that eager but masterful gleam in his eye, and suddenly I felt very tired and bored with the Newport Papas and all the jaunting about after stupid crockery. Suddenly I felt it would be very nice to have someone of my own.

I opened my mouth to say, "Oh yes—yes—yes!" Then I remembered. There was a cool five thousand pounds— twenty-five thousand dollars!—in drafts telling me not to be foolish. My home base was London, and I was far from home. The battle was not yet won.

At this juncture May came forward with a practical suggestion. "Wire Charlie Ansell, silly, and see what he says!"

I wired: "Have enough money to pay all expenses back to London, also offer of marriage. How will bet stand if I accept?"

Immediately came the cabled reply: "You win bet. Take money and man."

This seemed to settle things. At any rate, I thought I was set free forever from blue bowls. My error. When Papa heard that I was marrying the good-looking diplomat who had braved the savage Siberian railroad to overtake me in Japan, he sent me a little wedding gift. I had a premonition as I opened the box that I knew what it contained. I was right. It was a blue bowl. In my annoyance I hurled the treasure across the room and left its fragments to be swept up by the maid. Such youth, such ignorance! Today how tenderly I would glue those priceless fragments together!

It was the season in Japan when petals from the cherry trees come sifting down, making the ground beneath as softly white as snow. Once I had finally given myself over to the thought of marriage, I found myself slipping deeper and deeper under the spell of romance. Certainly the man who had pursued me half around the globe was a figure for any woman's dreams. Although he had no money, he owned an old name in Italy, and he was already well started on a brilliant diplomatic career. His whole being, I found, was aristocratic. I surrendered myself completely to his undeniable charm.

I cashed Charlie's drafts, gave my future husband a wedding present of the money to buy some polo ponies, and also what was left over—just about enough to buy a villa outside Milano, which he fancied as our future home. We planned that after we had spent several weeks in Japan, that honeymooners' paradise, I should go to America to visit my parents while he returned to his diplomatic duties and then made ready the villa. On my return to England he was to join me in Southampton and we would go to our new home in Italy together.

Then it was time to settle the formalities of the marriage. As the count was a Roman Catholic, it was necessary that I become one also. Situated in the edge of Yokohama stood a little mission church, and adjacent to it one of those little paper houses that served as home for the mission priest. It was there that the count took me for my instructions, which because of my convent training did not need to be extensive.

Within two weeks after my impetuous lover's arrival the wedding ceremony was performed. It was nearing the end of March. The tiny Franciscan chapel was very low, like the house the priest lived in. To enter, we walked down a path covered with white cherry petals. In a garden at one side a bent old Japanese woman, the priest's housekeeper, was planting vegetables. I was wearing a simple street dress, and on my way I had stopped to pick up a Japanese baby and be photographed. Wilson Porter came down from his big house on the bluff to be one of our witnesses; Louis Eppinger, director of the Grand Hotel, was the other; and in only a few minutes harum-scarum Belle Livingstone had attained the dignified title of the Countess Laltazzi.

Mr. Eppinger gave us a wonderful wedding breakfast, and Wilson Porter, who had offered us his house for our honeymoon, sent us off in rickshaws hung with wisteria and piled high with cushions.

No matter how many weddings a woman may have, I suppose there can never be more than one ideal honeymoon. This was it for me. Porter's house was a luxurious one, surrounded by cropped lawns, with sunken baths, rose trellises, and blossoming trees. His Japanese servants kept the rooms filled with fragrant white flowers. Everywhere, white. Nothing but white. For my breakfast tray every morning the gardener sent up his most exquisite spray of white roses. In this bridal atmosphere our happiness seemed complete.

We gave garden parties, including one for the Grand Duke Boris, then a dashing young blade who was staying on board his yacht in the harbor of Yokohama. In the beautiful house next to us on the bluff whom should I discover but my old acquaintance Harry Strong, and with him May Yohe. May, who used to sing popular songs in the music halls of London wearing a big hat and a polka-dotted dress, had taken the city so by storm that she succeeded in marrying the Hope Diamond. But she never seemed to like Lord Francis Hope, and when he lost both legs she left him.

In those halcyon days I listened to the old, old story told as only a highbred Italian can tell it. It was perhaps a finely mannered love the Count felt for me, but it was none the less deeply satisfying and he never seemed to tire of showing me extravagant attentions.

My new husband asked only one thing of me—to keep myself always impeccably groomed.

"I do not wish to enter your room, night or day," he told me once, "unless I am sure that you are appropriately dressed to receive me."

My clothes were part of my charm for him; he never wanted to see me other than at my most alluring.

All too fast flew the days, and when it was time for me to board the *Nippon Maru* for San Francisco, we both felt strangely sad at parting; unaccountably so, since the parting was to be for so short a time. But in my flower-filled suite on the ship we managed to make my send-off gay and hilarious.

"Au 'voir!" we kept repeating to each other as we lifted our glasses of champagne. "Till we meet in Southampton!"

Southampton!

9 *Strained Interlude*

When I stepped onto the docks of San Francisco ten days later, I found myself taking a look at my native land after a long enough lapse of time to enable me to gather a brand-new set of impressions. Oddly enough, everything seemed foreign to me. Customs officials I found rude in comparison with those abroad, and cab drivers disconcertingly familiar. The only link I could recognize between this strange country of my birth and the honeymoon existence I had left behind in Japan was the cloud of cherry blossoms spreading over the land. As I crossed the continent in the Overland Limited, the burgeoning trees seemed to be following me. When I left May in New York City and took the upstate train to Rochester, I found famous Cherry Valley weighted down with white beauty. Cherry blossoms, cherry blossoms around the globe.

After Father had retired from newspaper work on the Chicago *Dispatch,* my parents had gone back to Rochester, at Mother's insistence, there to build the home of their old age near to her family, the Liklys. I had helped finance the building of their little nest and I was eager to see them in it.

Also, I must confess, I was not unwilling to have them see me in it, now that I had a title. I was still unsophisticated enough to enjoy the idea of the sensation I imagined the arrival of the Countess Laltazzi would create in little unpaved Locust Street, with all the local newspapers printing blurbs about my globe-trotting, and Mother's neighbors peering through lace curtains at my Paris dresses.

As to creating a stir, my hopes were doomed to disappointment. Whatever the neighbors might have thought about my title, my family were distinctly not impressed. Father tried to be philosophical, but to him I had merely married a foreigner. As for Mother, she thought that having coronets embroidered on my panties was downright silly.

The only thing that pleased Mother was the fact that I was pregnant. Perhaps she thought this condition would at least keep me respectably quiet, less likely during my visit to shock staid and proper Rochester. I should have liked to talk about my coming baby, but my Victorian mother would only say, as if to close the conversation: "Belle, let's not talk about that."

In spite of these few disappointments, however, the visit may be said to have been on the whole a success. Later, in retrospect, I could see that from it there had come a general softening of attitude on the part of my parents toward the child they had never been able really to understand. It was a rewarding experience for me, for I had always been sincerely devoted to my father and I earnestly wanted to bridge the gap my long absence had created.

Finally it was time for me to leave them, and as we parted

the regrets were as real, I am sure, on my parents' side as on my own. May, waiting for me in New York, met me aboard the liner that would take us back to England on the last lap of my round-the-world trek.

During the trip I frequently compared in my mind this crossing with the first one I had made in the old *St. Louis.* How green I had been in those days, and with what little idea of the future that lay ahead. This time I was filled with thoughts of a future that seemed very secure and very glittering—a new life, a new home, a new baby. I counted the days till I should see my husband again, waiting for me on the docks at Southampton.

Instead of the count, however, it was his lawyer I found on the pier, and the news he greeted me with was shattering. Within the week my husband had died of pneumonia in St. Petersburg.

Affairs were in complete chaos, because of the fact that it could not be proved that our marriage in Japan had been legal. Although the ceremony had been binding from the standpoint of the Church, according to international law consular representatives should have been present. The money I had given my husband had been absorbed into his estate and would be swallowed up by his family. I was in no condition to fight a legal battle.

However, with my customary optimism, I believed I had enough to see me through the months preceding the birth of my child and after that, Micawber-like, I was sure something would turn up—it always had. I rose to the challenge, as I had done after the collapse of the Great Fingal Mine, and for the present decided to say nothing to my friends about my straitened circumstances.

Since my mourning would exempt me from wearing jewelry, I promptly paid a visit to Mr. Jay Attenborough. The first time I gave a cab driver that telltale address I spoke under my breath; eventually the time was to come when I would have been able to shout it without the slightest embarrassment. Pawning the pearls my "syndicate" had given me in happier days enabled me to take a suite at the Hyde Park Hotel. There, in the weeks that followed, all the old crowd turned up—the Guardsmen stationed at Knightsbridge, Tom Asten and his wife, Dick Dickerson and Frank Roudebush, Daddy Longworth, then in London, and many others. Their society was cheering, if expensive.

After I had pawned the Catahoi diamond, and Phil Davies' presents, even Jim Brady's diamond compact, I began selling my most expensive dresses and wraps. Some of my laciest and loveliest I cut up to make little garments and to trim a cradle and a baby basket. Just before the baby was due, I gave up my suite at the Hyde Park, bought some furniture on credit, and moved into a flat in Fortman Mansions.

Nearing Christmas in 1903, when I felt my confinement was at hand, I invited some American friends, because they seemed somehow the nearest I had to a family, to come in for a final celebration. The supper consisted of scalloped oysters and chicken salad, which I had prepared myself. For the first time in my life I found myself getting panicky, frightened enough to believe this might be the last supper I should ever eat. Late in the evening I asked my guests to give way for the doctor.

Next day I was holding in my arms a baby daughter, a fatherless being. It was Florent Lambert, that gay, gorgeous sportsman with whom I used to go to the Drags in Paris and who always came to see me whenever he was in London, who named my infant. I had wanted a boy, but with his wonderful, dramatic Belgian flourish, Lambert cried: "But no, Belle! This girl child will be the light of your life! You must call her Solange—sun angel!"

Solange she was.

It was not long after this that some of my old creditors

began to catch up with me—those in London who had been left only partially satisfied after the fall of the Great Fingal and the several Paris firms where I had rashly outfitted myself for my world trip. Now both old creditors and new ones began to turn on the heat. Debt collectors became my boon companions. I could not make them believe I was penniless. To such a statement they would immediately argue: "But how then can Madame afford to live like this?"

The answer of course was that Madame couldn't afford to move.

The men all looked alike—pale, chinless sorts in worn silk hats and shiny frock coats. They settled on my premises like Kansas locusts on the prairie. They clicked their heels on my doorstep as I entered or left. They waited long hours for me in my hall. They would have eaten off the same plate with me if I had let them. The women even penetrated into my bedroom.

"*Bon jour, chère Madame!*" they would gurgle. "*Vous êtes très méchante!*"

I became past expert in distinguishing a collector's ring on the bell from a friend's, and in keeping the old collectors from tangling with the new tradesmen. The list of my troubles that I poured into their deaf ears should have moved a heart of stone. But always we came back to the same question: "Can Madame possibly find the money by tomorrow?"

I began to recall stories I had read of poor debtors being thrown into jail in England, sometimes hanged. Finally the process servers began serving their diabolical writs. When I was knee-deep in summonses, I appealed to a lawyer. Could I be turned out in the cold? Over and over again he assured me that such a thing was most unlikely.

The most persistent of my creditors was Beer, my Paris dressmaker, into whose till I had poured so many francs. One day I came home to find that he had installed bailiffs in my flat, an army of them to lodge and board. The chief sheriff was very jovial, always ready to run errands for me and to give me tips on the races, but dislodge him and his henchmen I could not.

Fortunately, in the set I was frequenting it was no disgrace to be poor. I remember one day a very nice boy remarking in a crowd that he had just ordered eighteen dozen shirts from his shirtmaker.

"For heaven's sake, why so many?" someone exclaimed.

"Jove, my laundry won't trust me any more," was his explanation.

Everyone understood perfectly.

Of course the inevitable eventually happened. In spite of my lawyer's glib assurances, everything I had left was seized except the baby.

In this crisis my old friend Sir Donald Stewart, then Governor of East Africa and home on leave, came to see me. Sir Donald on occasion could be every inch the severe official, but whenever he called on me in gubernatorial mood I would always ply him with whisky and soda until he thawed into his usual genial self. I saw a great deal of Sir Donald while he was in London that time. Just before he returned to Nairobi, he paid me a visit and slipped into my hands an envelope containing a thousand pounds.

"I want you to have this," he said. "Somehow I have a strange feeling I may not come back again."

His intuition proved correct. Hardly had he reached Nairobi when he fell suddenly ill and died. I lost a devoted and generous friend in Sir Donald.

Now, with his gift money burning my pockets, my first thought was to increase the amount until baby and I were set for life, and the only way I could imagine making a quick profit was at the gaming tables. Oddly enough, a gambler never entertains the thought of loss. He can't afford to. No one who has never gambled can possibly understand the projects, plans, dreams a gambler can create on the turn of a card or the chance of a horse going to the post.

About this time my friend Nellie Grant was starting for Ostend. The thought came to me to go along with her and try my luck there. So, after I had bought some dazzling clothes and found a nurse to stay with the baby, we set out.

A book could well be written about Nellie Grant, later Lady Waleran, one of the most remarkable personalities in my list of courtesan friends. Her mother had been a charwoman and her father a policeman, and when they came to visit their daughter they were said to be old servants for whom she had a fondness and were treated as such. Nellie was known as past mistress of the art of not letting her wires get crossed. For several years four of the biggest men of the Empire played puppets to the strings she pulled, one of them a top-ranking admiral in the British Navy.

Nellie was a born general. Her executive powers came out to their fullest during the war, when she ran one of the biggest hospitals in London. A glance from her was like a spoken order. She allowed no liberties from her friends but kept them all under strict discipline. As for her lovers, she told them to speak and they spoke; to bring and they brought; to go and they went. From one she scooped up an armful of pearls; from another a handsome inheritance. When she finally decided to marry, she chose Lord Waleran, former Conservative whip in the House of Commons, then Sir William Walrond. From him she scooped up a name and a title.

At Ostend everything went swimmingly for me at first. A week at the baccarat tables and I was some five thousand pounds ahead of the game. Then—

Enter the villain—the man with a system. In this case none other than the American actor, lovable Nat Goodwin, at that time husband of Maxine Elliott, who with every good intention in the world confided in me his pet, never-failing system by which I could double my five thousand. In spite of all I knew about the bad reputation of systems I fell for Nat's, with the result that I lost everything but the proverbial shirt. Complications consisted of a huge unpaid hotel bill. There was nothing for me to do but hasten back to London, where I might hope to raise a loan. Meantime my beautiful new wardrobe would have to remain in the clutches of the hotel.

I arrived in London on a Friday afternoon, put my all-but-penniless body in a hansom, and drove off in the fond belief that in some of the accustomed haunts I would soon find someone I knew. Not so. I went everywhere. Not a familiar face. Suddenly I remembered that it was a Friday in August; everyone was out of town except those who pretended they were and stayed indoors. My blood congealed as I thought of my mounting cab fare. I lunched at the Savoy; no luck; I rode around some more; no luck.

But that night at dinnertime, when I turned into Romano's, there at last were a couple of men I knew—goldbug Arthur Collins, lord of Drury Lane Theater, dining with the American actor, Paul Arthur, noted for his anteroom filled with silk pillows on which silly women had embroidered their initials.

"Do sit down with us," Arthur begged. Little did he know the pauper he was inviting.

The evening I spent with them paid off handsomely, because at the end of it Arthur Collins lent me a tidy sum, enough to float me for some weeks to come. Quickly I sped home to my infant daughter and paid the nurse her overdue salary, after which she immediately gave notice.

Then a very lucky thing happened. The new nurse I engaged was a colored girl named Grace. Years before, Grace had been in W. J. Davis's theater in Chicago—dear to my memory; after she left me, she went to Lillian Russell when Miss Russell had become wife of Alexander Moore, American ambassador to Spain. Grace proved to be a greater treasure than emeralds and rubies. In the lean, uncertain days that followed, it was Grace who kidded me, encouraged me, and shamed me into keeping my morale always outwardly presentable.

"Why, honey, you'se no hen at all if yo' cain't scratch fo' jest one chick," she would say.

Thanks as much to Grace as to anyone else, I kept scratching. It was Grace too who promoted the idea that the real solution of my financial problems lay in another "to have and to hold," selected, naturally, from the millionaire class.

One day Grace came back in high spirits from her walk with the baby in the Temple Gardens. Rolling her eyes delightedly, she showed me a large bouquet that she said had been laid in the baby's pram by a handsome stranger. This tender overture was followed soon after by another of the same kind, and a third.

"No, ma'am," Grace always said. "I dunno who he is. But he sho' does have a sweetenin' smile."

Not long after this the stranger was made known to me, introduced by a Miss McNaughton whom I had lately met. I had heard of the famous Miss McNaughton and the sensational diamond set in one of her front teeth, but I never knew whether the idea of the diamond was adornment, bravado, or advertising. Miss McNaughton made two wealthy marriages, the first to a New York stockbroker, the second to a prominent Frenchman. The day I made her acquaintance I was disappointed not to see the diamond in evidence. She was then in London, and it was in her apartment at Clement's Inn in the Strand that I was introduced to a Mr. Edward Mohler from Cleveland, Ohio, who identified himself as the donor of the pram bouquets.

Mr. Mohler proved to be witty and amusing in a quiet way, and his winning smile was all that Grace had claimed. The smile seemed no less attractive when I learned the size

of the fortune he had inherited from his uncle, General Cald-
well of Cleveland, who had been manager of the Vanderbilt
roads and owner of the Nickel Plate Line.

Next day Nellie Grant and I lunched with Mr. Mohler.
Nellie was now preparing for a trip to Monte Carlo and again
I wanted to go with her, but that stiff-necked Ostend hotel
proprietor was still hanging on to my several trunks of new
clothes. When Nellie tactfully introduced my dilemma into
the luncheon conversation, Mr. Mohler quickly and eagerly
offered to get me out of pawn. He would go over with me
immediately, he said, to settle matters. I agreed with what I
hoped were blushing thanks, for I was very anxious to regain
my wardrobe.

In Ostend it cost my new friend a pretty penny to get
my trunks released, but as I knew by this time what a
very wealthy man he was, I had no scruples about letting
him pay the bill. I had no intention, however, of lingering
over the matter and so, under pretext of attending to the
shipment of my trunks, I slipped aboard the boat with them
and left Mr. Millions alone in his Ostend room.

When I arrived in London, a telegram was waiting: "Fly
away, little yellow bird, fly away home." Not without a sense
of humor, I thought.

Mr. Millions proved also to be not without a sense of determination, for when Nellie and I arrived in Paris two days
later, en route to the Riviera, there he was, waiting for us
at the Gare du Nord. For two days he had been meeting all
boat trains. He would like to join us, he said, in our trip to
Monte Carlo.

"You didn't think you were going to lose me in Ostend, did
you?" he smiled.

On the train Mohler assumed the role of perfect host, even
succeeding in softening Nellie's imperious manner, and by
the end of our journey the three of us had established completely congenial relations. I began to realize that I had acted

rather stupidly in Ostend in running away as I had done, and now, to compensate, I turned on all the charm I was capable of.

Beautiful Monte Carlo was ablaze with sunshine. Silvery, misty olive trees glistened on the hillsides; an orgy of rich golds radiated from the orange trees; tall palms threw their long shadows on the sunlit roads; masses of flowers tumbled over the walls. And spread out before all this perfumed loveliness was the sweep of dazzling blue water. The sunny corner on the rock that Monte Carlo occupies is so romantic that it is no wonder the ruined mariners cling to the beautiful reef on which they have been wrecked.

This time it was not my turn to be wrecked. Staked by the liberal Mr. Mohler, I promptly made enough to settle myself comfortably with Grace and the baby in a delicious little old pink-coated villa hidden from the main road in a cluster of bamboos. An old, tumbledown wall, over which rioted rambling roses, surrounded the place. Grace viewed the scene as a perfect setting for romance.

My household was made complete by the addition of Giuseppe. Possibly it was my Italian title of Countess Laltazzi that charmed him, but certainly I have never had a more faithful, or versatile, servitor. Giuseppe was a wonder. As chef he donned white cap and apron. If the bell announced a visitor, Giuseppe changed like lightning into a gorgeous green porter's livery and, running down the drive, with great ceremony threw open the massive iron gates and bowed the horses all the way to the door. Then he would disappear for an instant and reappear the perfect butler. In the afternoon he became gardener, or sometimes to relieve Grace walked a fretful baby.

Edward Mohler's infatuation continued to increase; wherever I went he dogged my footsteps. His constant presence inspired Grace with the conviction that he was the logical candidate for that wealthy marriage she insisted I must make. Casino winnings were fine, she argued, and there was no doubt that with Mr. Mohler's help I was having better than average luck, but Grace was a great advocate of social security.

"Marry dat man, Miss Belle," she would say, "while yo' can. Dat baby girl needs a papa."

I had to recognize there was much good sense in Grace's advice. Besides, I was beginning to feel drawn to Edward, in spite of the fact that sometimes I found him a trifle hard to understand. There was a little stiffness in his nature, which I attributed to his ultraconservative German-American family background. He was also very jealous, I discovered, and given to quick flare-ups. But most women find a little jealousy not too hard to forgive, and after all he was certainly devoted and he was rich. I decided to play "Barkis is willin'," and I began a campaign of what might be called suggestion. I made it my business to refer chattily to happy married couples; I trailed my victim past churches; I stopped in front of jewelers' windows wherever wedding rings were displayed.

Suddenly one day the victim disappeared, completely, leaving no word. I was mystified. Had I overplayed my hand? I was also furious; and after a little while I became worried. Then the old bugaboo—money—loomed up again. My winnings at the casino took a nose dive one day, and there was no generous Edward to stake me again.

No one, I am sure, but my loyal Grace and my gallant Giuseppe could have entered with such spirit into the hand-to-mouth existence that followed. For the next three months our lives became rather too faithful a copy of the original *Vie de Bohème*. Dandelion salad can pall. But Giuseppe's belief in my star never wavered, and when things became critical he voluntarily offered to lend me the whole of his life's savings. Still my luck remained obdurate.

I decided to write a book. Chancy as literature might be, it couldn't be worse than the gaming tables. My big fish had apparently escaped me, but if Giuseppe could continue to catch other fish from the Mediterranean, perhaps all of us might continue to eat until the book was sold. I worked day and night, furiously, completely absorbed by my new gamble, until finally the opus was finished.

Then one evening, as unexpectedly as he had walked out of my life, Edward Mohler walked back into it. He gave no explanation for his mysterious disappearance, and it was not until some months later that I learned what had happened. It seems that when he felt my matrimonial suggestions beginning to take effect on him and he began to consider seriously the possibility of making me Mrs. Mohler, he decided to take a quick run over to New York to check up on my record. Either satisfied that he could take a chance on me, or too much enamoured to care, he had now returned with the momentous question on his lips.

A trifle light as air, however, almost stopped the question forever. As he entered my villa, before our greetings had hardly been said, his eye fell on a flute lying on a table. Immediately I saw the jealous flush rise to his face.

"Who plays the flute here?" he queried sharply.

"Giuseppe," I lied. The flute really belonged to a good-looking young Englishman who had formed the habit of dropping in and tooting it at me.

"Ask Giuseppe to bring it out on the terrace and play us something," came the startling request.

My heart sank. Giuseppe was talented—but a musician? There was nothing I could do, however, except to take the flute to the kitchen in search of Giuseppe. For the first time Giuseppe balked.

"But you've got to!" I insisted. "I'm ruined unless you do— that means you're ruined too. Here—this is the way you hold it. Tell Mr. Mohler there's a key broken—tell him any-thing—only blow! Act as if the thing belonged to you—and smile!"

Poor Giuseppe! His smile was the sickest thing I ever saw. He trembled and he fumbled, and when he finally got the flute to his mouth, he produced the most appalling sounds. My goose is cooked, I thought.

But my suitor's infatuation was proof, as it turned out, against even this dead giveaway, for the next night, when we were dining out, the hoped-for question came. We were at the Reserve Restaurant at Beaulieu, so close to the sea that I could hear the plop-plop of the waves below.

After my unfortunate matrimonial experience with the count, I was determined that the Mohler marriage should wash. At this one there should be an American consul present, and furthermore I wanted it in England, where things are done right. I suggested to Edward that I send the baby to America with Grace for a visit with my parents and that we go back to London, when we were ready, for our nuptials. And so it was arranged.

This, my third wedding ceremony, was of the simplest, and its general atmosphere actually somber. Only Tom Asten and Billy Manderlick and a few other friends, including Dick Westicott, the American consul in London, were present, standing around as witnesses in a gloomy registrar's office. I was wearing a gray dress and a silver gray toque and carrying a mass of bright flowers. But after the cheerless business in the dismal foggy building had been finished, we joined the other guests for a lavish and frolicsome breakfast at the Savoy.

The wedding present I most prized was not, strangely enough, the expensive bracelet I received from my bride-groom but a small check, just arrived, which proved that my little book, written under such duress in the rose-covered villa by the sea, had actually found a publisher.

10 *Pillar of Propriety*

I'm sorry to pull this one out of the hat, but I actually did go on my third honeymoon alone. Well, not exactly alone. The North German Lloyd steamer *Kaiser Wilhelm der Grosse*, bound for New York, was well filled, and four of my good friends caught the same boat—Patrick Murphy, the wit; Dick Dickerson and Frank Roudebush, and Sir William Van Horn, one of the fathers of the Canadian railways. Billy Manderlick decorated my cabin with white carnations in honor of my bridal state, and the captain gave me a place of honor at his table. No bride ever had more fun than I did. To make up for my groomless condition, these four of the most entertaining men I have ever known kept me amused day and night as the great luxury ship sped across the Atlantic.

The object of my trip was to fetch Solange home from her

visit to her grandparents. She had crossed to America in faithful Grace's care, but since Grace could not bring the child back it was necessary now for me to go over after her. Of course I expected my ardent bridegroom to go with me, but Edward, to my astonishment, stated that he preferred to be left behind; that he did not wish to be introduced to my family or to introduce me to his own until he had had a chance to tame me a little!

At the very idea of any man expecting or even wanting to "tame" me, I was thunderstruck. Although I would have been the first to admit to a little "wildness," in the parlance of the day, it had never occurred to me that this was anything but an asset in life as I lived it. I had always found men seemingly amused and entertained at my very lack of the "tame" feminine qualities. Since I had left small-town conventionalities behind me in Kansas so many years ago, I had known nothing except complete freedom of action. Social laws that seemed to me dull and stupid I had always given myself full rein to break and I had never found any objection or opposition from my men friends. Edward's immediate hint after our marriage that as a husband he took a different view of my "wildness" came therefore as a total surprise. I decided he couldn't really be serious. But he was serious.

On my return to Paris I found that my Petruchio had selected a very charming cage in which to begin the taming and had spared no expense in gilding it. The house at 3 Rue Alphonse de Neuville, off Parc Monceau, was in the Louis XVI period, furnished in exquisite taste by the famous Jansen. The drawing-room walls were hung with green velvet, and the dining room was decorated with a gorgeous frieze of embroidered fruits. I remember that in one room leading into the gardens there were two very large Sèvres vases and that it used to cost ten pounds a week to keep them filled with roses.

Life in the fashionable American colony in Paris that summer of 1905 was a frivolous existence but a very pleasant one. Women looked like beautiful dolls in the fashion of those nights, with their tulle-wrapped heads and their masses of fluffy ruffles sweeping the ground. Paris was full of amusing places. Luncheon at the Madrid—a restaurant in the Bois— or tea at Armenonville; downtown to dinner at the Café de Paris; then perhaps on to the Ambassador for an open-air show. That season it was considered very smart to wind up the evening milking the goats at the Pré Catalan in the Bois. As the Pré Catalan suppers often continued into breakfasts, it was not uncommon for revelers to find themselves driving home in a radiant Paris dawn.

Although our social life was filled to overflowing, Edward from the first assumed a husband's right to approve or dis- approve his wife's acquaintances. One of the first aspects of my "taming," I found, was that I was expected to drop those whom he considered unconventional. This would have cut out practically everybody I knew. It is quite true that many of my friends had a tinge, or more, of the unusual. I have always preferred unconventional people. I know they often cause trouble, but they are usually an amusing relief from the bores of the world. Courtesans, divorcées, faggotts, gam- blers, alcoholics were all numbered among my circle. I sat in no judgment on their private lives; my only touchstone was the gay heart. Many of these Edward refused to allow me to receive in our home and I was obliged to resort to meetings on the outside, under the rose. Naturally I chafed under these restraints, though for some time I tried out- wardly to meet his wishes. When I saw how inordinate his determination was that his wife's deportment should be above reproach, I realized for the first time that, in spite of his veneer of European sophistication, Edward was basically a Victorian Middle Westerner, than whom there is no one more prudish.

There was another trait of mine too that he considered a

heinous fault. Like the other Katherine, I was well-known for my barbed tongue, which was capable of demolishing anything that got in my way. If a woman attacked me, I had no hesitation in retorting with brutal frankness, aiming my remarks always at a tender spot. Too, I have always found it easy to raise a laugh by catty comments, and Edward feared that unless I learned to curb this tendency we would both suffer socially. Poor Edward. He might as well have expected Niagara to reverse itself. Try as I might, I could not restrain the venomous quips that kept leaping to my mind.

Or perhaps, if truth were told, I did not try as much as I could have and should have. As I look back now, I can easily see why this was so. True, this was my third marriage and I should have proved the ideal wife, experienced in the art of making a husband happy. But my first two marriages had been in reality no marriages so far as affording wifely discipline was concerned. This was my first experience since childhood of the restraints of respectability, and infinitely harder to accept from a husband than from parents. It was difficult for me to understand why the natural exuberance of my manner, which had seemed so attractive to Edward before we were married, should now irk him so much. But his devotion to me continued strong, in spite of his criticisms of my behavior, and I sincerely did want to please him. Also I enjoyed my new position in Paris society, and being featured in the social columns.

As a part of Edward's yen for respectability we even had a pew reserved for us in the American church, and for the first time in my life I had the experience of being called on by the pastor's wife. Ladies of the congregation left cards and invited me to teas. Suddenly, without warning, I was aghast to find myself, if I didn't take care, about to become a pillar of propriety!

And so two years passed, the taming process not more than partially successful. Edward was alternately encouraged and discouraged with my progress, and I kept believing that I could eventually satisfy both him and myself by conforming outwardly to his wishes but at the same time maintaining private contacts of a more amusing nature.

Finally, after Edward decided that I was sufficiently subjugated to meet his sisters, he issued invitations to his three families of in-laws to visit us in Paris. My eldest sister-in-law was married to Charles Long, who was Senator Knox's secretary in Washington; the second to Theodore Livesay, an attorney for the Pennsylvania Railroad, and the third to a Dr. Pease of Boston.

Try as I might to live up to the Mohler standard of decorum during the in-law visit, I kept making one *faux pas* after another. The climax came when, forgetting that in staid American circles of that day certain events were supposed to come as a complete surprise to the entire community, I mentioned in the bosom of the family that I was *enceinte*. Too late I remembered how even my own mother, when I had wanted to talk about my first pregnancy, had carefully ignored any reference to my condition. I had become accustomed to the gracious habits of the French, to whom the expectant mother is sacred. In France even the streetsweeper, paying homage to a new life, bares his head and wishes the pregnant woman "safe delivery" as she passes by.

In the fall of 1907 my son Edward was born. I am certain that the happiest day I have ever known was that lovely September morning in Paris when I lay in my brocaded satin bed and gazed at the dear little infant the nurse had just laid in my arms. Edward Mohler *père* was wild with delight, and in return for my achievement presented me with the most expensive Russian sable coat he could find.

But sables or no sables, I was rapidly getting to the stage where I was bored to the point of explosion by my husband's ironclad demands for conventionality, and always the Mohler reputation to be reckoned with. I was becoming satiated with regularity; even economic security lost its charm. Since my marriage to a man of Edward Mohler's prominence all my movements had been followed by the Associated Press and it was getting harder and harder to break through the formality in which I was imprisoned and to reach those wide open spaces of freedom I had left behind. I was a square peg in a round hole. This was hard on the peg, also hard on the hole.

To settle my restlessness, Edward proposed a trip to America to visit both our families, in Rochester and in Cleveland. Always generous, he chartered a large section of one of the big liners to accommodate ourselves and our retinue of servants. Arrived in New York, he engaged a special train to take us upstate.

Here, at last, was a really triumphal entry into Rochester. Hometown girl had finally made good by a bona fide marriage to a bona fide millionaire, and none of your fancy foreigners this time but a real, honest-to-God American. Mother was wild over her new son-in-law. Doors of relatives were flung open, and bottles that had been reserved for christenings and golden weddings were uncorked.

From Rochester we went on to Cleveland. As we stepped off the train, a picture flashed through my mind of myself as a little girl from Emporia once alighting in the same station with Mother, bound on a visit to Mother's rich relatives. Then the little girl had been awed by the fine Likly houses; today the Likly relatives were awed by the Mohler millions.

Shortly after our return to France my husband took a beautiful villa in Beaulieu, near my romantic old pink-coated one. There, with children and servants, we used to pass part of each winter.

Summers found us installed in an old farmhouse in Normandy. Thirty-six years later, when American soldiers first set foot on the soil of France on D-Day, 1944, they landed at Ouistram, within a few miles of that tiny *port-de-pêche,*

Lion-sûr-Mer, that I know so well. Luc-de-Mer, the next village, had once been fashionable enough to attract Napoleon and his court, who foregathered there in the summers.

Our rambling old Normandy house was covered with tangled jasmine. Driving down the little winding road, we could smell our fragrant nest before we could even see it. It was an enchanting place, swept by the salt spray of the Channel. We called the house "Le Mauve" because of the sea gulls always circling over it. In June Le Mauve was knee-deep in fields of buttercups; in August apples ripened in its ancient orchards. Verdure ran clear to the water's edge.

I loved the spot. There, summer after summer, I took Solange and little Edward and "baby-farmed." In the old Normandy kitchen, with its huge chimney, we ate our meals— beefsteak and kidney puddings cooked over the open fire, and rice pudding made in huge crocks. I hung Normandy-red-and-white curtains at the little windows and painted beach chairs the same cheery colors. While the children were busy with their governesses, or flying their kites, I would walk along the shore looking for the biggest *langouste* I could find. *Langouste* as the fishermen cooked it, in salt water and seaweed in a great bubbling pot out of doors, was my favorite delicacy.

Days in Lion-sûr-Mer were very quiet. Spirals of blue smoke circling from each mouse-colored, quaint-roofed house showed that the village was as much awake as it ever cared to be. Village life centered around the open market where the fish was sold. Early in the season, when it was time for the fishing boats to start out, a great ceremony of blessing would be held on the shore, each man in his best blouse and altar boys swinging censers in the processional before the priests.

Every summer the children and the mothers of Lion-sûr-Mer held a *concours* on the beach in which they competed for prizes by building very large and elaborate structures out of the glistening white beach sand. For days everyone would work like mad. The two judges were the mayor of the little town and the owner of the chateau which towered just behind us, a Renaissance castle mellowed and gnawed by time and hung in moss. I remember the Jacob's Well that took a prize one year. And once I won, with a huge hat in which I had stuck a feather duster for an aigrette.

The Norman peasant is supposed to be the most cautious man on earth. With him, in season and out of season, it's *"Peut-être oui, peut-être non,"* as he always manages somehow to let one of his hands rest casually on the scales. The thing I liked best about him was his enormous vat of calvados—apple jack—fermenting in his back yard. Poor fellow, he needs his calvados when winter comes and the cold winds from the North Sea rip in over the Channel.

Christmases in Paris—how vividly I recall them. Early on Christmas morning I would drive to the *halle* for greens and trimmings, with the chauffeur and the maids entering spiritedly into the game of decorations. We would wind the stairs with garlands, hang holly, set great vases of red gladioli against the green velvet walls. I would make snow-covered villages, complete with lakes and mountains, for the children to play in. I can see now the great tree that towered to the ceiling, loaded with presents—big presents, expensive presents—presents for everybody—and the babies and the servants crowding around.

When one begins to reminisce about the good old days, there is always the tendency to become a bit lyrical. But I shall be honest enough to admit that even with my beautiful home in Paris, my charming villa in Beaulieu, and my romantic retreat in Normandy life was not all one sweet song. I ought to have been supremely happy but I was not. As time went on, my husband and I found less and less in common. In spite of all his generous indulgences, his domestic tyranny continued—in fact, increased. The trait of jealousy in his nature, which I had noticed even before marriage, now developed into almost a mania. Edward was jealous of everyone and everything. It was not only his professed fear of my disgracing the Mohler name that I now had to cope with but his rigid determination to monopolize me completely. He could not bear me to have any amusement outside of himself, not even a book.

His jealousy often took the form of an unpredictable temper—sudden changes from caresses to anger. Though his presents to me were costly, sometimes he would destroy them almost as soon as he had put them in my hands. An exquisite chinchilla coat which he bought for me he burnt in the furnace before I had even worn it. Escapades of my previous life that I had laughingly told him about he now dragged out of his memory to confront me with. Matters reached such a point that often in a restaurant if some of my friends approached he would make me keep my eyes on my plate until they had passed.

In this bad situation that was developing between us I was greatly at fault too, of course. My temper was every whit as explosive as his. Furthermore, I was giving lip service only to his canons of respectability, and in my heart—and in my private life—my nature was unchanged. I still stubbornly clung to acquaintances and amusements outside the Mohler pale, considering them my escape from domestic turmoil when in all probability they were contributing to it.

For example, I refused to give up my close friendship with Marian Winchester and such gaiety as I could smuggle with her and a group of our old friends. At that time Marian, living at 9 Rue du Bois, was the object of the Greek king's passionate devotion. George I of Greece, it will be remembered, was the brother of Princess Alexandra and thus brother-in-law of Edward. Poor Marian! Time later made havoc of her beauty, but not such woeful ruin as the plastic surgeon who promised to restore the beauty by lifting her face. Since the evil day of that operation, not one of her friends has ever seen her. The last I knew of Marian was that she had sought out exile and forgetfulness in Taormina. Perhaps she reasoned ironically that among natives who deliberately slash their faces to heighten physical charms she might still pass as alluring.

But on the night when Lord Lonsdale, Sir George Prescott, King George of Greece, and Marian and I went to the Ambassador to have one of those comic photographs made of our group, Marian was at her loveliest and most glittering. King George was blond and tall, with erect, military bearing. He and Marian made a gorgeous couple. After having the photograph made, we all went on to Jan Van Beers' for dinner and it was there that I dined with four kings.

Van Beers, who later painted my young daughter's portrait, was a fashionable Belgian artist, particularly celebrated for the flesh tones of his exquisite nudes. He was often spoken of as the modern Van Dyck. One of his historical scenes hangs in the Palace of Versailles, and his *Woman with the Mask* was purchased by the Czar of Russia. *The Kiss* is known around the world largely because of its postcard reproduction, which incidentally brought the artist immense revenue as well as fame. Van Beers was an intimate friend of the Duke of Marlborough, and whenever he visited England he spent much of his time at Blenheim. As a young man he had been the dandy of his day; as I knew him in his later life he was still tall and dapper, with a goatee and a tiny mustache. Like most Flemings, he was bold in humor, bordering on coarseness.

The dinner parties that he gave in his house facing the Bois were the most talked-of affairs in Paris. Only those present could have divulged—but rarely did—what actually happened. It must have cost Van Beers much thought and more money to work out his fantastic scheme of producing a lavish dinner without a crew of nosy servants watching all, knowing all, telling all. What he finally devised was a table with a disappearing and reappearing center. In today's theaters everybody is familiar with the phenomenon of the orchestra rising full-blown out of the depths, like Venus from the wave. But in that day Van Beers' de luxe automat was one of the seven wonders of Paris, strictly not on view to the tourist.

On entering Van Beers' house that night we found ourselves in a satin-lined *rotonde*, furnished only by an enormous, blood-red satin pouf. In the center of the pouf stood a tall Sèvres vase filled with an immense drooping bouquet of bleeding hearts. From the *rotonde* anterooms opened right and left for men and women. In the powder room for women was a wide frieze of sculptured cats—jumping, crouching, stalking, sleeping, flirting—all painted in lifelike tones. The men's room, I was told, was decorated similarly except with a dog motif.

While we were waiting for the others to arrive, our host took us on a sightseeing tour of the house, which he had done in exotic and sensual décor. From a window halfway up the stairs we could look down on his beautiful gardens. The top of the house was given over to bedrooms, studio, and picture gallery. Van Beers' room abounded in erotic Hindu imaginings—each bedpost seven separate intertwined carvings of serpents; each of the four walls filled with sculptured Balinese dancing girls, realistically painted in his famous flesh tones.

Although Van Beers was married to a beautiful woman who had been his model, his wife never appeared at any of his parties; so it was our host alone who, after the tour of the house had been completed, led us down again to the *rotonde* from which a door in the rear was soon to open into the hush-hush dining room.

Edward VII had gone to the theater that evening to see

Le Roi, an amusing take-off on himself, accompanied by the Marquis de Soveral and the Marquis de Breteuil, the latter always Edward's nominal host in Paris during the King's unofficial visits.

Finally Edward arrived with his party, which included one of the beauties from the theater. Then the young King of Portugal came in, ardent and glowing, with Gaby de Lys on his arm. She too had come straight from the theater and was still under those towering white plumes she always wore on stage. She made such a striking picture that whenever my thoughts turn to her today I remember her as she looked that night.

The plume headdress was so much a part of Gaby de Lys that when she died of cancer in Paris years later it was appropriate that her hearse should have been decorated with five enormous panaches of white plumes. The crowds that day of her funeral were so great that I could not get into the Passy church from which she was buried, not even into the street on which the church stands. By some queer whim, Gaby left her immense fortune to the poor of the City of Marseilles, which, like the City of London, is very rich. Strange that with all her money Gaby had never been able to gamble. I have seen her gingerly place a louis on the table and then grab it back. Selfridge of London was her sponsor at the time of her death. But besides Selfridge and the infatuated young King of Portugal, Gaby owed a great debt also to Harry Pilcer, who created her as a dancer. Later Pilcer lived in Hollywood, I am told, and was often seen with Fannie Brice. But I digress.

The fourth king to arrive that evening was Alphonse of Spain, a very young lad in his teens. His tutor apparently recognized that social gatherings of the Van Beers type were part of a sovereign's worldly education. However, he did take pains to call early for the boy.

When all were present, our host opened the door into the

dining room. In the center was a long, low table, topped with opaque glass through which shone the only light in the room. Around the table were immense satin couches, piled with cushions. Softly in the background the shadowy walls were festooned with garlands of flowers, Pompeian style, caught up here and there with satin ribbons. At one end of the room was a miniature stage, with a glistening, frosty-white curtain closely drawn. The thirty guests found their places and seated themselves about the table, their circle of faces dramatically highlighted by the glowing table top.

In the center of the table were three huge mounds of flowers. While we were admiring them, the mounds began to move and open and untwine into three bewitching young artists' models—nude, of course—who gracefully presented each woman with a corsage. After this delightful prelude, the center of the table, bearing the lovely sirens blowing farewell kisses, slowly sank from sight only to reappear almost immediately loaded with the first course of our dinner. Each man took from the mechanical butler the dish meant for himself and his dinner partner and poured the champagne. From the *rotonde* the music of an unseen orchestra drifted in faintly.

King Edward seemed to like his French actress's quips, for he laughed uproariously throughout the meal. The risqué always tickled his funny bone. It was odd in that setting, as French as the Folies Bergères, to hear the King's German accent, even stronger in French than it was in English.

"*Ja, ja, sehr gut!*" he would sometimes break out.

All the kings, in fact, were obviously having a wonderful time. A dinner party such as this was the perfect type of entertainment for sovereigns so well known that public amusement incognito had become literally impossible.

The feast was long, but in those days no one worried about a waistline. Finally, when the wonder automat brought up only a floral centerpiece and settled down as if for a long rest, the overstuffed guests settled down too and began to relax and take their ease on the silken pillows. Then at the end of the room a chic little *commère* and *compère* appeared on the stage and drew the sparkling white curtain on the first scene of a risqué, highly amusing revue which had been specially written about those present.

At the conclusion of the farce various members of the party, one by one, with apparently no pre-arrangement, slipped off the satin couches and stepped up on the stage to contribute to the evening's fun. Yvette Guilbert, the *diseuse*, sang her inimitable songs. She was wearing her accustomed get-up of white satin, demi-trained, short-sleeved, with long black gloves matching her black pompadour. Gaby de Lys sang and whirled that night for the young man from Portugal as she never had before.

Réjane, ugly and fascinating as ever, did not offer to take part in the entertainment. Sorel, however, recited from her place on the couch where she sat erect, disdaining the comfort of cushions. I always found Cecile Sorel a big bore at parties because she was as melodramatic off stage as on. I was always afraid that if I should speak to her I might start her spouting Molière. The cut of her jib reminded me of the Louis' and their wives and mistresses, her features as hard as if chipped from marble. The last time I saw Sorel was the day she called at the Hotel Claridge with Comte de Ségur to ask Fanny Ward how to have her face lifted. It would have taken a derrick to lift that stony phiz of hers. At her house on the Quai Voltaire, Jansen, *tapissier extraordinaire*, gave her at least one fitting setting: a dining room completely marble—floors, walls, table, and benches. On the benches were blue velvet cushions to match the veins in the marble. Lord Rosebery, probably the most distinguished and almost the richest of English noblemen, provided this Louis-faced woman with her luxury.

If Sorel was to me the least attractive woman present, Vera

Douglas was the most enchanting. I had met Vera long ago at the Hotel Cecil parties in London. She had just landed in England then and was making a fresh start in life. Back in New York, Kessler, agent for Moët Chandon, had caught her playing around, but instead of making a scene he had suggested that they take a trip to Europe. It was only after Vera had been several hours at sea that she discovered Kessler was not aboard—she had been shoved off alone. In London she was immediately liked. She was so well-mannered, reserved, and poised that no one guessed her Canadian father was a street laborer. Vera would float up to people in her delicate way and speak in such a sweet manner that she won women's hearts as well as men's. Eventually she succeeded Anna Robinson as mistress of the wealthy Australian Rudolph Henning, who gave her a house on the Champs Élysées.

Winter and summer Vera wore white—always with a pink rose somewhere enhancing her pink consumptive flush—and pearls. What pearls that woman owned! She had a mania for them. Queen Margharita of Italy had none finer.

It was Vera who was responsible for all the silver fox furs later seen in shop windows. Someone brought her a couple of those dirty-gray skins from Russia and she started wearing them. For a long time *couturiers* had competed for the privilege of dressing her, and now her introduction of the silver fox naturally made the horrible creatures the rage, connoting to most women luxury and well-being.

At the time this fragile girl from nowhere started the silver-fox fashion, she was in the last stages of her fatal disease. Only a few months after the Van Beers party, Will Sleater told me how he had been summoned by Rudolph to bring a selection of jewels from Tiffany's to Vera's house. Vera, propped up against her white velvet pillows, spent her last afternoon in this world running her thin fingers through strands and strands of pearls and holding the necklaces up against her throat, while Henning leaned on the foot of the bed and watched her, a deep, inscrutable expression on his face.

Only after Vera's death was it discovered that she had been all these years in close touch with her parents. Her coachman had been in the habit of driving her regularly to *poste restante,* where she received letters. Her entire estate, a million dollars or more, it was rumored, was left to these humble people.

But that night at Van Beers' Vera Douglas gave no hint that she dreaded the Grim Reaper. Though she shivered frequently inside her sable cape, lined with its ruffles of duchess lace, her laughter was as spontaneous as anyone's.

The supper party with the four kings was my first meeting with Van Beers, but it led to a friendship that lasted many years. He never grew old nor lost his verve, and his humor remained to the end as Rabelaisian as ever.

It was shortly after this party that my relations with Edward Mohler, which had been drifting steadily from bad to worse, took an acute turn and several times in moments of anger the word "divorce" was hurled at me. Then suddenly my husband unaccountably absented himself from home for three days. On the fourth day a woman, smelling intolerably of patchouli, called at the house with a letter addressed to me: "Dear Madam: Do not worry. Your husband has been safe with us since last Friday."

The writer I recognized as the mistress of an establishment noted for the comeliness of its many female inmates. I smiled over the delicate concern exhibited for a wife's anxiety, an attention that could occur only in a Latin country.

The next morning I read in *Le Journal* a lurid half-column devoted to the exploits of "an American millionaire named Mohler—a modern Rabelais." The article gave a detailed account of a supper for a bevy of beauties, the bill for which amounted to a thousand pounds. With a happy sense of liberation I now realized that I was chivalrously being of-fered grounds for a divorce.

But those were the days before the Paris divorce mill had been set up. To secure a divorce in Paris then was a compli-cated procedure. All claims must be bona fide; there must be no collusion. A suit for divorce on the grounds of unfaithful-ness had to be supported by direct evidence—something not too easy to provide. To insure justice, the evidence must be attested to by a relative of each of the parties. I appealed to Will Sleater and to Charles Long, my husband's brother-in-law, then in Paris, to secure some direct evidence, my hus-band still presumably in residence at the same patchouli-scented retreat. They in turn appealed to the Commissaire de Police.

A day was set, the forces of retribution gathered, prepared to secure the needed evidence in person, and then ensued a performance that was pure comic opera. A line was formed. In front marched the commissaire, carrying his long staff of office and wearing a great ribbon as impressive as the Order of the Bath slung across his pompous chest. After him came not one but four *huissiers,* each with writing pad in hand and pen poised. Followed the family witnesses, and finally the outraged wife. Down the street this ridiculous procession marched to a certain house with discreetly curtained win-dows, where the commissaire banged with his long staff on the heavy door.

"Open in the name of the law!"

The door reluctantly opened. A whispered conference with the mistress of the house and then, with all the formality of a lord chamberlain followed by his retinue, "the law" mounted the stairs. I was dimly conscious that a great tra-la-la was spreading throughout the house. M. le Commis-saire stopped before a certain door, gave more thundering knocks, and opened without further ceremony.

Each of the two startled beauties within grabbed a sheet

and draped herself *à la grecque*. I was impressed to note the extraordinary social poise my husband was able to display. Especially later as he left the house, when he bowed low over the hand of the mistress: "*Au 'voir*, Madame. You will excuse this intrusion, I hope. My deepest regrets."

My husband promised that he would not utilize his all-powerful money to defend his case if I would agree to remain on friendly terms with him after the divorce was granted. He further promised to pay me alimony of a hundred dollars a day as long as I did not remarry. I accepted his word for this settlement without question, though my French lawyers were astounded that I demanded no security.

Then came the gauntlet of the judges. One by one I had to pass the interlocutory judge, the conciliatory judge, and the final-beyond-recovery judge before the certificate of freedom was placed in my hands. At last I was out of the gilded cage, back into the old wild life I had so long craved. The bird was distinctly not tamed.

But I had evidently not fully understood Edward's stipulation that I remain "friendly." The first night after the divorce, when I arrived home with three carloads of roisterers whom I had gathered up to celebrate my freedom, I found Edward calmly installed in his old quarters. There was a noise of quickly changing gears and backing cars, and a thirsty and disappointed crowd melted into thin air, leaving me alone to be "friends" with my ex-husband.

11 *Most Dangerous Woman in Europe*

There is no doubt that a married woman gets used to the smell and feel of a man around the house and misses him if he leaves. Perfumes and toilet water are wishy-washy unless balanced by pipe and tweeds. Though I was glad enough to break matrimonial jail, I did find myself very soon missing a jailer. After my divorce from Edward there was a nobody-home sort of feeling that was no fun.

It so happened that I had recently met an Englishman, Walter Hutchins, who bore about him a tobacco-y aroma and who wore his tweeds, like all the English, as if he had been born in them and had never got out of them. We had met at some of my more private dinner parties, and I had been aboard his yacht, *The Daisie,* at Deauville. He was very, very British, with much Oxford fur in his voice. As soon as I met him, I had seen that he was made for the pleasures of life, and with my love of good times we could not fail to be attracted to each other.

His father was Charles Hutchins of Ravenswood, East Molesey, a banker and head of the London Counting House. He had grown up motherless under an elder sister, Alice, and his doting father had lavished everything upon him.

Walter was a bachelor, and when I mentally marked him for my next husband the noose was as good as over his head. He offered no strong resistance; in fact, he gave every indication of being more than willing. But the date we proposed for our marriage followed too closely upon the heels of my divorce from Edward to conform to the international laws between England and France. In either of these countries we should have had to wait a whole year for legalities. American laws, however, were more broad-minded. Why not skip across the ocean to be married?

Leaving the children in France with their governesses, I set forth with Walter. We arrived in New York on Labor Day, 1911, with not a justice of the peace to be found. Next morning bright and early, "propped" with a ring from Wanamaker's, we presented ourselves at City Hall where we joined an army of couples besieging the window marked "Marriage Licenses." They were a conglomerate lot, and Walter's spats and cane marked us from the herd.

Suddenly a big, burly form appeared beside us, and a loud Irish voice boomed: "Follow me!"

We didn't know where or why, but we followed—through corridors, and up stairs and down stairs, and in and out of rooms. Finally our Irishman stopped at a roll-top desk, opened it, sat down, and took off his hat.

"New form of affidavit, beginning today. Wanted to try it out on somebody. You looked pretty good, so I picked you. —Name?—Where you from?—Paris! Know Dick Van Wyck? Friend of mine.—Where you want to get married?—Little Church Around the Corner?—(Into the telephone.) Get me

Dr. Horton!—Either of you ever been married before?—Oh, you have? Husband dead or living?—Living, hey?—(Into the telephone.) Never mind Dr. Horton. Get me an alderman."

In a moment in came a shirt-sleeved man mopping a perspiring brow.

"Here y'are, folks."

We stood up, and Shirtsleeves opened fire with a volley of meaningless words. A hurrying, unheeding individual bumped violently into our backs.

"Watch it, dope, don't ya see yer interruptin' a weddin'?"

In such tender atmosphere was my fourth marriage performed. This was not my final wedding ceremony, however. Still the burnt child dreading the fire, I insisted later on two other ceremonies with Walter Hutchins, one in England and one in France. I would have married that man around the globe if necessary. The first was in England when, coming back once from a cruise, we left Walter's cutter at Deal and ran over to the pretty little town of Sandwich in Kent. Although a civil ceremony, this marriage was far from being the ludicrous performance of New York City Hall. I remember a vine-covered municipal building; a quiet room, woodpaneled, with dignified furniture upholstered in green rep. The fact that Walter was suffering from gout and had to be brought in in a wheel chair made no difference to me, with my mind bent on tying a knot that couldn't be untied. Afterwards in France, in a little *mairie*, I gave a third and final hitch on that knot, just to reassure myself.

Our American honeymoon was a potpourri compounded of elegance and stodginess. First there were visits to sophisticated friends whom we had known in France—Stanley Foster, vice-president of the Bowery Bank, at his beautiful country place in Babylon, Long Island; and Joe Mack in Detroit. Then a whirl of sight-seeing. Walter found Americans mad and uncivilized, though later he conceded they wrote an inspiring page of history in World War I. It was exciting to see my own country through the eyes of an Englishman, especially to discover that my English husband knew more about American history than any American I had ever met.

Of course I was eager again to exhibit my latest conquest in Rochester and to get the family verdict on what I had brought back this time, so it was not long before Walter and I were standing on the parental doorstep. Father, privately, demanded to see the certificates of my divorce and my remarriage. As for Mother, out came the Stars and Stripes and her stuffed eagle screamed again. Another foreigner! Englishmen, she declared, make very severe husbands; besides, the whole thing smacked of indecent haste.

The Rochester relatives, nevertheless, uncorked more bottles, bottles which according to American mores of the day were kept in hiding from the children. Such silly deceptions I found tiresome. Though there seemed to be an accepted notion that drinking was immoral, I noticed the men of the family often breathed peppermint and clove down my neck. Their lack of frankness irritated me. Yet as my newest husband's charm thawed all hearts, even Rochesterians', the visit was chalked up as a success.

After a leisurely cruise in *The Daisie* up and down the English and French coasts, it was time to get back to Paris and set up our new home. We chose 110 Rue de Ranelagh, a handsome house, well suited for extensive entertaining. There was a great music room, Renaissance period, with immense hooded chimney and stone walls hung with tapestries, where three hundred guests could dance. Our library contained several thousand books; I looked forward greedily to satisfying my hunger for reading.

The children, I discovered on my return, had been taken by Edward down to Beaulieu, so I set forth to recover them. Either the news of my remarriage had not penetrated to that remote spot, or my "friendly" ex-husband had chosen to disregard it, for when I sent word that I was coming, there he was at the station to welcome me as usual in a flowertrimmed carriage. The cook had outdone herself for supper; the children's welcome was unfeigned. It all seemed so natural, so like coming home, that I couldn't bring myself to mention at first that I was now Mrs. Walter Hutchins.

Next day, driving over to Nice, Edward showed me the villa he proposed to buy for me, so that I might never have to wander over the world without a home. Then of course the news of my remarriage had to come out. Edward made no comment. He only fell silent for a few moments, then stopped the carriage and stepped into a shop. When he came out, he held in his hand a pretty little jeweled fan which he offered me with an ironical bow.

"You may need this some day, when the fierce fire in your Englishman's heart begins to die down."

At that moment, however, the fire was burning so brightly that the fan seemed like an empty gesture. My new husband was wild over me.

As time went on, Walter became equally devoted to Solange and little Edward, who were growing fast now. He walked with the children in the Bois, told them stories, exercised a gentle discipline over them. His quiet comment, "I wouldn't be proud of that remark," had a far deeper effect on sauciness than my shrieks of temper.

As a mother I was a tornado. My children called me "The Dragon" because to them I always seemed ready to eat them alive for their naughtiness. This was not because I did not love them, in my way. I was simply not cut out to be a mother any more than to be a wife. Edward and Solange had everything money could buy—toys, governesses, tutors, amusements, clothes, horses—but they must have been under constant nervous tension, always aware of the threatening presence of a volcanic mother in the background with her incurable temper.

As my children grew up, I was intensely ambitious for them, but they were never interested in the careers and splendors I laid out for them. All my pet schemes failed because I was never able to establish a really sympathetic relationship with them. I was full of plans for making them happy, but when they weren't happy according to my schedule I was ready to lick the pants off them. I couldn't let them be happy in their own way because I thought my way was so much better. I made no allowances for childish laziness or carelessness but demanded perfection. I lacked the tenderness that my parents had shown to me; in fact, I have to confess that I have probably never given real tenderness to any human being.

Lacking the absorption in my children's lives that most mothers experience, I continued in my habits of extracting every ounce of fun I could out of my own life. My genial new husband allowed me great financial latitude. I never once inquired regarding the depth of his purse, nor did he ever volunteer information. I had been used to living on the scale provided by an American millionaire, and I assumed Walter was equally affluent. We talked sports, politics, gossip, stage, art, but he considered it bad form to refer to business after hours, even to his wife. Many have thought it strange that he should have been so reticent, but it was simply that from his English point of view finances were not a woman's province.

Walter Hutchins was an engineer of high reputation. He had once put a railroad across the Andes, and just before we were married he had completed the famous Renault works in Paris. He was not an ambitious man, but he had been meticulous in his profession.

The real passion of his life was yachting. Our yacht was kept at Southampton, a skipper and a head steward always aboard. In spite of the fact that I hated the sea, I was dragged off on many a cruise through the Mediterranean, to Malta, Naples, or Greece—wherever Walter's vagabond whim dictated.

We were very congenial in Paris, however, where almost every day I would join him on a gin crawl, beginning at Ciro's for luncheon. Afterwards we would go to the races, or to the bars where English and Americans congregated. Edward Mohler had been a prey to alcoholic sprees, and I was relieved to find that Walter was not. He drank steadily, but his affability merely increased with every Scotch and soda.

I remember a French doctor once making the routine inquiry: "How much whisky are you in the habit of drinking, Mr. Hutchins?"

The poor medico nearly fainted at my husband's calm reply: "Oh, sometimes two bottles a day, sometimes a lot."

It was after my marriage with Walter that I entered upon a new phase of social life which, although it took place in Paris, was nevertheless entirely unlike that I had known as the wife of Edward Mohler. No longer now was I under siege from the leaders of the "proper" set. After my divorce from Edward, the church ladies left no more cards. But I did not propose, you may be sure, to hang around the outside of the charmed circle of Paris society looking wistfully in, for I have never permitted myself to be snubbed. Instead, with Walter Hutchins' full approval, I created my own type of society, the sort that Edward would never have countenanced. In my *salon*, contrary to all conservative tradition, I jumbled together royalty, writers, actors, jockeys, scholars; the noble and ignoble; the wise and the frivolous; the industrious and the idle. Our house became the center of very extravagant entertainments. I gave carefully planned dinners and engaged the finest artists from the Odéon, or dancers from the Opera, to amuse my guests. The fame of my hospitality began to spread and, as some of my affairs were pretty free-wheeling, so did the stories of the wildness.

I think I can account for the sources of some of these stories. My husband had been a popular bachelor, the kind every woman likes to play around with and keep in her entourage. No doubt certain women missed him, and their jealousy over my capture of their pet may have prompted them to turn thumbs down on me.

Then there are always those women who have been married only once and who give themselves almost virginal airs over the woman who has been married more than once. And I, why I had had four husbands! Meow, meow! I was always on the ruthless hunt for men, men, men! I married them and squeezed them dry and left them! My extravagance would bankrupt a Rothschild—not to mention my gambling! In spite of the fact that practically every woman in Europe gambled, to hear the once-married ones tell it, you might have thought I was the only petticoat ever seen in a casino.

There was also Edward Mohler's old charge—that I associated with queer people: dopesters, cardsharps, impure women. My drawing room was said by the purists to be too mixed. True, as I have said, the off-color variety did flock around me, though I might not always join in their off-color pursuits. Gambling in our house in Paris, for example, was taboo, under Walter's specific orders. All the English and American set in Paris in those days lived high-strung lives. A lot of people I knew were taking dope. Some were of the immensely rich class who had to prance through a continual procession of merrymaking days and nights. Some were newspapermen who worked and played equally hard. But though my pace was as fast as the leader's, I never offered, nor was offered, narcotics.

But in spite of all the raised eyebrows I was often told that there would never be in Paris a more amusing *salon* than mine. Everybody loved it, except the prunes-and-prisms ladies who preferred to remain away. Certainly the men flocked there. I am a man's woman. I don't know why men like me, unless it is because I am tolerant of their peccadilloes, but they have always sought out my company, a fact that in itself is enough to get me hanged, drawn, and quartered by the sewing circle.

Among the women who did come frequently to my house was Isadora Duncan. There was one woman who dared to be herself. I knew her well and liked her. I also liked Aimée Gouraud and was invited frequently to her house, with its forty-two Buddhas and its dining room decorated like the interior of a church. Aimée's boudoir was done in black and white—black furniture and sixteen white bearskins on black carpets.

Isadora was a superexuberant being who wanted to give something to everybody. She was a *grosse mangeuse;* she loved luxury—and tripe. She believed she had lived in Greece in an earlier incarnation; this may explain her veils and festoons. She also believed she had lived in the days of Rabelais; this may explain other things. Many thought her affected. I did not find her so. She did no harm.

The simple souls who heaped anathema upon me and my *salon* did not realize that every time they uttered their damning comments they were only adding fuel to my fire and scalps to my belt. Their broadcasts of my daring entertainments, in terms of incredible dissipation, were of course the most effective publicity I could have had. Day by day the lists of my guests in the society columns showed more and more Mr.s and fewer and fewer Mrs.s. But my parties were never dull, and the wives' frowns were soon forgotten in the melody and jests of those wide-open nights.

One day a yellow journalist handed me the sobriquet of "The Most Dangerous Woman in Europe." When I showed the article to my husband, he snorted in amused disgust.

Little did I realize in those crowded, fun-filled years what this experience in entertaining was to contribute to my later life: that my celebrated "mixed" Paris *salon* was to serve as model, during Prohibition days in New York, for those other *salons* that would keep me perpetually front-page news, bring me international notoriety, and eventually hand me a jail sentence. At that time I was living far too flamboyantly and hectically ever to give a thought to the future.

12 *The War As I Fought It*

At the Brevoort Hotel in New York in August 1914, Walter and I were awaiting our sailing date back to France. We had just come down from Rochester, where we had been making arrangements for my father's care and comfort. My mother had died the year before, and though Father had tried living with us in Paris, he was too old to be transplanted; the experiment had not been successful.

Suddenly across the ocean flashed the dread threat of war.

In our long residence in Europe we had heard innumerable rumblings from the European political volcano, but the rumblings always eventually subsided.

My husband shrugged his shoulders. "Just a bunch of financiers trying to lower the stock market again," he said. "You Americans are a hysterical lot."

But the scareheads persisted: Belgium raped, France mobilizing. Headlines screamed: "Germans aim for Paris!" The British war machine commenced to revolve. Kitchener was calling his First Hundred Thousand, and even militant suffragettes were laying aside hammers and hatchets to don nurses' garb. No cables were allowed either way. What had become of my children?

Every time I heard a special edition shouted I would run out into the street and almost tear the paper from the newsboy's hand.

Day after day we tramped in and out of steamship offices, trying to get immediate bookings. Finally we learned that the French *Rochambeau* would shortly make a dash for Europe and would take us along. From hour to hour we waited word about the date of departure. We sail today—thank God. No, we don't sail—damn! We do—we don't—for nearly a week. Then came the hurry-up call to get aboard.

The boat carried twelve hundred reservists—French, Belgian, and Italian—Walter and I being the only civilians. Making their farewells on the dock, these men were a motley crowd of harmless civilians like ourselves. But once aboard, they clapped on their kepis and became in a flash belligerents. One fellow, after he had changed his headgear, threw his straw hat overboard; immediately every man followed suit, until hundreds of white straw hats were bobbing on the river like a great patch of water lilies.

Four battleships escorted us far out to sea, then signaled us to scoot. A call for help in midocean only made us go faster, the captain fearing a trap. Not a light, not even a match, as we sped through the black nights. Halfway across, a German was discovered on board by some French reservists, who unceremoniously poked him through a porthole. I began then to realize for the first time that war was no game.

As we approached Le Havre, we found the Channel full of vessels. An English transport preceded us into the harbor, and strains of "Rule, Britannia" mingled with the "Marseillaise." Troops, lorries, and great gray gun-carriages tumbled ashore from the transport. Everyone kissed and petted the huge war horses that were standing about waiting to be shipped to some front.

The station, brilliant with uniforms of many hues, was a babel of horribly twisted languages. English and French officers were showering each other with extravagant compliments that neither could understand.

Passenger trains made up of baggage cars and cattle trucks were pulling slowly in from Paris, all filled with homeward-bound American tourists packed in like sardines without benefit of oil. Some had had the good luck to draw a few inches of space on the rough wooden planks that had been thrown crosswise, circus fashion, to serve as seats. Germans fighting to get into Paris could hardly have been more frenzied than Americans fighting to get out. Tourist wives were noticeably changed. No longer commanding generals, they were now clinging vines on their life companions.

I saw one Manhattanite offering the passport official an insurance policy. He winked at me and whispered: "Lost my passport in the Gare St. Lazare. All I've got is this eagle-trimmed document. Think this guy'll pass it?"

The guy passed it.

Civilians, like beetles stuck on the ends of hatpins, had to stay where they were put. We stood about and witnessed good-bys of wives, mothers, and sweethearts until I felt I hadn't an emotion left.

Only sixty pounds of luggage were allowed for each passenger, so to get our trunks expressed Walter had to buy twenty-eight tickets to Paris. We were stuffed into an antediluvian railway carriage and apparently forgotten. Finally the thing wandered slowly and aimlessly out of the station into the cool country twilight, then stopped. I scrambled out and made off toward the engine. There I found the driver sprawled out on a bundle of straw, asleep. He had stood on the foot-plate of his engine, his hand on the throttle, for forty-eight hours, hauling soldiers. He was human and he was tired.

Trains kept passing us, loaded for the front, a song on every man's lips, a flag fluttering from every window, garlands of faded flowers and verdure strewn over heavy guns exposed on flat cars. In box cars, under swinging oil lanterns, horses nibbled hay; in the open doors men sat, feet dangling, waving greetings as we cheered them. On every train was chalked: EN ROUTE POUR BERLIN.

We cheered until our little engine crawled into Rouen. There we saw the first of those trains coming the other way, the long, silent hospital trains bearing the wounded and the dead. Uniforms, spotless only a few days before, were now torn and bloodstained, and dulled by powder smoke. The station had been fitted with hastily prepared beds, and in the dim light white phantoms of mercy crept about. A hush now enveloped our train. From then on, there was no cheering. We no longer even looked at those trains passing ours for the front. I became choked up with horror and hate of all that was war.

In Paris, once outside the Gare St. Lazare, I was struck by the calm. Belgian, French, English, and Russian flags looked almost gay against the blue sky. But one could see at a glance that Paris was no longer in hot pursuit of pleasure. Parisians were still eating and drinking out of doors in the soft summer air, but their voices were lowered and there were lines showing in their faces.

Boys who peddled papers walked the streets silently, pointing to the name of their journal written on a card and stuck in the front of their caps. The Governor of Paris had issued an order to prevent these street urchins from creating a panic by screaming unreliable news to a public whose tension was at the breaking point.

A few emaciated horses, too bony to serve as steaks, dragged old-time cabs after them. Occasionally a military car dashed through. Or a taxi, driven by some old man who had left his fishing net or his plow to come to Paris and learn automobiling in a few hours, would career wildly through the half-empty streets, scraping paint off passing tramcars. Every house shutter was drawn, as if Paris were a city of the dead. Paris, the bewildering, rainbow-tinted center of civilization, the home of the fashionable, the intellectual, the artistic, lay in the shadow of the advancing Hun. In the awful stillness we drew up to the door of our house.

The children were safe. Only one kitchen maid remained, however. All the other women servants had gone to their homes, and the men had been mobilized, even our elegant butler whose grand manners had often put mine to shame. How I blessed him now for his lavish buying, when I saw our well-stocked larder and cellar. Since the outbreak of war pessimistic Paris housewives had been laying in enough stores for a fifty years' siege. Practically everything had been bought up.

My first evening in Paris I dined in the half-mobilized *salle* of the Café de la Paix. German beer was masquerading as anything but Pilsener, and the Rhine wines, though safely hidden in the cellars, were blue-pencilled on the wine lists. I asked my friends what it had been like in Paris when mobilization first began.

Wives, they said, would often receive the papers first and bring them to their husbands at work. Each man would lay down whatever he was doing, take his hat, and say simply: "*Au 'voir.*" A few had evil presentiments and said "*Adieu!*" In the Champs Élysées a group of workmen were repairing the avenue. When they heard the call to arms, they laid down their picks and spades and one said: "*Et *nous aussi? Eh bien, venez boire une coupe, mes vieux!"*

In the restaurants war, the social leveler, had made itself felt. Dear gray-haired old ladies, who beyond doubt led narrow, respectable lives, chatted with dyed-haired, painted ladies who beyond doubt did not. Were the Germans still advancing? For thirteen consecutive days the monstrous boot of the Huns had kicked dust over the vine-covered houses of every French village in their path, and for thirteen consecutive nights the measured tramp of their double columns had kept the tassel of every peasant's nightcap quivering. Could our picket fence of bayonets hold them back?

Everyone in the restaurants knew everyone else, and no one knew anything. I devised a subtle method of my own for outwitting the censor. I looked up a naturalized German, who before the war used to say "we" and who always on fête days had his German flags well to the front. Now this same gentleman took pains to say "they" and showed the Tricolor. If his mustache rose like a barometer to the smiling point, I knew the Germans were still advancing. Before the Battle of the Marne the needle dropped to "Variable," and a day or two later we heard that Von Kluck had changed his route. When the mustache fell to its lowest point, it soon came out that the "theys" were in full retreat.

The Place de l'Étoile was a white city of hospitals. Huge white muslin inscriptions of *Société Auxiliaire de la Croix Rouge*, punctuated by red crosses, hid the names of many prominent German firms. Hotels owned or managed by Austrians and Germans rushed for the protection of the Geneva Cross when mobilization took place. Under the thick mantle of philanthropy they could save their property from destruction, and by leaving a clever spy in nurse's uniform in each establishment they could still render valuable service beyond the Rhine.

The great vogue at first was that every large private house

should be turned into a hospital. Many ladies, however, withdrew from the ranks of charity when they found they could not have their houses devoted exclusively to officers, and the epidemic of unbounded generosity was soon stamped out.

All the smart world tried to be in Red Cross uniform; those who couldn't make the uniform had to content themselves with armlets. Every fashionable Parisienne decorated herself and her limousine with the Geneva Cross. Historians no doubt will spill rose tints over the "noble work" done by those undisciplined, sensation-seeking women who wanted to enjoy the poetry of nursing rather than to perform any menial duties. At the hospitals some of the gentle bearers of the Geneva Cross were still wearing their ropes of pearls and their diamonds, so that they might be distinguished from the professional nurses. The writing of letters for some handsome hero, not too badly wounded, who would make his elegant attendant his confidante and eventually, it was hoped, fall a victim to her charms, was all the nursing some of these ladies cared to do.

Men became as mad over khaki as women over the Red Cross. Journalists, salesmen, jockeys, bankers—all from neutral countries—for some inexplicable reason began arraying themselves in khaki. English tailors were besieged by that neutral army made up of the cosmopolitan habitués of the Paris-American bars. Lieutenant-colonels grew like gourds in a night, with the Army List none the wiser.

One day I saw a friend of mine walking around in a full cavalry outfit, hoping, I suppose, that some day a horse might dash between his shapely legs. Another was in a khaki uniform, with a French kepi and huge automobile goggles. I inquired his rank and regiment.

"Oh, I'm an interpreter," he said. "I'm looking for anyone who wants Greek translated into English. Those are the only two languages I know."

I wanted to be useful and I found plenty to do. First I turned my music room into a temporary hospital which I placed at the disposal of the authorities until the immense new building in Neuilly originally designed for a *lycée* had been made over into a hospital. At the *lycée* nothing had been organized, and with other women I worked feverishly to fill the harsh, empty rooms with the necessities and comforts which wounded men would need.

The next thing I did was to go about through the quarter in which we lived, asking families whose food supplies were exhausted to come to my house to eat. Every day I rolled up my sleeves, put on a kitchen apron, and made a substantial noonday meal for all who came.

A fashionable tailor brought me his big, left-over pieces of overcoat cloth, and I got women to help me sew the pieces into blankets. These were used at the railroad stations to wrap the wounded men in when they arrived, wet and cold. I bought sewing machines and chamois skins, and the women and I made still more warm coverings.

All the gates of Paris except two were kept closed, and the Bois was fenced off, with sheep grazing under the trees. On Longchamps and Auteuil racecourses, mountains of hay were stacked under waterproof covers, ready to feed the immense herds of cattle which were being gathered to offset pangs of hunger during the threatened siege.

Sometimes the cry of *"Une Taube!"* made us rush to look. The aerial invaders were paying daily visits to Paris and so punctually that one boy claimed he could set his watch by the advent of the steel dove from over the Rhine. Besides bombs, the *Taubes* distributed little tracts: "The Germans are at your gates. Prepare to receive the victors." But the French continued to gaze up with curiosity, as though the *Taubes* had been sent to amuse rather than to murder.

The Germans were publishing in all their newspapers that Paris was sure to have a revolution. As a matter of fact, we

did have one, but of a kind that had never been foreseen—
a revolution in dress. Suddenly, without warning, the Paris
couturiers freed women's feet and legs.

All this was thanks to the popularity of the brawny Hie-
landers, with their thirteen and a half yards of kilt. What
a sensation those bonny lads created on the Paris boule-
vards!

"It's disgusting," said one old lady, "the way England has
let her suffragettes go out to fight."

But the piquant mannequins and the dainty midinettes
were enchanted by MacGregor and MacDonald. They
adored the Scotch plaids. Their slogan became "snips from
the kilties," and every little jade carried her scissors with
her and used them to advantage. I saw one six-footer running like a deer to cover in a taxi, and I didn't blame him
when I saw the indecent remnant of a skirt a crowd of
those girls had left him.

In a trice, voluminous short skirts for women were everywhere. For so long women had been skimping around in
gowns made only to stand up in that they were overjoyed
with the roomier skirts and freer legs. Now a fleeing lady of
fashion could take long swinging strides toward a safe
haven. This was indeed a garb born of the hour's need.

The threat to Paris became more and more acute. The
news that struggled through strict military censorship was
so scant that I again sought out my naturalized German.
He was radiant. When I asked after his health, he nearly
danced a hole in the pavement.

"I never felt better in my life! Everything is going our
way."

I knew "our" did not refer to the Allies.

My husband, as an engineer, had taken pains to explain
that "it couldn't happen here," that the German guns were
not powerful enough to put Paris under fire. He was so positive about it that I doubt that he would have believed the

attack had really happened if the *Temps* had not announced it. The Rue de la Paix, where streams of sunshine had bleached out the once-gay hues of the tricolored *affiches* on the closed shutters, had long been as dismal as a Sunday in Lent. Suddenly the luxurious shops were being blown in. Somebody began to publish little maps to show how to avoid the shells, and you could see the French going about trying to follow these maps.

The grimness of war began to bear in on us. Hardly a day passed that we did not hear of someone's son or brother killed. In shining metal breastplates handsome dragoons went up and down Paris streets, bearing to the bereaved the little card which read: "Be brave. Your country has asked of you a great sacrifice."

It was rumored that Lord Northcliffe, owner of the London *Daily Mail*, was becoming greatly affected by the war. He seemed to live in a settled melancholy. As he and Walter had long been friends, my husband suggested that perhaps we should do something to dispel his terrible gloom. I agreed to get together a dinner crowd.

To keep the fun boiling at a party, every hostess likes to have a good stooge. One of my favorite stooges at that time was Tectonius, the musician, who was also a *grand causeur* and a never-failing wit. I invited him and told him that we should expect him to play for us.

But Tectonius had an off night. He was anything but funny. All through dinner he paid attention to nothing but his plate. Lord Northcliffe was sinking deeper and deeper into his slough of despond. A pall seemed to settle over the party. I could hardly wait for the meal to be over, to get my guests into the music room and Tectonius at the piano. The magic of his music, I felt sure, would break this evil charm.

The great tapestried room was lighted by wax candles. A silence fell as Tectonius came forward.—*Boom!—Boom!—*

When the wind was east we could hear in the distance the guns of Compiègne.—Tectonius sat down before the piano. He sat so long that I wanted to shriek at him. And all the while—*boom!*—*boom!*—the distant rumble of the guns. At last, slowly his hands lifted and poised over the keyboard. Then, crash! and they began beating out Chopin's *Funeral March!* I could cheerfully have murdered the idiot.

It was while the Big Berthas were raking Paris that I received the four-day-old cablegram containing the news of my father's death. I have never grieved for anyone as I did for my father. He was the one friend who always loved and believed in me in spite of the differences in our characters.

Shortly after this, my husband received a call from Lloyd George to return to England to assume direction of the Woolwich Arsenal. He left immediately for his new duties and I soon followed him.

When America decided to come into the war, a service of thanksgiving was held at St. Paul's in London, attended by the royal family and all the diplomatic corps of the Allies. As I listened to the magnificent "Battle Hymn of the Republic" ringing out above the crashing of the massed bands, I was swept off my feet with a wave of patriotism.

My stay in England had not been particularly pleasant, and as soon as I knew the Yanks were coming I saw an excuse to chuck London and get back to Paris where I belonged. I wanted to have my house open and ready for the boys from home.

The advance guard of the Yanks, when they arrived at my door, found me in sweeping cap and apron. But Colonel Stanton, who mixed the cocktails, didn't care. I told him my plans for making our boys pack up their troubles in their old kit bags.

This was the beginning of the perpetual open house for the A.E.F. which I kept in Paris until the end of the war.

Our music room with its vaulted ceiling had always reminded me of a *salle de garde* in some medieval castle. But in the months that followed, the tall candles threw their dim light over anything but solemn gatherings.

Under the carved mantel that towered to the roof, a Negro jazz band, with Seth Low's jolly face over the drums, played the rhythms our doughboys loved. Here in this room any American soldier was welcome. French mothers, crowding in with their marriageable daughters, were sorely perplexed because they couldn't tell whether the officers or the men had the most money. General Ryan, that grand leader of the 69th, and good-looking shavetails like Dave Shryer and Donald McGibney were equally popular.

To amuse the men I brought in all the prettiest girls I knew, and the most fascinating stage stars. I gave a fête for the little butterflies of the Opéra, whom the war had so cruelly stripped of a livelihood. On special holidays, such as Thanksgiving, Christmas, or New Year's, sometimes as many as forty sat down to dinner. Always there would be surprises in the way of novel entertainment, and hang the expense.

Not long after my return to Paris, my husband was relieved of his duties at Woolwich and sent to build arsenals for the Americans in France. He surprised me by showing up one day in an American car which had been furnished him, driven by an American chauffeur.

Besides the Yanks, there was always a large number of British officers who made our house practically their headquarters and joined in all our fun. Of course many to whom we raised glasses in farewell never came back. To those who failed to return we merely raised another glass, then spoke their names no more. In every heart was the thought: "Tomorrow we die, but tonight we live."

13   *Taking the Bumps*

To me, the end of World War I could not easily be appre-
hended in the flood of press reports streaming out of the
famous Hall of Mirrors in Versailles. The realization of
peace came to me instead on a rainy day in Paris when,
from Jan Van Beers' windows, I watched the Woodrow Wilson presidential party detrain at the little Avenue du Bois
station. In 1919 American presidents were not the globe-
trotting, conference-table addicts they have since become.
At that time no president had ever before left the United
States during his term of office, and at the sight of Wilson's
lean, dignified, silk-hatted figure alighting from a Paris
train I was suddenly struck with the great significance of
what I was witnessing. Dramatically it was brought home to
me that the very presence of this man in France meant that
the long nightmare of carnage was over at last.

From then on, I felt a new freedom of spirit, a freedom to turn my thoughts once more to myself and my family. Fortunately, too, for family crises were in the making.

The first hint I had that Solange was grown up was her statement that she intended to go on the stage, a proposition which I strongly disapproved.

This was not my idea of a suitable future for my daughter. I had poured out money like water to give her the best education procurable in Europe. As a little girl she had been sent to Miss Russel's exclusive school in Westgate, England. Later, in Paris, tutors met each other coming and going through our doors. Madame Marcou neglected nothing to develop her musical soul; Phillip, the grand master of scales, taught her the technique of the piano. It was my dream that she should be fitted to make a proud marriage. Often in my mind's eye I saw her standing beside the massive Renaissance chimney in our music room, enveloped in a cloud of bridal tulle, with a wall of lilies forming a background for her pure, cold beauty.

But with all the ferment in our house during the war her attention was distracted from study. She had become fascinated by the clever artistes whom I had brought in to dance, and now could think of nothing but becoming a dancer herself. At her insistence I put her under such famous teachers as Aveline, of the Opéra, and Staatz, the ballet director, and eventually she acquired sufficient technique to secure engagements at the Folies Bergères. Morris Gest, who had been a frequent visitor at our house, even offered the child a part in *Mecca*.

But her heart after all was not as set upon art as she had imagined, and it was not long before she drifted into a romance which seemed to me even more unsuitable to her than a stage career. I objected with my usual tactless vehemence. She stood her ground. She did not realize how proud I really was of her and how much I wanted her to develop her fine native abilities. Our relations became more and more strained; they cracked the day she came to me and announced that she had chosen to marry the young man. In France a minor may not marry without the parents' consent, but this difficulty the young couple solved by being married in America. Beyond that I knew nothing of them; the break between us was complete.

I saw her again two years later, quite by accident. It was at Monte Carlo where Field Marshal Lord Ypres—General French, as he was better known—and I were judging competitors at a fancy dress ball at the Métropole. I had just awarded the first prize for men to Lord Northesk, who later married a beautiful Ziegfeld Follies girl, and after the prize-giving had gone with Lord Ypres over to the casino.

As we were wandering about the tables in the Sporting Club, I heard Lord Ypres whisper: "Look at that perfectly lovely girl."

I followed his eyes. There was Solange, a vision in a Nattier-blue period costume, with great pink roses.

It was the last time I saw my daughter while I lived in Europe.

After Solange's departure my spirits took a dive. My son by then was at school in England, and with neither of my children at home the great house at 110 Rue Ranelagh turned cold and lifeless. I took no more pleasure from my beautiful furnishings but plunged into a period of morbidity in which I relived ceaselessly the days when my children were young. Cute childhood incidents I had forgotten for years crowded through my thoughts. Again I held them in my arms while they slept, woke, smiled at me, and slept again. I nursed them through their baby ailments. I remembered their happy Christmases.

I tried to read, to study, to write, but I could not concentrate. For me there has always been only one way to forget

—through a turbulence of pleasure—so I returned to gaming. After the baccarat tables at Deauville had failed to stimulate me, I launched forth on the supreme folly and extravagance of my life—I began to run horses.

I know now that it is cheaper to live at the Ritz in silk sheets than to own a horse, even if he wins, and none of mine ever won. I bought three at Tattersall's in Deauville—Helen of Troy, Corset, and Baby. They were beautiful creatures and I thought I loved them all, until I found out how mean they were. Beautiful and mean. Baby always "also ran," but Corset never ran at all—she simply walked. Of course I was as green as a leek, or I should never have had those vixens foisted on me in the first place. I entered them in Paris and in Dieppe. I played wildly and lost constantly.

Throughout all this senseless extravagance Walter had maintained his usual silence regarding money matters. He broke the silence for the first time when he came to me one day, seated himself on a thirty-thousand-franc Beauvais chair, and said in his customary quiet tones: "Belle, we have no more money."

The shock this announcement produced in me is difficult to describe. I had had absolutely no inkling of any financial difficulties. In fact, as I have said, I had had no inkling, period, of anything pertaining to Walter's private affairs. Extravagant I had certainly been; but lacking any information to the contrary, how could I have known that I had been spending, not my husband's income, as I believed, but his capital? Had I only known, I could have retrenched, and I would have.

The debacle, I felt, was Walter's fault as much as mine. I considered that he had behaved with great irresponsibility in not taking me into his confidence. Yet, knowing him as I did, I could not help but understand why, with his particular background and temperament, he could have acted in no other way.

This, remember, was in the days when women were not even voting, and Walter was by no means the only husband who took the position that the man of the family should control the purse strings. It was a sort of unwritten law, especially in the higher financial brackets, that women should not have to bother their pretty little heads over anything as sordid as money. More especially was this true with the well-to-do Englishman, who, as everyone knows, tends to greater reticence and less sharing of business problems with his wife than the typical American. Walter's professional integrity was unquestioned, and he had a fine code of honor in everything that pertained to living the life of an English gentleman. In areas where he could rely on tradition he was in full command of any situation. But the loss of money was something unforeseen in that tradition; an emergency that caught him unprepared and extremely vulnerable because of his pride. Yet even if he had realized the breadth of my experience with the boom-and-bust type of economy, I doubt if he could have changed his course. He did not know the meaning of the word niggardliness. It was more consistent with his lifelong concept of the role of gentleman to play the game royally to the very end; then, if must be, to throw down the cards and leave the table.

So there we were—both completely ruined—and it was necessary to lay our plans for a moneyless future. For himself he proposed to return to England and his sister Alice until he could devise some way of recouping his fortunes. He had an invention on which he was working and in which he had much faith. He would leave to me whatever I could salvage from the sale of our possessions. We both agreed that it would not be practicable for me to think of going with him to live with sister Alice, with whom I had never been popular and who, when I was around, never took her cigarette out of her mouth except to say something disagreeable about Americans. She and I constantly attacked each other, like two great stinging wasps.

Quite calmly, without recriminations, Walter and I parted. There was no thought of divorce between us; personally we had always been most compatible and congenial. In fact, to keep up each other's spirits, we talked with phony cheerfulness about the day when "things would clear up" and we could get together again.

Meantime, I was once more on my own. Once more I had only my wits to live on. The shock was profound, though it was not till later that I realized how far-reaching its effects would be on me.

The yacht went first. Then good-by Corset, Baby, Helen of Troy—the devils. The house and everything in it and my car went next, all to the European director of the Swift Packing Company.

Giving up my Paris home was the toughest thing I had ever had to do. When the last servant had departed, I went on a farewell tour. I looked in the nursery, soon to be filled with the happy children of the new owners. I paused at my boudoir. I went down to the library, which I had loved so much.

In the dining room I had ordered the table laid for twelve. From under a Venetian lace cloth showed the gleam of yellow satin. Over the table were scattered lovely little marble statuettes. Venetian glasses were grouped before each place. I walked over to my place and turned down my glasses.

The horn of the car which had once been mine announced the noisy arrival of the newcomers and their large family of children. As I handed over the keys, I died a thousand deaths.

In other lean years I had always fled to Monte Carlo, so it was natural to follow again the gambler's homing instinct. With all my possessions turned into cash, I lost no time in taking a villa in the Avenue des Fleurs, only two minutes from the casino.

Nothing had changed. Grouped around the tables were the same stolid croupiers in their funereal attire, with their sphinxlike faces and steely eyes, all light and shade stamped out of their expressions by the frightful monotony that men of their profession are forced to endure.

There was the same army of what the French call "*pique-assiettes*"—"pick-plates." They are the wrecks who, once they have lost their fortunes, stand about in the Temple of Midas waiting for invitations to luncheon and dinner. Anyone arriving in Monte Carlo without his own circle of sin in those days could always gather up a duke, sometimes a prince, at least three duchesses, besides any number of honorables—all at the disposal of any party-giver as chair decorations. They are well described by their name. They not only pick the plates, they also pick the best seat in the car and a front seat in the box at the opera—in short, pick themselves a good time generally. With armor plate where their feelings ought to be they cling desperately to any vestige of old-time glory.

Some of the women wrecks have snow-white hair, which they probably hope may lift them out of people's harsh memories; some are divorcées who have made only a hop, skip, and a jump at marriage. Many spotless white villas hide the spotted reputations of famous beauties and kings' favorites of bygone days. In the excitement of a place like Monte Carlo, derelicts need not remember; and the turn of a wheel or a card keeps them alive one more day.

Some men can gamble and keep their heads, and make a living out of the casino. They are not really gamblers but businessmen. But women gamblers—what a joke!

A woman gambling for a man is the finest player on earth. She will sit in the game with a face as blank as though it were carved in marble and with no pity play the boob for everything he has—wealth, affection, position, even freedom—and take them all on bluff. Not so in a game of chance. There she reveals exactly what she is holding. In baccarat, if she has a five, she invariably hesitates and seeks with her eyes some telepathic counsel from the other players who are at the mercy of her judgment. She can never prevent the warm glow of satisfaction from mounting to her cheeks when she sees the banker is baccarat; nor the limp, irritated look that clouds her brow just long enough for the dealer to know that the ten-spot he has thrown her has ruined her hand.

Knowing all this as I did—for I was as sophisticated as any follower of chance—I can account for my conduct only on the theory that I was temporarily insane. Only a lunatic would have risked what I did. Maddened by shock and loneliness, I became utterly reckless.

In earlier days when I had come to Monte Carlo with Walter, he had always made me promise that when the money I brought with me into the rooms was gone I would not borrow, but wait until I could go to my bank the following day. This was to prevent me from falling into the clutches of the moneylenders and stampeding myself into a panic. Gambling women are easy prey for loan sharks, with luck at low ebb and hope riding on mountainous waves. They crave money as a morphine addict craves his daily drug. Money they must have at any price. Looking constantly at quantities of bills and coins stacked up before their eyes, they lose all sense of values and pledge their incomes for years ahead in order to have a few more hours of play.

This time I found myself in the *Cercle Privée* one afternoon without money. I was standing looking on when a *fille de joie* came up to me and whispered that my dear number 17 was coming up at the roulette table back of me. I smiled and pointed to my empty purse, whereupon she hastily took out three thousand francs from her own purse and pushed the notes into my hand. I accepted and sat down to play.

As if by magic, 17 took cover from the ivory ball and appeared again only after I had played my last louis. I was terribly upset to be in debt to a perfect stranger.

Explaining that I would not be a moment, I flew up through the gardens to a restaurateur and borrowed three thousand francs for the girl and three thousand more for myself. Unluckily I passed back through the overheated, smelly, stuffy Kitchen, and there, pushed and jostled by the mob, in my haste to get my money in on time I lost the six thousand francs before I even reached the Private Circle.

Then I was literally hot and bothered, as I rushed through the gardens again. My face was flushed, my hair disheveled. Again I told my plight to the kind restaurant-keeper, who wrung his hands in sympathy.

"Give me your diamond earrings, *chèrie*," he whispered.

I tore them off. He flew to the cash desk where his wife, like all good French restaurateurs' wives, was ringing up the profits, and returned with a fistful of bills—seven thousand francs.

Anyone might think that I could have kept my eyes on the ceiling in order to return unscathed through the Kitchen. But no. And at the sight of the first table my confidence was back as big as ever. I got a seat, but that was all I got. No matter whether I staked hundreds or thousands. I lost my *coup*. No matter what color I played I was always wrong.

As I threw down my last note, I looked around to see who was giving me the evil eye. A very nice American boy was standing behind my chair. I could sense his concern.

"Tough luck," he said.

Before I could catch myself. I had whispered: "Have you any money?"

"A *mille*," and he whipped it out.

I threw the *mille* after the rest and turned around to ask for more.

"Why, that's all I have, and I must get away early in the morning!"

He looked so startled that I dug around in my bag once more. There was one louis I had overlooked.

"Come," I said. "The roulette table."

I threw the small chip over the heads of the players and announced 21. The ball, which was already spinning, fell in my 21.

My nervous creditor grabbed my elbow. "I'll settle for that," he gasped.

But I shook off his hand and told the croupier to let it all ride. Everything was silent except for the whirring sound of the little ball. A click and the voice of the croupier—21! I scooped up my winnings. Fearful that I had the mad idea to play everything back for a third turn on 21, the boy snatched his thousand-franc note from my hand and made off, waving it above his head.

Three persons that one afternoon had been drawn into the confused meshes of my panic, and before I was cured others followed in their train. But this was not the extent of my folly.

I had recently received my parents' legacy, and as the weeks went by I pushed that on the table too. In effect, I shoved out the little house in Rochester with the furniture inside it, and the garden with its thriving fruit trees. Eventually, in the ruins of my heritage, I was sitting behind woman's favorite mask, a smile, and thinking—not regretfully of my abominable actions—but of where I might get

more money, no matter from whom. Waiter, harlot, stranger
—it is all the same to the gambler.

Ornaments disappear rapidly from the throat of a gambling woman. The costly pearl collar is replaced by a
platinum chain, which gives way to a black ribbon to which
is attached some valueless object. Soon I was reduced to the
black ribbon—badge of destitution.

The game had got me. I was stony broke.

When a woman goes broke in Monte Carlo, she leaves—
on somebody else's money. My friends, who had been concerned over my heedlessness, had frankly intimated their
doubts that at my age I could escape falling into the "pick-
plate" class. Ten years before, yes, when I had had some
pretensions to youth. But when a woman is middle-aged,
chances for a profitable flirtation are pretty slim.

Fortunately I had been testing my fading charms on a
wealthy manufacturer from Leicester, England, with excellent results. When the crash came, it was thanks to him
that I was enabled, and emboldened, to tackle London once
more, where I optimistically installed myself in the expensive Princess Hotel.

Walter, I discovered, had not been able to improve his
fortunes and still wanted to continue with his sister. There
was nothing for me to do but go on taking the bumps. I
was back in the risky life I had always loved. But with what
a difference!—twenty-five years' difference in age.

The war had made drastic changes in London. Few of
my old crowd of girlhood days were in town. It was a new
troop of young bloods who rallied round that winter of
1923, all broke, all taking the bumps. One was young
Childers, whose father had been Lord Chancellor of the
Exchequer. Plowden was the son of London's wittiest magis-
trate; Pat Guthrie the son of a very wealthy Edinburgh

woman who had disowned him. After I left the Princess I lived for a time with another beachcomber, Lady Duff Trisden, whose mother owned Stirling Castle and whose brother was a colonel in the Black Watch. But no matter how dark the financial futures of this crowd might be, their chatter was unfailingly bright. Ernest Hemingway, sitting in the Select bar and listening to Lady Duff Trisden and Pat Guthrie, might well have been mentally scribbling them down in his novel *The Sun Also Rises.*

How the other half lives, indeed! Which half? We poor rich who had the nerve, not to say the dishonesty, to live at swank hotels often had to rack our brains to raise tips and bus fares. One of the circle of indigents had an aunt with failing eyesight and a charge at Claridge's. Often the crowd would have preferred a change to the Savoy or the Ritz, but Claridge's was an ironclad necessity.

Most frequently we ate by being invited into homes. Every day I had cocktails at the Savoy or the Hyde Park with Mrs. Mappin or Mrs. Donner, both of whom I had met at Monte Carlo. Mrs. Mappin was a woman of great wealth, petite and charming. She was the daughter of the Topping who built great docks, such as those at Liverpool and Sydney and Singapore, and her husband was one of the Mappins who gave Londoners their zoo. At the Hyde Park or the Savoy bar, I could usually find someone from whom to wangle a dinner. As I always took care to keep my appetite under control and not to overstay my welcome by a cheery fire or to mention how strapped I was, I continued to receive enough invitations to keep me from starving. Dinner was often followed by suggestions for a bridge game, and there were occasional winnings.

As time went on, it became harder and harder to keep up appearances. Sometimes bluffing for a good meal had to give way to the reality of a pub on Northumberland Avenue, where for a bob you could get a slab of beef, some greens, and a hunk of cheese. The phrase "struggle for existence" began to take on a grim meaning. I learned the interiors of all the moneylenders' offices and with what an air of benevolence the spider will devour the fly. I borrowed as long as my honest face could get trusted.

Coming down by easy stages from the Princess I eventually arrived at those creepy, awful hotels in the vicinity of Charing Cross Station. Here, listening to the talk of the little tarts in the lounges, I learned that their best pickings were the men who missed trains. In those squalid hotel rooms, greasy walls bore witness to many a drunken brawl. One day in a dingy, flyblown coffee stall, I met a waiter who used to be maître d'hôtel at the Métropole in Monte Carlo. We looked at each other in startled recognition, then both of us burst out laughing. Mrs. Mappin, who met me afterwards little realized, as I stepped in and out of her Daimler, from what gutters my feet had just come.

I learned to be very careful that no one offered to drive me home. Sometimes a bachelor with whom I had dined would insist on seeing me to my door. Then I would have to give a decent but fictitious address, stand in the entrance, and wait until he was out of sight.

The worst embarrassment I suffered was from my rich friends who met me in the street and took me home with them. On one of these occasions a friend asked her maid to go and fetch me a hat. Naturally the maid resented giving to an outsider what she regarded as her own loot, and she brought out something that looked like a nesting parrot. The little stuffed bird cocked its head, with its one remaining bead of an eye, down over the rim at me as much as to say: "You will visit these rich friends, eh?"

Next day when I passed the mutilated veteran who used to let me look at his papers every evening without buying one, I asked him how he liked my new hat.

"Keep it on, sister. It'll hand some poor bloke a laugh."

So parrot and I went merrily on our way.

For those who can no longer afford any roof, the Embankment offers many fine arches to curl up under. In St. Martin's-in-the-Fields one could sit for one night only. The longest part of those bedless, roofless summer nights was just before dawn. Often I would walk to Covent Garden in the gray morning light to watch the flowers being coaxed into life. Embankment nights turned cold as winter came on, and just before dawn I would go to warm myself in Charing Cross Station where early trains of workingmen poured out their torrent of humanity.

One day my chest began to pain. I went to a hotel in the Strand, where I had stopped in the days when I had had eight shillings for a night's lodging, and asked for the manager.

"I haven't a thing but what I am standing in," I said. "I'm sick, and I think I'm going to be sicker. But I can give you pawn tickets for a fur neckpiece."

The pawn tickets were waved aside and I was given a room. For six weeks I lay with double pneumonia, my only nurse the maid who brought me a cup of tea now and then. When I let Walter know my plight, he came at once to see me, and often thereafter. He was still broke, but trying to market his invention. My son, he told me, was still in school.

One day when I was getting better, I lay looking out across the uneven rooftops with their odd chimney pots. Suddenly a scrawny black cat appeared on my window sill, peered inside with feline curiosity, and jumped on my bed. As I stroked her dirty black fur, I thought: Here's my luck again. I'm going to find a way back to Paris.

After I had recovered, I dropped in one day to see Daddy Longworth, now married and living on Adelphi Terrace. Lord Thomas Dewar, famed for his White Label Whisky, happened to be there.

When I told Daddy I wanted to go back to Paris, he said: "Here's the man who will take you. He's going there tomorrow."

Lord Dewar was very courteous. "I'm sure I owe you a great deal," he said, "for the advertising you must have given my whisky these many years."

He owed me nothing, but he gave me what I needed: a generous sum of money. Before I left with him next day for Paris, I called on my husband.

"Would you like a divorce?" I inquired.

"No, darling, I love you just the same," he replied.

14   *The Literary Bug*

Back in my adored Paris, where even in the poorest *café* a jest is given for a jest, my feeling of luck persisted. The war had brought as many changes to Paris as to London, but in going around to the old haunts I met several former cronies. At the Ritz bar I bumped into Jack O'Brien, from the United States, and many other foreign correspondents, including Jed Kiley, Walter Duranty, Floyd Gibbons. When I met Basil Woon, writer and authority on the Paris not described in guidebooks, he greeted me warmly.

"Where have you been, Belle? I've been looking for you. Ray Long of *Cosmopolitan* wants some articles from you on the European scene."

"I ought to be able to produce those," I said. "Especially now that I'm living over in Montparnasse."

In Montparnasse, the home of literary Bohemia, one could exist almost literally for a song, and here I had taken refuge, hoping that the money Lord Dewar had advanced me would tide me over until I could redeem my fallen fortunes. In that famed section I found a lovely pavilion in Rue Verrie, with a large studio, a library, a bedroom, and a terrace garden outside the studio with iron doors opening on the street. I had often visited the Latin Quarter, and now I anticipated a good deal of pleasure in studying its offbeat inhabitants at close range.

The pleasure was all in the anticipation. Looking back on my experience there, I remember the description a man once gave me of delirium tremens. A huge snake, he said, had coiled itself on his chest. After hours of agony he managed with a mighty effort to push its cold, heavy body off onto the floor. He heard it fall, then watched it uncoil and slowly crawl through a window and disappear, leaving behind a trail of green slime. Though Montparnasse is no longer on my chest, its slimy trail will always drag across my memory.

In the old Montparnasse, in the days of the fabulous grand dukes, it must be admitted that gaiety and affection, though very pleasant, had their price and were marketed in a businesslike manner. But Montparnassians of the Twenties burned incense neither to Eros nor to Mammon. The women were not, as one might have supposed to look at them, prostitutes—that is, no more than were the men; they were neither frankly commercial nor looking for romance. No one fell in love, no one fell out of love; and to my knowledge no one ever got out of debt.

"Food, food, lots of food," was their war cry. A band of Forty Thieves, made up of would-be writers and artists, notorious ladies, and overindulged sons at the end of their financial tether, soon descended upon me, fed in my free eating house, and as long as I loaned—that is to say, gave—my money freely, accepted me into their ring and allowed me to trail them everywhere.

During the year in which I sailed up and down the uncharted river of degeneracy, tying my bark sometimes at the Dome, sometimes at the Select or the Rotonde, I gathered all kinds of data on these people until at last I was able to explain them to myself.

I saw that I had wandered into the land of exhibitionism. While I have no doubt that here and there might have been found Montparnassians who were serious in their work, the great majority, as I encountered them, were not. These were not nice young artists, here to share each other's crust, to love, to dream, to paint or write; these wanted only to be seen talking endlessly, drinking, and wearing the beret that distinguishes the Left Banker. The debauches in which these triflers indulged nightly I could have understood of serious artists who needed relaxation after a hard day of creative work. But these poseurs never did anything except to sit around in the *cafés* and boast of what they were going to do, idling the whole night through until the scrubwomen arrived in the morning. I sat around with them and listened to them holding forth in language no soldier would tolerate in his barracks without throwing his boots at the speaker. When foul words staled, the exhibitionists would begin to shed their clothes.

There were probably no more disillusioned, no more hopelessly wrecked denizens of the Quarter than the English and American girls who had been sent to those fake educational dens in Paris which rooked fond parents in the name of culture. It was no wonder that intelligent and spirited girls revolted from the meager fare offered by broken-down nurses and inferior governesses and that, in search of something to fill dissatisfied days, many of them wandered into Montparnasse. They could not know that they were escaping from a shoddy school milieu into an equally shoddy one of art.

The reckless waste of youth was heart-rending. One after another I watched the tragedies of beautiful girls in their teens, glimmering like fireflies for a moment, then lost in the darkness. One hotel was nicknamed "Hôtel des Suicides."

It is in Montparnasse that the wily dope-vine gropes for its victims, its dainty tendrils clutching for a green bough to reduce to deadwood. The studio dinner parties constituted the Quarter's greatest menace. They seemed very exciting to the unsophisticated girl, who imagined that in the low lights and the thick haze of cigarette smoke she was seeing how artists really live. Often these parties were given ostensibly to help a less fortunate artist. Everyone brought his own liquor and paid liberally for the skimpy meal provided by a nearby *café*. The studio was usually bare of furniture and guests sat on packing boxes, trunks, and floor. No cloth graced the table, and the shortage of glasses often obliged four or five to drink from the same tumbler.

After the concierge had been forced to call for quiet, there would follow whispered invitations to other studios where opium could be smoked. Unless a girl was willing to expose herself to the jeers and ridicule she had heard flung about all evening at the uninitiated, she would accept—just for once.

I was very fond of one lovely English girl, an artists' model, a child of seventeen. She used to burst into my pavilion, fling a bunch of roses in my lap, kiss my cheek, and whirl out again. One night she came in to show me her costume for the fancy "undress" ball of the Quarter. It consisted of a flimsy, transparent cape.

"For heaven's sake!" I gasped.

"Do you like it? I made it myself."

"It didn't take you long," I said. "What are you anyway?"

"Spring!"

"A pretty early spring, I'd say."

There was hardly a leaf or a ribbon to clothe her pretty, childish body. In a few minutes a band of students grabbed her, shouldered her, and away they all went, laughing.

Two days later, as I was sitting on the terrace of a *café*, I saw a worn-out horse dragging a dilapidated hearse in which lay a plain wooden coffin. There was not a flower, not a mourner.

"Going west ninth class!" observed a waiter, unfeelingly.

"The little English model," grunted the fat Dutch proprietor.

"Not that child who went to the *Bal Bullier* as Spring?" I cried.

"*Oui*, Madame. She shot herself on her return from the ball."

"But why—why?"

"Why not?" shrugged the Dutchman. "Just a cow less."

Nearly choking with hatred of his heartlessness, I tore to the old woman's flower stand on the corner and bought the biggest armful of flowers I could carry and ran after the hearse. I overtook it just as it was turning into a plot of unconsecrated ground in the Montparnasse cemetery, so near to all the mawkish gaiety the poor child had escaped.

At last, in 1925, the articles Ray Long had commissioned me to write for *Cosmopolitan* were completed and accepted and I was in possession of a flatteringly large check. As there was now no further economic reason for lingering in the squalid atmosphere of Montparnasse, I promptly shook the dust of that detested crossroads of exhibitionism and tawdriness from my feet and returned to the Right Bank, where life immediately assumed normal proportions again.

All this time, during the year or more I had spent in the Latin Quarter, the words my husband had spoken the last time we met in England had been lingering in my mind: "No, darling, I don't want a divorce. I still love you."

His tone had certainly seemed sincere, but nevertheless I had sometimes felt a nagging doubt. Was it really only money that kept us apart? Finally, I decided that being now in funds, with money no longer a bugaboo between us, I would put him to the test. So I wrote him a letter.

He came at once.

In the months that followed the publication of the articles, as I read my complimentary reviews and listened to the praises of my friends, success as usual began to go to my head. I began to assume that I might be another George Sand, and that the world might still be my oyster. In fact, I eventually became so bitten by the literary bug that in the summer of 1927 Walter and I took an old-world chateau on the edge of Fontainebleau where I could be quiet and write, as the foolish saying goes. And high time, too, for by then the exchequer had dwindled alarmingly.

The house was a rambling, lofty-ceilinged affair that had been reconstructed from the stables of La Grande Mademoiselle. Each generation had added a room here and an ell there until the mansion now fairly sprawled through the Forest. Modern plumbing was still an unknown art in the town of Fontainebleau. True, there was an intricate, if archaic, maze of waterpipes in the house, thanks to which we often found little lakes and rivulets in such out-of-the-way places as our drawing room or library. During a storm the Forest itself—loose stones, bits of fallen logs, moss, and underbrush—rushed in whirlpools and eddies through our dining room.

A senile rooster with a rusty voice crowed the hours from one A.M. to daylight. At dawn, the French artillery school left its barracks and rattled past, off to play at war in the

Forest. Later a town crier with his drum hawked the latest village news under our windows, interrupted from time to time by the sonorous horn of the newspaper woman as she trundled day-old papers up the drive. Finally twenty students of Walter Damrosch's school of music would start playing all around twenty different compositions. The only completely quiet inhabitant of Fontainebleau was the fish vendor's pet turtle, which took his morning walk down the main street to announce the price of fish. On his back was inscribed POISSONS FRAIS, followed by the daily quotation.

With no more disturbance than these provincial activities Fontainebleau seemed to me an ideal retreat for creating. Retreat it proved to be, but in the insane-asylum class. My cellar stocked with good, persuasive wines and liquors to reconcile all prejudices, it was not strange that the world and his buddy descended upon me.

Being only thirty-five miles from Paris, my house was an ideal escape for all my turbulent, word-mongering friends. Hardly would I take my own heroine out of her swaddling clothes to coax her into my manuscript than the clang of the gatekeeper's bell would force me to drop her again. Real writers and would-be writers kept arriving day by day from Paris.

"Why, Belle, this is simply delightful!" they would gurgle, and then telephone to other geniuses craving to be far from the complexities of urban living. Promptly more guests would arrive, bags, pets, and typewriters.

My gates apparently chalk-marked, faces I had hardly seen before arrived from I knew not where. My willy-nilly guests rushed up and down the stairs and swarmed over the premises like trout in a mountain stream. Some, in the ecstasy of this newfound haven, sang at the tops of their voices. I called the show a circus, and believe me it was no one-ring affair. In lieu of a calliope we had a young and budding pianist; noisy performers went berserk and whirled through their acts in a bedlam no self-respecting canvas-top would endure.

My weakness for the members of the Fourth Estate, whose stock in trade it is to be entertaining, has always been more than the friendships I have formed among them. It is a deep-rooted and genuine affection reaching back to the time when I called a newspaperman of another day "Father." It was only natural then that my forest retreat should become a rendezvous for foreign correspondents. Jack O'Brien of the United Press would telephone that he was coming down for a "whiff of ozone from out that fern-carpeted Forest." What he actually meant, of course, was a whiff from old bottles mellowing under sacred crusts of cobwebs and dust in the wine cellar. Floyd Gibbons often called to ask about the prospects of "cawn pone with poke chops an' good ole-fashioned gravy, down yo' way." Another gastronomic guest, Count Karl Bülow von Dennewitz—who never referred to his title, but was just "Denny" to his friends—then on the Paris *Herald*, would wire for the potluck that he well knew would be excellent.

Basil Woon led caravans to rest at our house over the weekends; Hank Wales, Ralph Heinzel, Jed Kiley, Minott Saunders, George Slocomb, Walter Duranty, Lawrence Hill, William Daniels, Tor Arosorano, and John Fitzpatrick the pianist were among the weary and travel-stained who sought refreshment.

That summer of 1927, as I walked the traditional ways of kings and queens in the old town of Fontainebleau, I began to feel a premonition that Fate was again at my elbow. But it was not until later, when I looked back, that I realized how well she was marshaling her forces to bring to a close an old life and to create a new one.

By the end of summer, prodigal entertainment had made a deep hole in our resources, and the inspired manuscript that would have redeemed our fortunes had not yet been

written. Neither had any of my husband's moneymaking
plans materialized. This time we did not try to conceal from
each other our realization that our days together might be
once more coming to an end. Again the soft cushions were
about to be pulled from under me.

As usual I cared little. I had never allowed myself to complain when the wheel spun around to a nonpaying number;
never thought of throwing my poetic body out of a window.
Fate, I had always found, never closed one door without
opening another. So when I received one day a letter from
Ray Long asking for another manuscript from me, this time
on the American scene, I saw in his request the opening
door. Ray suggested that I come to New York to rediscover
my own country.

"After so many years in Europe," he wrote, "you must
have completely lost your perspective on America."

His letter gave me a new yearning—that of the expatriate
for her native land—at a time when I thought every yearning had long since been satisfied.

But saying good-by to Fontainebleau would be no easy
task. Besides my husband and my host of Bohemian friends,
I had two devoted acquaintances in that little French town.
One was the Baroness de Vaughan, whom Leopold of the
Belgians had made his morganatic wife. She was one of the
most radiant personalities I have ever known; a born courtesan who had all men at her feet. The other special acquaintance was Georges d'Esparbes, *conservateur* of the Palace of
Fontainebleau. Though he was a celebrated scholar and an
authority on Napoleon, his erudition sat lightly upon him.
Small, dynamic with laughter, he loved conversation, *cafés*,
and the clinking of spoons and ice in tall glasses of that opal-
escent liquid known as absinthe. In short, he was just such a
Bohemian as George Slocomb described when he wrote of the
Academician, Raoul Ponchon: "He loved wine, laughter and

rhyme, which is the minted coin of speech." At the time Marie Dressler made one of her pictures in Fontainebleau, she spoke no French and M. d'Esparbes no English. But when Marie called "Hello, darling!" to him from the Palace gardens, the rich warmth of her voice conveyed the "darling." In the evening, when he came to tell me about the incident, he was still beaming with pleasure.

Through those impassioned discussions of literature in which the French delight to indulge, my proposed book had been developed in Georges d'Esparbes' library at the Palace. When I confided to Georges my decision to go to America, I told him how much I should miss him as a listener and as a critic.

"The only unhappy moment I shall ever spend with you, Georges," I said, "will be when I say good-by."

"And that good-by," he answered, "must be said at a farewell dinner in the Palace."

What a farewell to the Old World it was! That last evening I dressed early and walked with my husband through the deserted park, skirting the pond where the old carp lazily finned their way, to our host's apartment in the left wing of the Palace. There on a table in his library I found ice and the various ingredients for a real American cocktail.

"Just waiting for the American priestess to say a few incantations," Georges said as we entered, "while she mystically sprinkles the gin and twirls the ice."

I had never been quite able to educate the Baroness and Georges down to our American cocktail. They were always ready with a long diatribe against it, the gist of which was that mixed drinks injure delicate palates. But nary a word could I ever get from them against their *Trou Normand,* served right smack in the middle of dinner. This strange libation is nothing more nor less than a large glass of applejack, tossed off before the game course. Our cocktail may be potent, but once you slide into that Normandy Hole your feet are caught in quicksand and you may land under the table if you are not careful.

After we had finished our cocktails, attendants dressed in the livery of Napoleon ushered us into the dining room, up the broad stone stairs by candlelight instead of the less romantic electricity. The soft yellow glow lent to the mouse-colored walls a sad and faded luster.

The Baroness was more lovely than usual that night, and her beauty did not escape the aging eyes of the dean of American painters, Alexander Harrison, who was seated opposite her. M. Briand, the statesman, had his cat with him. I adore cats, and I always liked him for loving the soft, furry little creatures. Maréchal Lyautey of the nearby garrison was present, and with him half a dozen handsome young officers. Newspapermen and artists made up the rest of the gathering. From the very Gallic conversation induced by my potent cocktail, I doubt if even a *Trou Normand* could have kept the ensuing effervescence at a higher level.

Going home, we descended the horseshoe stairs, accompanied by Georges, into the Cour des Adieux, and as I met the evening aroma of the Forest a pang shot through me. The friendly, silent trees, the flowers cuddled in their beds under cover of the night dew—everything was so calm, so peaceful.

"Georges," I said, "only half of me is going to America. The other half will always be here in Fontainebleau."

Next day my writers broke camp. Good-bys echoed through the halls. I didn't stop to check the inroads on the wine cellar; simply turned the key, and walked for the last time past the flowering juniper bushes which stipple the ground under the old oaks in the forest.

Back in Paris I blew into the Ritz to say good-by to Frank, the barman, not forgetting Peter and the big boys at the door, all of whom I had known as little boys. Then I dashed a few good-bys to myself down my throat and hurried off to the Gare St. Lazare. Under the vaulted roof of the old station, amid the screech of whistles, clanking of brakes, raucous cries of porters, and rumbling of trucks, lost in a haze of steam, a diminutive locomotive patiently stood puffing and waiting to pull the boat train out. A dignified but poignant farewell from my husband—a last farewell! we were never to see each other again—and the Transatlantique pulled out for Le Havre, to the accompaniment of shouted good wishes from assorted journalistic friends who had gathered to see me off.

On the way to Le Havre the train ambled, as trains do in France, through the apple orchards of Normandy, where I had passed so many summers. Looking at the apple-laden trees, I thought of all the calvados that would soon again be filling those little stone jugs in which the conquering worm is at last defeated. The trees made me think of those giant oaks that held up the sky over Fontainebleau and I wondered if I should ever return to walk again under their thrilling silence, except, as Stevenson says, "at night in the fondness of my dreams." When I realized those great friendly branches were no longer spread above me, for a flash I was lonely as a hawk.

Part Two
SPEAKEASY

1 Return of a Native

I have always thought that the passengers who make their way up to the bow of a departing liner must be looking across the waters to new shores for happiness, and that those who linger by the stern rail are leaving their happiness behind. I was among those at the stern, when I crossed to America in 1927, for I was leaving behind a whole lifetime of pleasure in Europe. Looking aft until the fading light on the shores of France melted in the haze, I seemed to see the once-gilded towers of my past, like the lost town of Is, sinking into the sea, and I could even fancy that I heard the ghostly music of their bells.

I knew that both my son and daughter were somewhere in this America to which I was returning. My son had completed his education abroad with a course in engineering at the University of Frankfurt-am-Main. Now he too had come to America and was living with his father and the second Mrs. Mohler in Cleveland. Both of my children had chosen to go their own ways, and I had accepted their decisions. I had no intention of being a death's head at their feasts or a Lazarus at their gates.

Parsimonious souls, looking at my empty purse, were already censuring me for having thrown away so much money in a wild torrent of spending and giving. True, I had swallowed the sugar-coated pill of Rabelaisian philosophy—that life is its own justification and we need not live depriving ourselves of anything. "Belle Livingstone, that chatelaine of castles," criticized the press one day, "lets fortunes trickle through her restless fingers." On the other hand, another newspaper had editorialized: "In our eagerness to lay away money for a secure old age, we forget that old age needs other things besides cash in the bank. It needs memories of laughter and song, of days and nights of carefree, youthful happiness. We don't need to go the whole way with Belle Livingstone, but there are worse crimes than improvidence."

Darkness settled over the Atlantic, and still I stood leaning on the taffrail, lost in reflections. The steward interrupted these reveries to say that he had placed my deck chair and my maid's on the lee side of the ship. I was startled when I heard my fifty-two-year-old voice say "Thank you." So different from the lighthearted, frivolous voice that no doubt said the same words thirty years before when I was crossing eastward in the *St. Louis*.

Fifty-two, and fat. Gone was the seductive hourglass figure. Gone the protection of a wealthy husband. More than ever I needed my wits.

Toward the end of the voyage I began to watch from the bow of the ship, and at last one glittering morning in September I looked again upon the New York skyline which was to form my backdrop for so many years to come.

Gazing at the big metropolis, I heard no warning voice telling me I was to be a prisoner in its purlieus. Instead I likened the high buildings to the towering walls of new destinies which I had to scale. I remembered that the world will always speak to one who has pluck.

I strode down the gangplank and crossed the pier shed to the large letter under which were stacked my Vuiton bags.

"Got any liquor?" asked the customs official, as my French maid wrestled with the straps and locks of eleven trunks.

I had brought along a considerable supply of brandy and champagne, but the silent, disapproving glances of my abstemious Marie, together with my own serious thoughts, had somewhat dried up my thirst. So I had left the stock of liquor, nearly intact, in my cabin. I thought I was entering a nonalcoholic Volsteadian state, and I did not want to begin by breaking American laws of Prohibition.

"All I had left over is back there in my cabin," I replied.

The official gaped, thunderstruck. A hurried look at the stateroom number, and he and a policeman were off. After a hiatus of some fifteen minutes in examination of my luggage these pawns of Prohibition returned, their satisfied faces showing plainly that they had made unofficial disposition of my liquid gold.

A porter grabbed me. After enigmatical chalk marks had been scribbled on my luggage, I was hustled toward a cab stand. Here I told the cabman to take me to the old Brevoort on lower Fifth Avenue, choosing this hotel first because it was French and second because I had stayed there with Walter on my last visit to New York, that frenzied summer of 1914.

"How much?" I asked the driver on arrival.

Either he spoke Icelandic, or else he came from one of

those new countries that crop out on maps after any war. I didn't get a word he said; nor did I comprehend the cabalistic figures indicating rates to which he pointed on the side of the taxi. I was baffled.

"Here, help yourself," I said finally, offering in my hand all that remained of my cash estate.

The man's face lighted up as he grabbed a generous handful. I looked down to find I had exactly two dollars left. The repercussion of those two dollars was to hit me later on.

Undaunted by my diminished capital, I walked confidently into the lobby and registered. As I took the proffered pen from the nonchalant desk clerk, I could see by the look in his eye that he neither remembered nor cared that I had once before lived at the Brevoort. Impulsively I signed "Belle Livingstone" instead of "Mrs. Walter James Hutchins," suddenly recalling the luck I had had in New York before under that fortune-seeking name. The clerk called "Front!" and a bellboy caught flying keys mid-air and herded me into the elevator.

The musty old furnishings in the suite made me feel even more at home than a personal greeting could have done. In the alcove, as polished and shining as a fire engine waiting for an alarm, stood a huge brass bed with its short cotton sheets—reminder of home sweet home in my first stodgy little flat back in the Nineties.

It was an exhilarating September afternoon; I stood in the entrance of the hotel wondering how to begin my rediscovery of America. Suddenly my heart gave a happy thump as I spied the old white-haired Negro doorman of the brownstone house across the street. He was a bit of my past, for all during those hectic days in 1914 when extras, each bearing more and more terrible war news, were being shouted every few minutes, I used to sit at our windows in the Brevoort watching this good soul undisturbedly polishing brass and sweeping steps. In those days he did more to calm my nerves than all Walter's reassurances. Seeing the old man now, I accepted him as a fortunate omen. I wanted to wave at him, but like a ship in the night I passed him by and boarded a bus.

Taking a nickel from my purse, I offered it to the conductor. Instead of accepting the coin, he pushed at me a stubby, gunlike apparatus which looked for all the world like a steel frog with a hard, uncompromising mouth. The contraption sucked the money out of my hand and swallowed it with a clink. Fascinated, I watched that gluttonous little monster gorge itself on more and more nickels. The grim silence of the conductor made me recall, with a touch of nostalgia, that on Paris buses a ready word was always to be had in exchange for the ready coin.

At Forty-second Street I got down from the bus. I wanted to cross to Times Square and take a look at dear old Broadway, where I used to sail in and out of theatrical offices with all the assurance and vanity of youth. In the subway I was told to take a shuttle to Times Square—but how to find that shuttle amid such a scurrying mass of humanity! Women were stepping on my heels and men were dashing hither and yon, briefcases in their hands and a time-is-money expression on their faces.

"How much?" I asked the man in the change booth.

"Just a humble buffalo, sister, and step on it."

Back in the land of the free—free with sass! I thought, returning to my purse the remainder of the diminishing two dollars.

As I stepped through the clattering turnstile, I experienced the first good spanking I'd had since my Kansas upbringing. But where was the train? I grabbed at the first man who passed.

"Follow the green line, lady!"

"Where?" I yelled after him.

Another man rushing by shouted: "On the ceiling!"

I crawled into the buzzing swarm. If I took my eyes off the green line I lost my way; and if I took my eyes off the crowd I was apt to lose a foot. I followed the crowd up some steps and, my backsides smarting from a final thump from the final exit turnstile, stood blinking like a mole in the daylight. My shoes were so scuffed that I looked about for a boy to restore their shine. A dark-eyed, swarthy lad standing by a shoeshine chair sensed my thoughts.

"Drop a jit in de slot, Babe!"

As the brushes flew around and around my shoes, I began to wonder if all business in America was now conducted by dropping jits in slots. In the very next chair sat a pretty but vapid young girl, chewing gum highly and widely if not handsomely. What mileage she was getting! How her jaws must have ached! I recalled Bruno Lessing's line: "You may think they are thinking, but they are not; they are just chewing." I noticed the quick tempo of the passing feet and the expressions of the faces that belonged to the feet—worried, sad, vacuous, purposeful. All these people were going somewhere in a tearing hurry; they were not loitering, as the French are likely to do. All at once I hated the crowds and wanted to get away from them.

After some deliberation I recalled that Mary Brush William, the writer, lived on Fifth Avenue near my hotel. Anticipating the cloistered quiet I should surely find in a private home, I decided to call on her and slipped again into the sea of passing faces. But this time no more nickel-grabbing, greedy frogs should gulp my money. This time I'd walk.

I found Mary at home and was ushered into her living room. A bedlam was roaring out of her radio—commercials, songs, weather reports. She made no move to tone the thing down, so we were forced to shout above it. While I was doing my best to top the brassy din, periodically some other mechanical contrivance broke loose in another room and chug-chugged for a full minute. After this had happened several times, I could no longer control my curiosity. "What in the name of God is that?" I shouted.

"Oh, that's our electric refrigerator," Mary yelled back. "It used to wake us up at odd hours during the night, but we're used to it now."

As the automatic elevator dropped me to the street, I realized that I was experiencing in full force the technological triumphs of America. On every hand were new and wonderful devices to simplify living and produce more leisure. But where was the leisure? Americans seemed to have changed since the war into a restless, hurried, brash-mannered people.

Back in the Brevoort I found Harold Dunning waiting in the lobby. Harold was a delightful nomad who belonged to no time or place. He simply flew over this world like a big black crow, picking up anything that sparkled—especially wineglasses. In Paris, whenever he had picked up too many glasses and was out of money, he used to drive up to our house at any hour of the night, stick a match in the doorbell, then crawl into the cab and wait for someone to bail him out. But at this period, *mirabile dictu*, Harold was enjoying the luxury of a motorcar and a country house. He had acquired these fleshpots by pounding out fiction by the ream—the kind in which the heroine is left dangling over the cliff until the next installment. In a word, he had become a prosperous pulp writer, packing each page of his typewriter paper with thrills for thousands of readers doomed to lead drab, uneventful lives.

"Have you had dinner, Harold?" I asked.

"Not a drop," he replied.

"Seeing you dining but not wining," I said, "will hand me a great laugh."

"That laugh, Lady Hutch, you will never have. Just a step or two from here I'll buy you a *fine à l'eau*."

He took me to Julius's at Tenth Street and Waverly Place,

the first of the many speakeasies I was to become acquainted with in the days to follow. As we entered, a yell was rocking the dingy hole. Surveying the surroundings, I saw a bare, shedlike room along one side of which was a rickety mahogany bar. What a discolored Latin Quarter, I thought. The only novelty in the place was a large, white cat called Whisky who served as cashier *à quatre pattes*. If a customer's change was heard to ring on the bar, up would come Whisky, take the silver piece in his mouth, and walk with it to the cash register.

Henry de Wolf, a handsome young artist I'd known in Paris, made a landing at our table. With him was Bill Preston, a newspaperman I'd also met abroad. During the evening I noticed much more drinking than I had ever seen on the terraces of Paris *cafés*, yet the camaraderie of drinking was missing. Even my companions offered little toward pleasant conversation; they simply sat and drank.

"Nobody here seems to be having much fun, Harold," I observed.

"It's the rotgut we're drinking," Harold replied. "Wait till the bootleggers have squeezed enough bum alcohol into your juniper juice and etherized enough beer for you, and you'll find your palate will be vitiated too by the lousy stuff."

"I don't believe I'll do much drinking," I said, putting down my glass of very bad gin.

"Oh yes, you will! You'll drink if only as a gesture of revolt against the white-ribboners. Those fanatics have made people drink who never thought of drinking before. And repealing the dastardly law won't help much either. I tell you, Belle, America won't be sober for three generations."

Harold ordered another *fine* and lapsed into cloudy silence. What a monumental truth he had just spoken! I had to smile when I remembered that in Europe we'd actually thought it impossible to get anything to drink in America.

There at Julius's, that first hectic night, I learned all the

secrets of the strange process by which barrel shavings were
turned into whisky, and the procedure for manufacturing a
high-powered and barely potable brand of gin. I learned too
the new American slang being coined in the speakeasies. Expressions of wonder reached their climax with "What do you
know about that!" Positive decisions were accented with
"You said it!" and differences of opinion by snarling "Ba-
loney!" or "Applesauce!" Aside from these clichés I noted
also the stepped-up pace in expression, the wisecracks, the
racy idioms, and for protective coloration I deliberately set
about to cultivate a new manner of speaking.

That night and succeeding nights, a Livingstone exploring
driest America, I hounded Bacchus down dirty steps, between open garbage cans, into half-lit dank cellars where
grotesque painted figures floundered around on gold-splashed
walls. Beneath the figures on plaster, plastered figures on
hard benches worked desperately at trying to have a good
time in an atmosphere heavy with smoke and the fumes of
horrible liquor. Overfamiliar waiters in dirty shirtsleeves
served drinks from flooded trays and then dropped down at
the table for a friendly chat, for everything in Volstead days
was free of formality. Even the rats—zoological variety—sat
on their tails and waved from the corners. On the tables were
smelly, liquor-soaked, checkered tablecloths reeking of stale
beer and the cigarette ashes which had sifted through them
for many a day. I was astounded at the contrast between the
civilized drinking in Europe and the vulgar guzzling of these
dull-eyed, raucous Volsteadian rebels. The prevailing tendency to get drunk, no matter on what or with whom, seemed
to me a profanation of the Bacchic spirit.

Paris is always spoken of as the wickedest city on earth,
but compared with New York of the Roaring Twenties she
was a dear old lady in billows and ruffles of lace. I had always remembered New York as it was when I was a showgirl
in *The Milk White Flag*. In those days brains had to rustle as

well as silk petticoats, and conversation had to glitter. But Andy Volstead had brought in a queer kind of mores as well as a queer kind of gin. I came back to find that "This Freedom" was the slogan of the "warm babies" and the "hot mammas." In the Nineties music reminded me of sprites dancing in a sunlit meadow; the jazz of the Twenties sounded to me like a mob of hoodlums romping overhead on a tin roof.

Still, those nights in the evil-smelling speakeasies were less dull than the afternoons I spent throwing myself over the teacups with some of my old beaux who emerged from the Union and University Clubs and came to call on me. Seeing them after all these years startled me. Were these weary dotards the same men who had filled my girlhood with the appetite for more and more amusement; who had cultivated the budding gourmet in me as they casually called for strawberries out of season and offered me my first pierced peach in champagne? The years had piled up on me too, but I offered up thanks that I could still laugh and be merry, even if the peach in my champagne had turned into an oft-used olive in a Martini.

Returning to the Brevoort from a Village haunt late one night, I found my maid in the street in tears.

"Madame's door is locked!"

"Of course. But the key is at the desk."

Marie shook her head. "*Mais, Madame ne comprend pas.* They have taken the key away!"

"You mean we are locked out?"

"*Absolument, Madame.*"

"But why? What has happened?"

Then it all came out. After some questioning I learned that Marie had incautiously given her confidence to the headwaiter at the Brevoort and had told him of my dwindling resources. That two-dollar financial balance of mine didn't look good to the management.

I stood there on the curb in lower Fifth Avenue in the early dawn and did a little fast thinking as to where I might turn for help. The situation was too dime-novelish even for my tastes, and to complicate matters I had this totally disorganized Frenchwoman on my hands. Suddenly I remembered Charlie Goddard, a friend of mine who was stopping at the Vanderbilt. At this I shook a little hope into Marie and we set out for that distinguished hostelry. Charlie was the promoter of the chain of Schulte cigar stores, one of the big trust kings of the country. I had known him in my showgirl days in New York and only that summer at Fontainebleau we had renewed our old acquaintance.

I strode into the Vanderbilt lobby, picked up the house phone, and asked to be connected with Mr. Goddard's suite. Calling at such an hour was a gamble, but I had to take it. Charlie answered.

"This is Mrs. Finnegan," I chirped, "of the clan of In-Again-Out-Again-Finnegan."

I could sense Charlie's defense instincts switch on, but his curiosity was spurred and I was asked to come up.

Charlie himself opened the door. His shrewdness told him that something was amiss even before I had time to explain my predicament, and he began to criticize me mildly for having left a good home in Europe. I explained the misfortunes which had beset my husband and told Charlie why I was in New York.

Finally he ordered his valet to call the Brevoort and have my bill charged to his account and my trunks sent to the Vanderbilt. Next he telephoned downstairs and instructed the clerk to put me in a room.

"She's all right, but I'm not responsible," was his ambiguous recommendation.

2 *Park Avenue Whoopee*

"Be sure to live on Park Avenue, Belle," Jack O'Brien had said that day he waved good-by at the Gare St. Lazare. "Park Avenue is the Manhattan Yukon where the gold-diggers rest on their shovels."

Now, installed in the Vanderbilt, I recalled Jack's advice and congratulated myself that I had so quickly and painlessly reached my El Dorado. But alas, the din! Any calm that might still be in New York I had left down on lower Fifth Avenue when I made my tragi-comic exit from the Brevoort. Here, in midtown, the roar of the big metropolis came through my windows and penetrated my walls: the machine-gun rattle of riveters, the throbbing drone of planes, the sputtering backfire of trucks, the persistent whistles and hoots of the river boats, the vituperative honks of taxis.

One morning as I lay in bed sorting out the noises, I was

startled by the ear-splitting wail of a siren piercing through all the other sounds. In Paris, during the war, such an ominous shriek was a danger signal that used to send everybody scuttling to safety in a Zeppelin cellar. Frantically I seized the telephone.

"What am I supposed to do?" I chattered to the operator.

"Relax," said the blasé voice. "It's only Jimmie Walker clearing his way through traffic."

After such a fright I decided I needed a man-sized drink and, knowing I would find one in Charlie Goddard's suite, I dressed and went knocking at his door. What a sight! Here was no stage set for ten nights in a barroom but rather ten bars in a bedroom, and here it was that I got my first real taste of "whoopee"—vintage Roaring Twenties—in the land of the free and the mad.

I walked in to find Charlie swathed in a bathrobe of Turkish toweling and being variously anointed, manicured, and massaged in the process of being brought around after another night on the pleasure circuit. An amusing colored masseur, well-known to all the tycoons, finished rubbing Charlie down, and then the barbers and the manicurists took over. Meanwhile, a nurse, a secretary, and sundry waiters, bellboys, and yes-sir-men of every description hovered over him.

Charlie was a man who had to have everyone's undivided attention. He was wont to make expensive gestures before his little court, such as suddenly calling Paris or London and talking in five and six figures. That morning a brisk, dapper man came in and took an order for two Cadillacs to be shipped to Charlie's chateau on the Riviera. Throughout the forenoon more and more people continued to arrive, and all helped themselves freely to the bonded liquor laid out on a sideboard. Senator Ham Lewis of Illinois dropped in and with his witticisms stole some of Charlie's show.

Among the arrivals was a man who may have been a bartender, because as soon as Charlie spotted him he announced we were all about to take an alcoholic trip to the beach at Waikiki with the aid of the newcomer's Honolulu cocktail. The drinks were to be tall and frequent.

"Pete," he roared to the head bellboy, "get me a Hawaiian orchestra. Get me all the gardenias pushing up between the pretty fingers of that little florist downstairs. I want tropical atmosphere—gobs of it!"

The singing of the Hawaiians, the wild laughter after each of Charlie's jokes, and the rattling of glasses carried the morning well into the afternoon to the accompaniment of a cataract of liquor. Eventually the party reached that state of apotheosis in which everyone was magnificently alive to his own importance. Before this beatific self-idealization could be swept away in the continuing flood of drinks, I left. All the happy little burrs were still clinging tenaciously to Charlie.

All but one. When I took my leave, a quiet, well-dressed man who had been sitting on the end of a divan, holding a briefcase on his knee and refusing all drinks, accompanied me. As we walked to the elevator, I asked by way of conversation if he were Mr. Goddard's legal adviser.

"Hell, no, sister. I'm his bootlegger."

This remark was evidently expected to produce some manner of answer, so, without any real interest, I asked if bootlegging paid.

"Sez you," was the cryptic rejoinder.

My new friend then offered me as a present a bottle from his briefcase. Here, I thought, was a really interesting American, a member of a new and lucrative profession. I wanted to talk further with him but explained that I had only one room and therefore couldn't ask him in.

"That's the bunk," said he, contemptuously. "Since old Volstead gave us guys a leg up, that moral stuff is out. Why, the only place a guy can drink today is behind closed doors, and

I'll tell the cockeyed world there's a souse behind every one of them. Look in any store window. Nothing but cocktail sets. Every magazine you pick up is runnin' a drinkin' story. If you don't believe this burg is wet, get an eyeful of all these briefcases you see in everybody's mitt."

Food for thought!

On returning to my room, I received the first of those last-minute invitations with which New York hostesses fill their houses at a telephone's notice. A ship acquaintance named Mildred was calling from her apartment on Park Avenue.

"Put on your glad rags for dinner tonight, Belle, because we're going places!"

At the appointed time I was ushered into Mildred's rose-dipped sanctuary, with its low lights, low taborets, low chairs, and very low music. The scent of some exotic perfume announced that my hostess, a Titian miniature, was fluttering out to welcome me. For some minutes we chatted, awaiting the arrival of the broker who was to take us out—"to make whoopee," as Mildred put it.

He arrived, and at once Mildred's sensible, matter-of-fact personality changed. She became completely infantile. The broker had under his arm a fine seascape that he had bought for the apartment. As he presented it, Mildred clasped her hands together, cocked her head on one side, and cooed:

"Ooooooh! It must be awful good—it looks so wet!"

In a soft silence her Japanese boy brought her wrap. She slipped into it, looking like a little ball of fur, and rolled us all toward the door.

"I wanna be goin' places and doin' things," she lisped.

Soon we were doing things at Yar's in Fifty-fourth Street.

"Ain't he purty?" asked Mildred.

I looked at the murals—arctic scenes, with a huge polar bear in the foreground. I thought she meant the bear. No, she meant the broker. Like Long Island locals leaving Penn Station, the same phrase left her lips every few minutes.

"Some chicken livers *en brochette,* Baby?" asked our host.

"I didn't know the naughty chickens had livers," Mildred giggled. And to me: "Ain't he purty?"

With a highly polished forefinger Mildred playfully counted the buttons on the broker's coat. "Rich man, poor man, beggarman—oh, let's go back to the rich man!" And she clung to the button until it nearly came off. "Oh, what a shame to mess up the pretty asparagus! Ain't he purty?"

Between eating and kissing and raving over his Baby— about whom he was crazy, as everyone within earshot soon knew—my host finally finished dinner.

"Whoopee! Now let's go shee Tex Guinan! Whassay? Wanna shee Texsh, Belle?"

Coming across on the ocean liner, I'd read about Tex in a magazine article and ever since had been wanting to see her. In only a few minutes we were at her club.

In we strode, and when our party was sighted off Rock Candy Mountain, all the brass and drums cut loose. But even that din could not drown the bawling of our supersouse. We were almost blinded by the spotlight, which, directed momentarily on us, diverted attention from the floor show. Texas' dancers paused behind the flimsy covering of the big lace fans which served as costumes while all eyes were trained on our Whoopee Chief with his big and little squaws trailing single file after him to his ringside table.

As the show resumed, Tex swept across our vision, ablaze from wig to heels in flaming reds. She jumped on a chair in her fiery taffeta dress and her red satin slippers and waved to the figurants on the bright frieze of night life, wisecracking in her megaphonic voice. Her wit fizzed like sky rockets. I had a suspicion, however, that the cheerio of her own evening would come later when she read the tally of the total receipts. Though eventually Texas and I were to be linked together as protagonists supreme of New York night life, that evening I felt no psychic premonition of it.

Except for the continuous yelling of our Chief, our party would have gone unnoticed. On and on he roared above the pandemonium, bellowing out his signals for the etherized cider that passed for champagne. More and more he drank. At last he reached the giving stage. He gave the beautiful cigarette girl a kiss; gave the musicians hell for not playing his choice of music all the time; wanted to give Texas a lot of new ideas for her show; gave the party at the next table a pain in the neck; and finally tried to give me away to a young man who looked as though he might die of fright at any moment. And above all the din Mildred kept chirping: "Ain't he purty?"

When we finally rose to leave and our noisy escort went to get his coat, my fur-wrapped friend slipped her arm through mine and asked in a perfectly normal, well-modulated voice:

"Aren't you tired?"

All evening I had been expecting that if Mildred ever recovered her reason she would start raving about this man's making such an exhibition of us. Now I couldn't resist asking why she didn't.

"I've learned, Belle dear, to let 'em yell. They're his lungs he's shouting with, and it's his money he's spending, so why not let him have a good time?"

While I was undressing later, Mildred's "Let 'em yell!" kept ringing in my ears. I thought: Well, I've had a close-up this evening of the man in Wall Street who does smart things all day and silly things all night. In the good old days, the gold was near the surface and hearts were generous. I pitied the modern Mildreds when I saw how hard they had to blast to get a nickel out of these East Side mines.

Next morning the synthetic champagne had taken its toll of me. I felt as faded as the gardenias on my dressing table, their snowy petals turned to a nasty brown and their bright silver ribbon tarnished and frazzled. In this state of low spirits I was cheered by the announcement of a caller. It was Madeline Boyd, a Frenchwoman, then the wife of Ernest Boyd. Madeline had a cultivated understanding of everything except mankind. She would walk into a room, sit on a chair, and refuse a drink, all with the same assertiveness. A "No" to Madeline would die on your lips. So when Madeline announced that morning that she was going to introduce me to some "very nice" people in New York, I docilely gave my bark into her hands, and I must admit that while she stood at the helm she piloted me through some beautiful nights.

One occasion that I particularly treasure in my memory is that of a dinner given by Douglas Parmentier, whom I titled "Sir Douglas" because of his amalgamation of attractive qualities. He had that rare quality of politeness, of genuine interest in all that was said, that transcends mere affability. The Parmentier dining room was floored with large black-and-white marble squares, and the black oak dining table all but hidden under sheaves of American Beauty roses. The adjoining library was done in pale grays, colored and animated only by the books and bowls of roses and the beautiful gowns of the women.

I recall that Mr. Hartman, editor of *Harper's*, was present that night and, like all editors, an attentive listener. This particular evening he had good reason to listen, for Ernest Boyd and Sam Hoffenstein were fencing exceptionally well and amusingly. All through dinner the two wits crossed words. Lovely, ethereal Emily Vanderbilt contributed to the brilliant company by her silence. When I came to know her better, I told her she was the first woman I had met in New York who didn't dislocate interesting conversation. Perhaps it was because of this talent of hers that she was always to be found in the company of artists, whose gifts she must have appreciated and whose spirits she must have soothed. If only she had chosen, she might have been the "quiet genius"—the Madame Récamier—of her day.

One of the first country houses I visited was that of

Odette Myrtle. The party included Jean Hermet, Achmed Abdullah and his wife, and Frederic Worlock and his wife, Elsie Ferguson. I must have taken my cap and bells with me that day, for I clowned so well that I got myself invited to another dinner, this one in the New York house of Mr. Wyckoff, a broker.

Here Elsie Ferguson was at the head of the receiving line. The cocktails, though good, were very formally served. The gold plate leaves me without words to describe it. Whether it was the formality, or the gold plate, or some unreceptive personality in the party that stiffened me, I don't know, but all my gift for frolic deserted me and I went upstage with the rest of the guests. Something had knocked the jokes completely out of me. Worlock even poured his own champagne into my glass in an endeavor to strike some sparks out of me.

"Do, for God's sake, redeem yourself, Belle!" he whispered.

But it was no use; I was a flat tire.

A few days later I was at a dinner party given by Dr. and Mrs. Jelliffe, where the other guests were Dorothy Parker, Robert McBride, and Henri Bendel. As we were gathered in the drawing room for cocktails, a rosy-faced little man rushed in, grabbed me, gave me a loud, smacking accolade on each cheek, at the same time whispering in my ear: "Don't say you don't know me!" It was Tommy Smith, who confessed later that he had told the doctor and his wife he had known me in Paris. Tommy was a *grand causeur;* hostesses loved to have him at their dinner parties.

It was Tommy who took me to tea at Dorothy Parker's where I met Buddy de Sylva and his wife and Gene Markey. That evening we all dined together in an Italian speakeasy under the very eaves of City Hall.

When the holiday season arrived, Skipper Madeline Boyd came in one day to tell me that we were weighing anchor to sail to Bob Chanler's for a New Year's Eve party. Emily Vanderbilt and Douglas Parmentier were to be aboard; also Ernest Boyd, Tommy Smith, Sam and Edith Hoffenstein, and the very delightful and amusing Val and Bibi Dudensing.

Of all the Whoopee Chiefs of that era, Bohemian Bob Chanler was perhaps the most outstanding. For popularity he depended on his own vivid personality rather than on his maternal Astor ancestry or his large fortune, though it was the latter that permitted him to offer unstinted hospitality to the artists and writers whom he loved to gather about him. Bob kept perpetual *table ouverte* for intellectuals, both heavyweight and lightweight. To be included in the Chanler gatherings was an invisible decoration among the New York intelligentsia. Had Bob lived in Renaissance days, he would have been styled a patron of letters. Around his immense circular dining table every night could be found diverse artists gorging themselves at Bob's expense and talking feelingly and eloquently about their freedom from the lure of Mammon and their contempt for the golden calf.

So much has been written about Bob Chanler and his eccentricities that I am going to confine myself to his holiday party in 1928. The house in East Nineteenth Street was lighted up like a Christmas tree, both inside and outside. Paul, Bob's little Filipino boy, took our wraps. In a very large room, the walls of which were hung with Bob's own portraits of sundry friends, we found our host seated majestically in a large chair on a dais. Beside him were taborets for anyone he might invite up near his throne. His sonorous voice first thundered out a welcome to our party, then bellowed for the Filipino:

"Paul! Bring us some wine. My God! How these people can drink! Paul! Paul!"

The boy smiled a knowing oriental smile, intimating that Bob's comment was supposed to be merely a pleasantry, and my crowd, who knew everybody, moved off to circulate among their friends, leaving me alone with my host. As Bob sat on his dais surveying his satellites, each of them in turn served as whetstone to sharpen his sadistic wit.

"Looks like Coxy's army, doesn't it, Belle?"

At that moment a young thing came up to pay her respects and was greeted with this thrust:

"You must sit up nights studying how to be as stupid as you look."

In a fluster of embarrassment the girl retired. I found myself blushing with her. Bob spotted another guest and beckoned him to the throne.

"Where have you been keeping yourself?"

"I've been ill, Mr. Chanler."

"You look as if you had galloping leprosy now," Bob sympathized.

To relieve the poor boy's distress I asked Bob the name of another young man sitting on the other side of the room.

"Who?" taking a squint as though he might be getting a perspective for one of his portraits. "Oh, he's the sap who takes photographs of snowflakes. Last year he photographed the cinders flying out of Vesuvius." The next moment he groaned. "Oh, my God! Here comes that young ass who read relativity and went mad. What do I care whether the umbrella falls down and hits him on the head, or he goes up in the air and hits the umbrella?"

The boisterous New Year was now clanging its bells in earnest. Suddenly a wild female apparition came dancing and shrieking into the room in a mad clatter, her white, skull-like face pierced by two coal-black eyes, a slash of scarlet for a mouth, the whole surmounted by a crazy mass of grass-green hair.

"The Lord protect us, Bob, and who would that be?" I asked. "The Phantom of the Opera?"

"Oh, her?" Bob chuckled. "Van Vechten calls her 'The

Dance of Death.'" He gestured widely at the portrait-filled walls. "Dead people—all dead. Everybody's dead today. You're dead."

I had no chance to ask him to explain this dismal philosophy, for just then in came Pat Leary, who had made several millions simply by getting a little crinkly piece of tin to stick tightly on a bottle mouth and who carried himself with all the assertive bearing of the typical Whoopee Chief.

It was not long after his entrance that Emily Vanderbilt brought me my wrap and whispered that we were leaving. Sheep-like, I trotted after her down the stairs, beneath walls painted with vivid snakes slithering through lush verdure, their glistening eyes following our every step. Out on the street I learned that we had been invited to a party at Pat Leary's suite in the Élysée.

At Pat's apartment cases of champagne littered the floor. Pat's whoopee vanity made him too an arclight for the literary moths, and tonight both the light and the moths were lit. For three days and three nights, with the blinds drawn, the carousal continued.

No one knows how long it might have gone on had it not been interrupted by Bob Chanler's giant form appearing in the doorway.

"Rats!" he snarled. "Never let any of you pretend to me again you are my friends! For years I've provided you with a free clubhouse. I've been your Wailing Wall. I've listened to your arguments and your pretensions and your hard-luck stories. I provided you with entertainment for a happy New Year's Eve, but every one of you was ready to follow a pied piper out of my house. Rats—that's what you are! Rats!"

There wasn't enough intelligence left among our party to remember our street numbers, let alone find the proper answer to Bob's philippic.

Next morning, back at the Vanderbilt, supported by a brandy-sour, I tried to recall where I was before that incredible lost weekend at the Élysée. Eventually I was able to remember an interesting conversation about an idea of mine that I had had with a man named Franklin Berwin, known to his friends as "Tiger," whom I had met earlier through Mrs. Jelliffe.

During my stay at the Vanderbilt, I had been drawn into New York's whoopee world, where I'd met four of the biggest chiefs, each with his own form of vanity and pomposity. Park Avenue was far more torched up than I had pictured. I began to see that big business, Wall Street, society, and literary Bohemia had all been drawn into the mad Volsteadian maelstrom which sucked down alike money, morals, and mentalities.

Couldn't I make money by supplying whoopee-mad Americans of the better class with an escape from themselves in a setting more tasteful than the sour, rat-infested basements they had been frequenting? I thought I could do something new—draw an intellectual thread through New York night life by providing a meeting ground where might congregate the best minds and the best purses; where high hat might meet high brow—they seldom are found on the same person. In short, I would create a kind of superspeakeasy that would in effect duplicate my former Paris *salon*. Certainly with my years of experience in entertaining and my reputation as a hostess I had all the qualifications. I needed only a pot of gold to set me up in business.

Just before that Bacchanalian New Year's party of 1928 Franklin Berwin had been rash enough to listen to my idea. The day I went down to Wall Street to get the money from him, stocks, like Samson's columns, had commenced to shiver and tremble. But Tiger was as good as his word, and the promised finances were forthcoming. The whole nation was on the biggest spending spree of its existence, and in the grip of the whoopee psychology of that era who could possibly have foretold—or would have been believed if he

had—that the great financial crash of all time was only a
year away?

Shortly after, I left the Vanderbilt with all my luggage
and with my bill marked "Paid in full." I'd had a grand
time on Park Avenue, and in the few short months I'd been
away from my villa at Fontainebleau any misgivings I may
have had over leaving the lovely old world for the giddy
new one had vaporized completely.

3 *The Philanthropic Speakeasy*

The so-called plan with which my speakeasy career was opened was as completely lacking in common sense as in commercial foresight. The idea I had propounded to Franklin Berwin was to form an association of intellectual and affable spirits, each able to put up two hundred dollars. This sum would make a member eligible for eating and drinking privileges for one year. Any kindred soul who could not put up the two hundred dollars would be allowed to eat and drink just the same.

The idea was as beautiful as that of the League of Nations, and much more convivial. It survived almost as long. It was not original; François Rabelais had had a similar idea centuries before.

The first problem was to find a house. In my Paris home, the velvet carpet on the broad stairs leading to the *salon* had borne witness to many guests. In New York I had little doubt that my rapidly growing circle of friends would soon wear another such path if I could only provide suitable stairs and *salon*.

On all sides I had heard praises sung of Benjamin Wood's little mansion on East Fifty-second Street which Ben had bought during one of the intervals between his many marriages and had christened "One Man House." I decided to acquire this house, in spite of the fact that everyone who had ever had business relations with him had told me that Ben was so hard you could drive nails into any part of his body without his feeling them.

When I arrived to have tea with the owner, there was nothing about the exterior of the house to suggest the surprise that awaited me behind the reticent and simple façade. An English butler opened the door. Before me spread a vista down stone steps into a lofty Renaissance hall with an Italian marble floor and vaulted Florentine ceilings. At the far end of the hall great doors opened on an exquisite miniature garden that could have challenged any of its size for euphony and cadence. Beyond a fountain, with its statuette standing in a basin of sparkling water, was an old colonnade that in perspective seemed to extend a long way; in reality it covered only a few feet of space. Upstairs was an English library and in the rear a charming breakfast room, all the gayer because of an array of colorful old glassware through which the sun—or failing the sun, an artificial moon—shone to entrance the eye. Beneath a zodiac frieze of silver and delicate tones of green, the walls were paneled with pictures of ships. I began to understand why my friends had tried to dissuade me from tackling the old Titan to give up this expensive toy on which he had lavished so much money and thought.

But my cupidity must have made me persuasive, for I succeeded in talking Ben out of, and myself into, his beautiful little *bonbonnière*. I wanted the house so badly that even the staggering price of nearly two thousand dollars per month, plus two hundred for the butler who went with the lease, failed to daunt my spirits. Then and there, in that beautiful setting, was born the first and only free speakeasy in New York; and there began my career as night-club owner.

Like Rabelais, who plucked his *moutons à la grande laine,* my good angel Tiger Berwin proved to be a wonderful shepherd for finding the sheep with the golden fleece. The glittering list of those present at my housewarming was ample proof of his skillful herding from the social, artistic, and literary worlds. Everyone of any note was there.

I am afraid I did not co-operate well in the plucking that day. I remember that Henry Raleigh, well-known illustrator, asked how much he owed for his bottle of champagne, but I waved away with a magnanimous gesture the idea of anything as vulgar as money, reminding him that he was in a *salon,* not a saloon. This reply was too startling for Raleigh, and rather than discuss the matter further, he thrust twenty dollars into my butler's hand and rushed out of the house.

The news of my enterprise burst like a star shell over the astonished city. Good food and good wine served without checks! Of course there were expressions of spleen from competitors. A resistance to the new idea was also reflected in the press:

> When a parched gentleman craves vinous or spirituous refreshment, he sashays into a speakeasy, imbibes his brace of bracers and departs. That's what speakeasies are for. The modern "speak" is not a literary or artistic *salon,* as Belle Livingstone, author and *bonne vivante,* chooses to call her establishment.
>
> Out-and-out speakeasy proprietors, who have been serving liquors without literary frills, are usually lenient with their rivals who happen to be caught. But not with Belle Livingstone.

They hope she "gets the works." A literary *salon!* Hypocrisy heaped on lawlessness.

Fool's paradise as my *salon* later turned out to be, when the long-wool sheep, or solvent members, became scarce, I was nevertheless divinely happy those first few months. In Europe, where I had had chefs whose food and wines were capable of reviving the most jaded palate, I had acquired not only the art of entertaining but the passion for it, and in those early days at One Man House I seemed to be living again in leisure and wealth. I even believed what Harry Hershfield wrote: "Belle is going to make something of those two breadless arts—Wit and Wisdom." As to any possible consequences of operating outside the law, I was strangely indifferent. How did all the others manage? I reasoned. There must be a way. It was not long, however, before I had a narrow escape.

Very soon after the news of my housewarming had been bruited abroad, my butler announced two men who insisted upon seeing me. A little mystified, but intrigued, I had them shown up to the library. They introduced themselves by saying that they had met me at the Silver Slipper, but as I didn't even know such a place, I decided they must be off the scent. Never suspecting, however, who they really were, I chatted casually until another caller arrived, a young man who came upstairs gaily waving an obvious package at me. At this I invited all three into my breakfast room where I mixed gin rickeys for the young man and two Federal agents from Washington. As it turned out, the fact that I gave, rather than sold, the drinks saved me. Uncle Sam apparently had no law against the philanthropic drink.

In spite of the baronial hall and comfortable library, the intimates of the house, as time went on, were more likely to be found grouped about some succulent dish in the kitchen. Late at night, after a big party, the "best folk" always seemed to find their way downstairs, where they dispensed with butlers, gravitated to the icebox and the kitchen range, and sang lustily to the accompaniment of sizzling sausages and scrambling eggs. Or sometimes the *pièce de résistance* would be ham steeped in champagne; on other nights a plain, old-fashioned English beefsteak-and-kidney pudding. Around the kitchen table—their big spoons *en air* like hungry schoolchildren—would congregate some of the most rollicking wits in New York. Clare Briggs and his wife Maggie, his devoted shadow, were often of this crowd. Little did I know that this witty cartoonist, with his merry Puckish smile, was to become one of the dearest memories of my life. Clare was full of charm; one labeled him "best folk" at once.

In the months that followed it was only natural that Texas Guinan and I should become acquainted. I liked her from the first. One night at a dinner party to which Clare Briggs had invited Ring Lardner, George Buckley, and Texas Guinan, Clare and Ring arrived a little the worse for Lambs' Club highballs. Texas was her usual sober self. Ring proceeded to fall asleep in a big chair; the rest of us had our dinner.

After dinner Texas, who always loved doing something unusual, had an idea. She sent her car for Nerida and the nine-foot python, then performing at her club. When the snake arrived, Texas took it and laid it around Ring's neck. Texas' perfume, or our laughing, woke him up. Feeling the chill of the snake, he looked down at it, started slightly, and then smiled wanly. Clare asked him if he'd like a drink.

Ring glanced sideways down at the snake again. "N-no, no——"

Very gingerly he touched the torpid, gelid neckpiece, looked at us, and tried to smile again. I said he'd better have a glass of champagne.

He gave us a searching glance, as if to ascertain whether

we saw what he saw, and then said weakly: "I think I'd better have just a cup of coffee!"

The English butler who was serving the coffee needed all his early training in self-restraint as he leaned over Ring to ask how many sugars, please.

Finally George Buckley, being like all men a friend to men, stepped up and took the horrible "dream" from around Ring's neck. When Ring saw the snake was real, he drained a highball in relief and laughed as hard as anyone present at what was perhaps the meanest practical joke ever pulled.

It was on another one of those *sans souci* nights that A. B. Harris, the Billboard King—one of my long-wool sheep— invited a crowd of us to go to Texas' club for supper. Texas, grand showwoman who believed that everyone enjoys the effect of a splash entrance, treated the arrival of our party to a fanfare of noisy brass and spectacular lighting effects.

Hardly were we seated than a young man came over to our table and speaking with a foreign accent, possibly Russian, introduced a portly Mr. So-and-So of Oshkosh, Wisconsin. "Ver' prominent—ver' influential." The Russian was one of those self-appointed introducers to be found in every whoopee resort who derive an obscure satisfaction—and some refreshment—from bringing together utter strangers.

Mr. So-and-So from Oshkosh had a drink and withdrew. After an interval, the Russian reappeared with another Mr. So-and-So, this time from Twin Falls, Idaho, also "ver' prominent—ver' influential." The Russian quietly assimilated another drink. Mr. Twin Falls boomed out some unintelligible witticisms, slapped the Billboard King on the back, gargled a glass of champagne, and he too vanished.

I looked around to see what the Russian would do next, and there he was, approaching with his third offering—a little gray-haired man whom he presented as Professor Somebody from Toronto, Canada. As usual the visitor was "ver' prominent—ver' influential." As a matter of fact, the professor looked as if he might be both.

His face was intelligent and studious, though blurred for the moment by champagne; clearly he was not the customary whooper-upper. Clare looked at him with interest and made a place for him at the table. During the comparative quiet of a torch song, the little man revealed that he had wandered into the whoopee world by accident and like most newcomers into those realms he was bubbling over with joy at his discovery. He confided that he was on the faculty of a Canadian university, was seeing the States for the first time, and had left a devoted wife at the Algonquin. From time to time, when something struck his fancy, he would mention his wife.

"How Mabel would enjoy that!" he would exclaim. "If Mabel were only here! Wouldn't Mabel like Miss Guinan!"

By degrees everybody at the table began to share his concern over the absence of Mabel and to feel sorry that so rare and convivial a spirit should be confined within the gray walls of the Algonquin. Someone suggested that Mabel be fetched; but because of the late hour we were afraid the club would be closed before we could return. The Billboard King, being a resourceful man, then proposed that we take Texas to Mabel. The little professor was flabbergasted by the devilish daring of the idea.

"Texas wouldn't do it," he said, round-eyed.

"What'll you bet?" asked Harris.

"Fifty dollars."

"You're on," and Mabel's husband and A. B. Harris shook hands.

The Billboard King then called Texas aside, and in a moment, to the surprise of the professor, Tex agreed not only to go herself but also to take the whole show including the hostesses.

"Won't Mabel be tickled!" chortled the professor.

A whole caravan taxied through the rain to the Algonquin. The little man, now somewhat uncertain on his feet, led the crowd into the elevators and up to Mabel's room. Opening the door and putting a cautionary finger on his lips to warn everybody to keep quiet—the surprise must be complete—he disappeared and left us in the corridor. In a moment ominous sounds began to issue from within. We all stood tensely silent in the hall until, moved by some obscure involuntary impulse, or pressure from behind, those in front opened the door.

In the center of the room stood a grim, gray rock of a wife, lecturing in no uncertain terms. The *joie de vivre* of the professor was certainly not being shared by Mabel, who gave the revelers one momentary, frozen glance and returned to the pulverizing of her errant spouse. Some of the dancers giggled, others studied the pictures on the walls; finally everyone made a confused exit and started for the elevator. There the professor joined us, a crushed fragment of his former exhilarated self. Downstairs at the desk he wrote a check to the Billboard King for fifty dollars and handed it over without a word. For an anguished moment I feared the Whoopee Chief would refuse it, but Harris was not without instincts. He saved the little professor from complete discomfiture by accepting it.

The next morning was Easter. I had no more than pulled the heavy curtains to shut out the sun when the phone rang. It was Texas asking me to accompany her to St. Patrick's Cathedral.

"I'll pick you up in my car," she said, "and after Mass we'll have a quiet little lunch at the Ritz."

Texas' showmanship never operated to better effect than that Sunday morning. Every move was timed to perfection. When we arrived at the cathedral, the huge police squad was already on hand to manage the yearly crowd. As Texas stepped from her Rolls, every one of those cops, with a merry twinkle in his eyes, called out his salute: "Happy Easter, Tex!"

A battery of cameras did not disconcert her. At the door she nodded to her press agent, who was on hand to tell reporters what she was wearing. Even the big show the Church puts on for Easter did not detract from Texas' stage effects. Those who had come to pray looked up to gasp as Tex, beribboned, beflowered, sailed up the center of the magnificent scene.

After Mass we walked in the Easter parade down Fifth Avenue among the publicity-craving crowd looking for the thrill of seeing their pictures in the papers next day. Finally the big event was all over and we turned into the Ritz, where Tex had ordered a quiet table in a corner.

That Easter was the first time I had ever been alone with Texas. Whenever I think of that luncheon, I always recall the shrewd conversational grenades, packed with Irish wit, that Texas threw into my dreams that day. Thinking twice as fast and around ten times as many corners as most persons, she almost made me regret I hadn't gone to school on the other side of the tracks.

"What's the big idea, Belle?" and she leaned across the table. "Two hundred dollars a sucker and everything on the house! You're not making a dime out of that place of yours. If you had a fortune of your own, like those folks who pay themselves to sit in an office all day—okay. But no kidding, you ought to incorporate and grab off some dough."

"You don't understand, Texas," I answered. "I want to live as I did in Europe, and this is the only way I can do it. A bank balance means less to me than having a *salon* again."

"My God! Oil the wheels of profit with that speech!" she cried.

"You see, I take pleasure in surrounding myself with people who can talk as well as drink," I went on. "Look at my magic list of patrons."

" 'Magic' is the right word," Texas held to her point. "Now you see 'em, now you don't."

The idea of two hundred dollars per wit and perhaps, and my coffers empty, was no doubt Texas' reason for inviting me to this lone luncheon. She must have hoped to open my eyes to the crass stupidity of my ways by giving me a friendly piece of her practical mind. To her the dollar was indeed almighty, and her very expressive eyes conveyed more clearly than words the fact that she thought me a fool.

I wanted to bridge over the difference in opinion which separated us, so remembering that Texas was basically very religious, I said as we left the table to return to my house: "Maybe my guardian angel will hover over me."

"If you don't clip his wings," was Texas' final jab.

My library was a bower of Easter lilies, and Easter callers were already beginning to arrive—Clare and Maggie Briggs, Bill Kraus, McKay Morris, Sam and Edith Hoffenstein, Bob and Muriel Johnstone, George de Zayas, Lewis Gallantiere, Donald Brown. Before Texas and I could greet them all, the butler announced that a gentleman who claimed to have taught me history would like to see me.

I knew that I had lived history, but had I studied it as well? Or was someone playing a joke on me? The caller turned out to be none other than the professor, once of Emporia but now of Yale, who long ago had been Mother's idea of the perfect husband for me. I remembered him immediately, and that he had once tried to kiss me.

"Yes," he admitted, "on your back porch in Emporia, when you were scooping ice cream out of a freezer for a church social."

At this I gave him the long-delayed smack.

"Not the voice but the kiss of experience," I said, "and now instead of ice cream we'll have champagne to celebrate."

Years later, after One Man House had become a restaurant serving a modest table d'hôte dinner, I asked a friend if she would mind dining with me there. I was in the grip of a nostalgic longing to look again on its familiar scenes; I wanted to relive some of my happy days there.

On our table was one candlestick holding one candle; one vase with one rose in it. There were no men in the place—just the drab sort of women who deprive themselves of everything, even a daily cocktail with which to stimulate their gray existence.

What memories the place awakened! In place of the one fading rose on our table I saw blooming trees, fresh from some flowering orchard, that had been brought in to fill the great hall with the fragrance of spring. I saw Bob Johnstone sitting at the piano; tall, personable Charlie Stewart dancing by the French windows that opened into the garden; John Ringling sauntering down the stairs; behind him Lillian Leitzal, looking like a Dresden doll as she skipped off the last step onto the marble floor as airily as if it were her circus net into which she was stepping; Charlie Goddard calling "Hello!" from the top step, and every other step clear down to the bottom, with his fierce and commanding affability.

There was Donald Freeman of *Vanity Fair*, impish and vague. A roar—and Bob Chanler came in with his following. I could hear him talking and laughing long before I could see his fine Dumas *père* head towering above the group. Then there was Pat Leary, never far off; Donald Brown, the handsomest of all my long-wool sheep, and with him Louis Winslow and his Rover Boys from the Racquet Club.

I could hear again Texas' throaty voice, and see Ray Long dashing up the marble steps to bring Texas downstairs. I saw Jimmy Quirk, Karl Kitchen, Ring Lardner, and George Buckley grouped around the dear and inimitable Clare Briggs. I heard again the beautifully modulated voice of Heywood Broun and saw his adorable, diminutive wife,

Ruth Hale, chatting with lovely Alice Brady. I visualized the statuesque and beautifully gowned Mrs. S. Stanwood Menken talking to flowerlike Emily Vanderbilt, and Tay Pay O'Connor having a spot of tea before the fire and enjoying the sight of his notable contemporaries pleasantly "jingled."

There was Floyd Gibbons, making his usual theatric entrance, and with him Count von Dennewitz. And standing at the head of the stairs, viewing the scene before entering it as a participant, was that great Western gentleman Bob Scripps.

Suddenly I felt as if I were in a carriage following a hearse. Suddenly I realized how many of this cavalcade of celebrities who once made New York nights merry had now passed into the eternal night, "leaving behind them the memory of a great banquet zestfully and gustaciously relished." Never before had it been brought home to me so forcefully that the penalty of living too long is that of seeing one's friends filed away in their caskets.

As in a dream, I relived those final days at One Man House, when the long-wool sheep who had paid their two hundred dollars had long since drunk up their dues and the treats were then on me and, as Tex had warned, the joke as well.

I remembered the day when, completely disheartened because at last I became aware that soon I should be forced to close my *salon*, I had turned like so many others to Tex's velvet-lined club for solace. No sooner had I arrived than I was summoned to the telephone, and a brogue one rarely hears outside of Ireland boomed through the receiver: " 'Tis the City Marshal's office spakin'. Will yez please come home so we can put yez out?"

Next day the Temple of Wit, as newspapers facetiously styled my *salon,* was officially insolvent.

4 *Silver Mattresses*

Everything salable in One Man House was sold to pay the piper, and then ensued a long transatlantic correspondence with my husband on the moot subject of my return to Europe. I felt that my lodestar in America had not yet set. Walter doubted my ability to hold my own in business with the smart New Yorkers.

"Those Americans will eat you alive. Call it a day; chuck it, Belle. Fair dues! As a wife you're no good to a man on the other side of the Atlantic!"

I was faced with a choice between his desire for my return and my desire to stay in America. My financial well had run entirely dry. In my purse nestled his letter and ten cents. A hot July sun was soaking down on the big city that all of a sudden had become awfully dear to me. Even though, like the proverbial moth, I had been pretty badly singed, I still wanted to go on fluttering about the great New York flame. I really couldn't leave it—just yet. I decided to postpone the reunion with my husband.

This decision was a more significant one than I realized at the time. The postponed reunion was destined never to be realized; within five years I was to be widowed again.

Broke again—but vanquished? No one can feel vanquished while walking on Park Avenue. On that wide, wealthy way self-pity dies and ambition revives. As I was walking down it that day, the sun shining, big cars purring by, and the people all striding briskly and confidently, before I knew what was happening a rosy cloud was slipped under my feet and I felt myself being lifted into the ether. The white buildings towering to the skies were once only someone's ambition; the New York Central trains burrowing underground another's. On a bright sunny day on Park Avenue something good just has to happen. It happened to me.

At the end of the first block I began to perk up; in the second block I began to imagine myself in the money again; in the middle of the third I was so rich in confidence that when I saw a little empty house at 384 Park Avenue I decided to acquire it. Just like that.

The owner of the house I discovered to be the very exclusive Robert Goelet, and still on my rosy cloud I opened negotiations with him for a lease. Since my husband's name was well-known to Mr. Goelet, both men being noted in yachting circles, it was not difficult to wangle a deal. Little did lessor or lessee realize that this little house, with its innocent exterior, was soon to be the subject of lurid stories on the front pages of papers around the world.

While the ink was yet wet on the lease, with little more to my name than comb, toothbrush, and soap, I moved into my new mansion on the Diamond Trail. I had nothing on which to sleep except newspapers on the floor, but as the weeks passed, with each Sunday's edition my bed grew more comfortable. A friend who brought me home one night offered to go in and turn on the lights for me. I told him my lights were turned on and off by my Maker. I don't think he understands to this day that I had only the moon to light me to bed.

In all the basement "speaks" I had visited, the only monies apparently spent on decoration were for a blower and a pot of bronze powder that some waiter in his odd hours blew on wet walls. I determined to set my new club apart from competitors by giving it a silver lining—applied perforce by my own hands—and as word of what I was doing spread, all my friends rallied round, prepared to join in the fun of making something out of nothing. Whenever anyone asked how he could help, I sent him over to Third Avenue for a can of paint and a brush.

The social Goldsborough sisters, Lucinda and Ellen, contributed hours to decorating what was afterward known near and far as the Silver Room. Having no money for furniture, I next hied to Third Avenue, bought some old mattresses, and covered them in silver cloth. There was still some silver paint left from the walls, so we painted the floor silver too. This last touch, born of necessity, only enhanced the charm of the room.

The murals were painted to make fun of myself before others could do so. On the west wall I sat, old and gray, with a bottle of gin in my hand and a tear in my eye, telling of *my* day. Mustachioed men of my era typified the time when a kiss without a mustache was like a potato without salt. The silver satin curtain across the end of the room was painted by the clever colorist Amy Hicks to represent the ocean I had crossed to learn the more refined taste of the grape. On the east wall I was stepping out of the Café de Paris, the greatest night club of all time. On the south wall I was shown at Monte Carlo, with voluminous feather boa and rake, sweeping in enough gold to buy myself a title and bask in the mirrored reflection of my coronet. On the ceiling I insisted that my talisman, a huge yellow sunflower, be painted. A silver room limned with biographical satire.

Various artists who roamed in and out wanted to have a hand in decorating the bar. One day the very good-looking Franklin Hughes brought his brushes and painted a large, silly-faced cow on the wall, and under it: *C'est une vache.* This forerunner of Elsie Borden so tickled my sense of humor that I let him finish the job. Even the critical, difficult-to-please Bel Geddes said that only a good artist could have made anything out of such an ugly room.

Finally everything was ready except the two most costly items, a piano and some liquor, both of which had to be managed without money. The responsibility of the piano I shifted to Donald McGibney. Today Donald could buy a piano factory, but in those days he had to use all the tactics of Molière's *Gentilhomme* in pulling a piano out of a hat. Then it was my turn to put out feelers for a bootlegger who would trust me.

The first one I tackled was a big, husky chap. I showed him over the place and told him about the eight hundred dollars' worth of liquor required for the housewarming, adding softly that I should need credit.

The gentleman expended a knowing leer on my silver mattresses, swung his cigar to the other side of his mouth, and said: "Lady, how do youse get that way?"

I saw that it would be necessary to clear myself of false imputations, so I decided to explain my astonishing furnishings to the next bootlegger in order that he might not judge me by my silver mattresses.

The second man listened attentively to my story and reflected deeply. "All right," he finally announced, "I'm going to gamble on you."

Proof that this gambler-bootlegger was a smart one is the fact that he now sits behind an impressive desk in Chicago, a prosperous man of affairs.

From his vantage ground at Fifty-third and Park, the policeman stationed there could see the liquor being unloaded in Tony's, Mary's, Murphy's, the Jungle, and a dozen other speakeasies, as well as in my place directly on the avenue. This post must have netted its incumbent a handsome fortune. When the officer went off duty, he would stroll around to all our places to inform us how many cases or sacks he had seen unloaded that day. All of us understood his pleasant, genial ways. One night my bootlegger arrived late, explaining that he had been driving around an hour to escape the pay-off.

The opening of my Park Avenue oasis took place on a Sunday afternoon in the late fall of 1929. By dawn the next day wrecks were piled high, and the bodies had to be carried out and deposited in limousines convened in front of the house. My beautiful velvet carpets were deep in cigarette ashes.

Princess Milikoff must have read my mind and understood how disturbed I was, for she invited me to her apartment at the Ritz Towers to recuperate. The fun of the second day was supplied by a note from Heywood Broun which I found on my return to the club: "Belle dear: It is the first time I ever found a speakeasy unlocked, unattended, and untenanted." Sure enough, I had gone out and forgotten to lock the door, leaving the rest of my liquor at the disposition of anyone who might have cared to turn the doorknob and walk in.

For some reason the place caught on, and every night thereafter the little house was full of sounds of pleasure— the young laughter of lovely debs; the strumming of some talented musician; the deep, rich voice of Libby Holman surprising everyone from a corner cushion; the *Rhapsody in Blue* when Al Segal sat down at the piano.

Among the sounds I must not forget the excited barking of dogs which model husbands whisked across to my place for a smoky night airing—and a nightcap for papa. The place became a fashionable kennel. Wives little suspected that their diminutive Ping Wangs or Chin Lees got only what air they could sniff up their pushed-in aristocratic noses during that dash across the avenue, tightly clutched under the hubbies' arms. Not until they read in Walter Winchell's column that Park Avenue husbands were beginning to beg rather than to resent taking the pooch for his night walk did they know that, as Walter put it, "the dogs were often useful in leading the blind husbands home from Belle Livingstone's." The best purses opened the evening and the best dogs closed it.

To me a cash register has always been an overrated monitor of honesty which never succeeds in preventing dishonesty. To keep my place free from such vulgarity and at the same time to give it a more clublike atmosphere, I compiled little ten, twenty, and fifty dollar books of tickets which patrons bought on entering. Afterward, anything that was ordered required a ticket, even a match or a glass of water. The tickets were in royal blue, the design a silver Liberty Bell on which the address 384 formed the crack. Small enough to go into a vest pocket, the tickets were used to signal across the opera or the stock exchange or a crowded thoroughfare to make known that the holder would be on a silver mattress on Park Avenue that evening. But their greatest virtue was that the books were very easily lost or mislaid, so that with these come-high tickets I was always ahead of the game.

These high-priced books and low-down mattresses were probably the only clever ideas that my most unbusinesslike mind ever conceived. Any man who had lost his springy youth would rather sit a whole evening on a mattress than have anyone witness his horrible struggles to get to his feet. When a stifled grunt, or the crackling of a starched shirtfront, or perhaps the spinning of a trouser button on the silver floor announced in the semilit room that some elderly gentleman had made a landing on one of the mattresses, I knew that there he would sit and sit and buy and buy, until he had bought enough champagne to give him the courage to believe he could hop to his feet and trip out of the room. "Trip" is right.

The silver mattresses were a sensation. They startled all New York, including the police department, who regarded them as equivalent to an unsolved crime.

"Is it a hop joint?" I heard them whisper. "Is it a bordello? Naw, it can't be. Look at the nice, respectable, well-known people sittin' on them mattresses, will ya?"

The stairs were a worse hazard than the mattresses. So many customers fell down those stairs that I used to say there might as well be only two steps, the top and the bottom. One night a well-known architect fell flat on his face.

"Robert!" I screamed to the head boy. "Pull this body around in front of Tony's while it is still warm!"

Perhaps it was the threat that worked. At any rate, "the corpse" opened its eyes and spoke.

That autumn there were a number of young Russian grand dukes visiting in New York and one night several, including Archduke Leopold, visited the club.

"*Le tour des grands ducs, Madame,*" Robert whispered, as he passed by me with a magnum of champagne.

Whereas Americans break glasses by accident, Russian gentlemen break them by design and are rather magnificent when smashing. When I saw the Cossacks swinging to their songs and heard the breaking glass, I had to rub my eyes and tweak my ears to make sure I was not dreaming that I was back in Europe during those brilliant days when the grand dukes *were* grand.

Since the place was ablaze with light, and music and laughter poured from the door whenever the beautifully dressed women and their escorts streamed in or out, I should have known there would eventually be a visit from the police. But having walked in on an avenue where in those day angels feared to tread, I felt safe in my exclusive location. One night, however, to the accompaniment of all the noise effects with which a raid is staged, the law rushed my door, leaped over my bar, and drove away with a van full of waiters and barmen. This was my first real run-in with the authorities, but it was just a pinwheel presaging the big fireworks to come.

Everything was to happen to me in that little house. On the day when some young friends of mine were married, they came up after the ceremony, with the best man and the matron of honor, to have a glass of champagne. I had just waved good-by to the wedding party and was closing the door when two strange men ran up the steps and pushed themselves inside. I was alone in the house.

One of the men pushed a gun in my face. "Who's upstairs?" he said.

"No one."

"Go find out," to his partner. And to me: "Where's your roll?"

"My bootlegger doesn't let me keep one," I replied.

This was the truth. Although abroad I had always kept my money in a bank as a matter of course, when I first started in business I derived a curious pleasure from handling the stacks of bills I had earned myself, even though by lawlessness and risk. Mornings, after the last customer had gone and before I went to sleep, I used to lay out my heavy "jack" —"centuries" and "grands"—on the bed in fancy designs as if I were planning a patchwork quilt. My bootlegger once surprised me in this little game, thought the risk—to him— of keeping money in my room too great, and insisted that I put the cash in a bank. I could see now that he knew what he was doing.

When the partner came back and reported he had found no one in the house, and the two were convinced there was really no money to be had, they settled for drinks. My staff, who came in later, did not know until the men had left that they had found me drinking with a couple of stick-up artists.

Shortly after this came an attempt at a shakedown. Two men appeared at the height of the evening and showed me a little case holding the badge of a Federal agent. Lord Derby, a very important Englishman visiting New York, was up in the Silver Room. I knew that he was about to go, so I asked the agents to hold back the raid until he left. In reply one of them took me aside and hinted that for five grand they wouldn't raid at all. I didn't have that much, but said that if they would call the next afternoon I could manage two thousand, an amount which they agreed to accept.

On the morrow I telephoned the Seventh Division, and Officers McGowan and Keiser came over and marked the money. Sure enough, at three o'clock a cabman called for the envelope. The two detectives went along in the cab, but no Federal man was at the appointed place to receive the money.

Tiger Berwin, still helping me to find patrons, told me one day that he was going to bring a young and very lovely matron to the Silver Room. She was one, he said, who liked smart Bohemia; and if my place appealed to her, she could bring in the Long Island hunting set.

"Mind," Tiger said, to save himself any reproaches, "I don't say she *will* like it. But if she does, you are lucky."

I was lucky, indeed. She came with Tiger, looking even more beautiful than I had been led to expect, and from that day Carol McIlwain became not only a steady patron but a loyal friend.

I remember once she nearly killed me with kindness. It was during one of those periods when I was looking worn to a frazzle and Carol insisted that I come out to her place in Locust Valley over a weekend for a rest. Her car would pick me up at ten o'clock on Sunday morning. About eight that morning the last husband departed with his Pekinese. In the car I dozed until I reached Carol's house.

This was my rest. We went into a beautiful, inviting library, with long French windows opening on the drive. Everywhere were deep, comfortable armchairs yawning for tired bodies, but Carol and I and all the house guests stood around an immense tray mixing eye-openers instead of eye-shutters.

Then the procession of the curious started. All those who hadn't dared to go into a "speak" for fear of raids came to have a good look at the woman who dared to operate one. The Ping-pong balls bouncing on the large table in the next room began to bounce on my nerves as well. Horseback riders cantered up the drive; more and more people kept arriving by motor. After lunch practically everybody in Locust Valley was standing around the tray. The horses by now had joined in the fun, and one was actually in the room. Radios blared, couples danced, fresh trays were brought in.

I looked around to see if there wasn't a chair I could throw my tired body into, but all the chairs were filled with Carol's hunting dogs. A prize cat or two cuddled up in the window seats. After dinner I begged one of Carol's friends who was going to New York to take me back with him. How peaceful and quiet my Silver Room seemed after that outing! I have wondered ever since why the Long Island set, who have such Roman holidays at home, come to town and pay for synthetic whoopee.

My first full-scale raid occurred one beautiful night in early spring. Earl Carroll was in the bar, up to his neck as usual in beautiful chorus girls, and Adele Astaire and her fiancé, Lord Cavendish, were with me in my little private library. Gathered in the Silver Room was the usual galaxy of the frisky, the arty, and the wealthy. Suddenly a guest of a few nights before, McNamara by name, appeared at my door. He had sung for us then, in a more or less melodious tenor, but was now returned, hat pulled over his eyes and coat collar turned up, as guide for the raiding party.

The debs, all excitement, fluttered about and ran up and down stairs in a dither. I heard one coo to her escort: "But how thrilling! Why, the place is alive with Federals!"

During all the confusion, I happened to remember that I had left in my desk drawer a purse containing twelve thousand dollars. Under the vigilant eyes of a Federal man who had been posted in the room, I took out the purse and handed it to one of Earl Carroll's girls, saying to the mystified beauty: "Here's that bag you left with me at the beginning of the evening."

Earl, standing nearby, made a sign that he understood.

When the house had been cleared of all guests, and while the Federals were busy packing and carrying out cases of liquor, one of the men removed his hat and addressed me.

"You don't remember me, Mrs. Hutchins."

Startled, I looked at the man closely for the first time and recognized, to my complete amazement, the Paris veterinary surgeon who used to pull my horses' teeth.

"I'm sorry to see you in this racket, ma'am," he said, shaking his head, and he sadly ushered me downstairs to take my first ride in a prison van.

In the small hours, while I was waiting for a bondsman, the matron came to my cell to say that a famous friend had telephoned that he was taking care of my package. Earl Carroll told me later that when he saw my batch of bills he gave them to the celebrity to put in a safe.

My bonds paid, I came back in the cold, slate dawn of a Sunday to find not a drop of liquor in the house. A search through the cellars showed that the conscientious investigators had not stopped until they had ripped the boarding off the walls. Even the innocent vermouth had been removed.

The first thing I did was to send out a batch of telegrams to my clients:

"Come back home. All is forgiven. We get raided Mondays, Wednesdays, Thursdays, and Saturdays. On off nights we have a gang war. Never a dull moment at Belle Livingstone's."

I had a succession of legal defenders. And speakeasy lawyers, I discovered, like Philadelphia lawyers, were a breed by themselves. Many who before Prohibition, I'll be bound, had to borrow a postage stamp to mail a summons, lapped up plenty of gravy during Prohibition. I was never in business for myself, but for my lawyers. And what a dance they led me! If I expected one to come by land, he was certain to come by sea. They would build a catafalque right before my eyes without saying it was for me. Once a lawyer tried to make me jump my bail by planning to shanghai me on a plane to Canada. A taxi driver who overheard his conversation with a bootlegger sent for Fanny Ward, who took me in charge, gave me salt water to get rid of my knockout drops, and stood by until it was time for me to go to court. But whether my lawyers pulled fast ones or slow ones, their scissors were always busy with my greenbacks. The only difference between most of them and Jesse James was that Jesse had a horse.

As time went on, if I had stopped to wipe the smile off my face and become serious for one moment, I would have had to confess that the increasingly frequent visits from the authorities were beginning to tell on my nerves. Somehow I couldn't distinguish the gentlemen from Washington from other gentlemen. I simply couldn't detect the detectives. I remember that charming Mr. Ryan who called one evening. He said he had formerly lived in 384 with his family and wanted very much to look at his children's nursery once more. In the Silver Room he pointed out to me, quite tenderly, where three little cribs had stood—and then showed me his badge.

Another night a short man whom I had never seen before sat down beside me and asked if I was Belle Livingstone. I looked in his hand for the little badge that I expected him to flash. In my mind's eye I saw my bar swarming again with Federal minions while their chief paid his respects to me. But this gentleman made no movement until Robert brought in three quarts of champagne, and then he pulled one of the taborets nearer to us and poured me a glass.

With all the gaiety of a trapped hare I asked: "Where did you say you are from?"

When he said "Pleasantville, Kansas," I was all at sea. As we were sipping our first glass, Cameron Rogers came bounding in, flung himself down on the mattress, and upset the champagne. Old Pleasantville, however, not in the least disconcerted, grandly ordered three quarts more.

After all my recent Federal troubles I just knew this couldn't be on the square, and when Pleasantville offered my secretary a thousand-dollar bill I made her give it back because I was positive it was marked money. Much more champagne flowed, and I told Les Copeland at the piano to play anything that sounded even faintly like Kansas. I even suggested "John Brown's Body" because I was sure we would all find ours moldering in the hoosegow before morning. Imagine my amazement when, after tipping all the attendants fifty dollars each, Pleasantville paid his bill and departed without producing the little case with the badge.

After he had gone, I rushed back upstairs and breathlessly asked of the whole room: "For heaven's sake, who could that have been?"

"Why, Belle, don't you know? That was Mike Meehan. He beared the market yesterday for seventeen million dollars."

Oh, ring out wild Belles! I collapsed on a silver mattress which might easily have been turned to gold if I had only known.

In those insane days, when everyone seemed to have lost his reason, Harry Thaw, whose mental stability had been questioned by alienists in defense of his killing of Stanford White, proved to be the sanest person who ever entered my club. He never had more than two bottles of champagne at any one sitting. My maddest customer was a well-known Philadelphian who used to bring his fishing tackle and fish all evening. Charlie Butterworth, who used to pal around with Heywood Broun, always chanted on arriving: "The name is Butterworth—not Buttercup, Butterscotch, or Buttermilk."

Dwight Fiske, famous entertainer, became an unchanging friend. He was tireless in giving of his great talent to add chic and artistry to my place.

In 1930 I experienced a personal calamity in the death of my old and dear friend Clare Briggs. There was a man who had a place in the heart of anyone who had ever seen his cartoons. When I knew I would never again see his bright smile, I wanted to shriek at Fate for taking from us this civilized, joyous, witty man. There are certain souls so vital, so powerful in personality, so necessary to their friends that it seems almost impossible to conceive going on without them.

Returning to the club after Clare's funeral, I was so depressed over the dismalness of his burial rites that someone in the crowd asked what kind of funeral I would like for myself.

"I want my friends to gather around a long table," I said. "It will have to be a long table that day, for all the drinks will be on me. On the table I want roses and mimosa, flowers symbolical to me of America and France, the two countries that share my love. Then, as a reminder of these days, a few sprigs of the juniper bush, and in among the flowers *beaucoup* glasses of champagne. No hymns; only the colored man's song 'Look Down That Lonesome Road.' No prayers; only stand and drink to my last great venture. Then break the glasses."

"Why don't we rehearse Belle's funeral?" suggested Freddy Kinkade.

So, pulling out roses and mimosa from the vases in the club, my friends laid the flowers on the bar and placed glasses among them. Gordon Taylor, famed singer of spirituals, happened to be present, and at Freddie's urging he sang my loved song so beautifully that everyone began to cry. In the midst of the tears over my "funeral" Maggie Briggs came in and, standing, we all drank a bumper to Clare's memory.

After Clare's death I had little heart to carry on the Silver Room. So when my second *salon* was closed by order of the court and a little note from the real estate office of the fastidious Mr. Robert Goelet, who had been getting more and more fidgety as raids and sensational newspaper stories had multiplied, I watched with complete indifference as the vans, filled with furnishings, instead of barmen and waiters, were being driven away.

Even the house itself has now disappeared. With the change of times, Mrs. Goelet had a beautiful theater built where my Silver Room once twinkled.

5 Country Club in Manhattan

The night before I left my Silver Room, Mrs. Bartholomew of Boston told me her husband was giving me a car; also his chauffeur, Percy. Thinking this was one of those glowing offers made when the giver is magnanimous with wine, I replied that I hoped Mr. Bartholomew would include gas and a garage and thought no more about it. To my astonishment I found myself next day the recipient of a beautiful limousine with a fat Percy at the wheel.

This handsome car called for a handsome ménage, just as years before Teddy Roosevelt's fine dishes had called for a mahogany dining table. So, on the corner of Sutton Place and East Fifty-seventh, I moved into a perfect little maisonette with patio and tennis court.

One might suppose that by now I had had enough of raids and arrests, but no. It was not long before my lawless nature began to yearn again for the excitement and profits of my new career.

Nearby, on Fifty-eighth Street, was a building, formerly the home of the Murray Anderson School, which seemed to me ideal for another club. I walked past it by day and dreamed of it by night. The ornate wrought-iron gates, I mused, would be useful in keeping out both Federal agents and undesirable thirsties. Besides, they gave the place the appearance of a fortified castle and would create in me the illusion that I was again a sort of chatelaine. But how could I suborn the Chase National Bank into renting me this property, after all the publicity my last two places had received?

The answer was a holding company, which was duly formed, and as evidence of which I received three impressive gilt-lettered books—stock book, certificates, and minutes— along with an imposing seal. I was now incorporated, as Texas had long ago advised, and had as partners three dummies.

The feeling of security which these legal formalities afforded me did not last long after some of my alarmist friends got to work on me. I tried not to listen to their croakings, knowing that the stoutest heart can be absolutely licked by fear; but the more aggressive forced me to pin back my ears and listen in spite of myself.

"You'll be behind the eight-ball unless you hook up with one of the bootleg kings," they warned. "My God, Belle! Look at poor So-and-So, found over in the Jersey meadows all trussed up like a fowl. And didn't you read about the guy they cemented in a barrel and dumped in the river? When you are going home some night in your highly enameled car something will go *putt-putt-putt*. Better have details arranged with your undertaker."

After enough of these cautionary remarks I decided that perhaps it wouldn't be amiss after all to seek some protection. So I went in quest of that reputed big, fierce Attila of bootleggers, Owney Madden. True, the police couldn't find him, but, green as a leek, I had the temerity to go from one place to another where I imagined he might be, asking for him. Owney, of course, never once emerged from his smoke screen.

Then one night, in the midst of my fruitless search, an attractive young man named Jimmy dropped by for a cocktail. On telling him of my afternoon's hunt for Madden, I was dumbfounded to learn that Jimmy claimed some mysterious connection with the underworld by which he could contact this powerful booze baron. As Jimmy was very young and still among the great unlicked, I didn't give overmuch credence to what he said; next day, however, he telephoned that Owney Madden would call on me early that evening.

Never could there have been a greater contrast than that between my mind's portrait of a beetle-browed thug and the actual man who was ushered into my little library. Owney proved to be a dapper, wiry, well-turned-out Irishman, a sportsman type such as one might see at the smart Punchestown races in Ireland. I sensed that he valued a joke for what it was worth, although he laughed only with his eyes. Both Owney and the man who was with him, Frenchy, refused anything to drink. They merely listened to the outline of my new project and then made an appointment to meet me on the morrow at the house on Fifty-eighth Street.

Tommy Guinan, Texas' brother, arrived with them. The house was still unfurnished and I felt Owney was not impressed, but I remembered the scaremongers' warnings that I must get some biggie's permission to open. It was now or never, and holding my breath I plunged: Would he like a piece of my club? Small wonder his eyes danced in amusement, knowing that he could take all of it if he so pleased.

"If you don't want a piece, is it all right if I open on my own?" I faltered.

Screwball! he must have been thinking. But Owney, always

a man of good manners and few words, merely raised his hat as he withdrew with his followers, saying: "Lady, go as far as you like!"

This issue of paramount importance being settled, I went on with other practical building details: plastering more clauses in the lease; laying an extra dab of mortar on the Building Department; cementing the good will of the Fire Department; filling each keyhole with putty.

Between times, I was spending every spare minute poring over books of design and decoration. As I turned back the pages of history, the sophisticated, bored curves of French design under Louis XV suggested themselves as a humorous setting for the unsophisticated New Yorkers of the Volsteadian era. As to colorings, I decided to indulge my patrons' mood of pleasure-seeking in bold splashes of red, gold, and orange. Those who remember *la grande salle* of the Fifty-eighth Street Country Club will recall its beautiful orchestration of colors: the gold-cushioned seats from which deep magenta ascended, losing itself in a rich orange, to fade away in a last note of pale yellow in the dome. Immense satin pillows on the seats took on all these tones. From the golden crown over the royal box—reserved for the first families of New York and distinguished visitors—fell gold cloth tufted with vermilion velvet.

The house was so large that I could easily segregate my customers according to age or mood, so I took the two rooms overlooking the ballroom and made them thoroughly collegiate, the walls decorated with monkeys from the brush of Orry Kelly. I chose monkeys because the young set of that era were so full of energy that I could compare them only to the wild apes I had seen in the jungles around Anarajapura in Ceylon. Truly it was like being in a monkey house to be at some of their uninhibited New York parties.

Vernon McFarland made a real contribution to prankishness in my bar when he arranged some trick lighting upside down, or rather, downside up. Pucklike, he shot lights up from below in a way that enabled such expert judges of feminine form as Flo Ziegfeld, Earl Carroll, and Ray Goetz to sit behind in the shadows and view the charms of unsuspecting ladies. Perfections and imperfections alike were exposed. Even with my failing sight, I could easily distinguish Valenciennes lace from *point de Paris*.

My favorite barman in Paris sent the champagne bottles that pyramided up each side of the bar: splits, pints, quarts, magnums, jeroboams, and methuselahs. To signify how wet the playground was, I had put on my wine list a replica of the famous statue of Manikopis in Brussels. We could indulge in this Gallic humor behind closed doors, with the giggly water up to the thirty-dollar high-water mark and still rising. Carol McIlwain gave me the Ping-pong room and the backgammon room ready to a chip. There was even a miniature golf course with a brook in which bright goldfish swam merrily.

At last it was time to write the invitations, and I telephoned Everett Harré to bring all his most gushing adjectives. When he arrived, I placed a bottle of brandy before him with which to coax the muse and left him. Here is the Harré masterpiece:

126 East 58 Street
October 25, 1930

Will you join me as my guest at the gala opening of my new Mecca of Merriment on October the twenty-ninth around ten P.M.?

Come to my opening and behold the lifting of the lid from my Pandora's box of surprises! Savage, uncensored dances of the jungles of Africa! Titillating, tintinnabulating, goose-creeping, delicious horrors of the Grand Guignoli! Continental bizarrie as will be cayenne to the jaded mental tongue and will pep up stomachs leathered on syntheticism and minds impotentized by banality!

In an atmosphere of the piquant and beautiful it will be my aim to bring together the aristocracy of Park Avenue and of the intellect; to bring back to our time something of the camaraderie and the joyance of the Venetian carnivals, of the Florentine fiestas, of days when an opulent and colorful aristocracy fraternized with shining artists in poetry, philosophy, drama, and art!

My opening will be a gesture to recover, for those qualified to appreciate or to afford it, the spirit of undiluted, unsynthetic, and pristine joy!

Please don't fail us!

Cordially yours,
Belle Livingstone

The great day arrived and I was ready. Every window, from the top to the bottom of the building, was curtained in frothy lace. Outside, the large sarcophagus was filled with flowers and verdure and lighted by two Grecian lamps glowing like coals above it. It was time for me to be squeezed into the sausage-skin dress of ivory velvet, specially designed for the occasion. There was no old-fashioned bedpost handy to which I could hitch my corset strings and pull, as we plump girls of the Nineties used to do to get our hourglass shapes, so several of the boys gathered in my room to lend a hand. Pushing, pulling, tugging, and laughing, they finally got me inside the beautiful creation, with its yards of tulle trailing around my feet.

The designer of my royal coronet of diamonds assisted at the grand levee to see that it was properly placed, and lighted by the sparkling wit of the young stylists, the sparkling crown was balanced precariously on my few remaining locks of hair. The last touch to my queenly toilette was given by placing around my neck a long string of synthetic pearls. Holding a wine glass in lieu of a scepter, I must have looked very much the part of the owner of a night club.

With everything in perfect order, my waiters, each as formally correct in attire as any European Boniface, swung into their places like the first line of chorus boys in a musical. In the Old World there is a very fine but distinct line drawn between the dress of customer and *serviteur:* a handkerchief peeping from a top pocket and a boutonnière are prerogatives of the customer only. Even my musicians were young and attractive. I didn't want any old baldheads in my orchestra, no matter how well they scraped or tooted. The only thing old that I wanted in my club, besides myself, were my old customers.

By midnight a steady flow of limousines seemed to be discharging the entire smart world of Manhattan under my canopy. Thirsty souls had to fight to get anywhere near my bemirrored bar, shining in the ebony blackness of the large barroom. Above the bar gleamed a silver likeness of Bacchus caressing the grape, illustrating Dryden's lines:

> Flushed with a purple grace,
> He shows his honest face.

The mob, following the god's suggestive example, caressed their glasses and flushed as purple.

Suddenly a voice at my elbow startled me. "Again as always, I see, the *Belle of New York!*"

I wheeled.

"Do I rate a glass of champagne, Belle, in memory of those faraway days in London when you used to bathe in my wine?"

It was the Duke of Manchester who, when I first met him was a jolly young stage-door Johnny. In fact, it was the *Belle of New York* girls who made the first inroads into his fortune.

My welcome was exuberant. "But, Kim, how in the world did you know I was in New York?" I asked.

"My car got tied up in your traffic! When I asked my

chauffeur what was going on, he told me Belle Livingstone was opening again. Naturally I had to come in!"

This was the night when I introduced Harlem to Park Avenue, and society columnists next day reeled with the shock. I had threatened my "Congo dancers" with death in boiling oil if they spoke so much as a word in Harlemese, so they obligingly leaped down the stairs gibbering like the pack of savages I had billed them. Some were in masks, others wore horns; all were covered with little more than the few bits of straw they called skirts. How the society boys lined the stairs to see the dark-skinned girls at close range!

The procession consisted of a bronze African, with more rolls of fat than any idol ever bared, leading a tribal collection of wives, the whole followed by horn-crowned evil spirits, with a witch doctor in long feather train sweeping up the entire ballroom. Around and around the "savages" whirled in a frenzy, letting out the most bloodcurdling yells, while the tom-toms beat a tattoo. A hardened old bank president pretended that the rhythmical thumping of the tom-toms cast a strange, magical spell on him which he was powerless to resist. I knew it was the naked, well-molded, sepia figures that had pepped up his mind, deadened for years by column after column of dollars and cents. But he insisted it was the tom-toms and really let himself go in a most unpresidential ecstasy.

Next on the bill was a snake, some eight feet long and as thick as my forearm, which had dined for the winter on its usual guinea pig. It slithered through its act to sensuous, mesmeric strains. No female torched at the piano or shouted from the floor, but, while the orchestra rested, little Jerry Smith played in the Monkey Room.

Youth was certainly served up there, not only with wine but with beauty and talent. Libby Holman, reckless and ravishing, with an army of admirers, liked the collegiate balcony; there also Miriam Hopkins floated about in a haze of blue smoke, like a bit of silver thistledown. The popping of corks punctuated the hum of voices as the lads and lasses held carnival far into the dawning.

Instead of announcing by megaphone and flash of spotlight the arrival of an important guest from abroad, or a star of stage or radio, my orchestra leader had been instructed to play a few bars of the national anthem of the foreign visitor, or the hit tune of the star. In this way I acknowledged and honored my guests without disturbing their dignity.

The Duke of Manchester was not the only overseas visitor that night. That dashing Life Guardsman of my days in London, Sir George Prescott, dropped in to show me how extremely kind the years had been to him, and Harold Anderson, another Britisher whom I had not seen since I was a young girl in London, showed up with a pretty companion. I could see by Harold's happy face that there had been no lapse in his frivolities.

Then there was the Archduke Leopold, accompanied by two Russian noblemen. As the archduke bowed low and kissed my hand in farewell, he said: "Be sure to keep a fool at your court, Belle, and Swiss Guards at your gate."

"Enough fools," I replied. "I wish I had the Swiss Guards!"

An unexpected visitor was John Rockefeller, accompanied by Mr. Pratt. I wondered whether Mr. Rockefeller had come for a survey of shocking conditions as he had seen them headlined. Certainly he did not come for a drink, because he had no refreshment whatever.

But the real excitement of the evening came when my secretary rushed up and whispered in my ear: "Al Capone has just gone upstairs!"

This was too good for me to miss, so I casually drifted up to the Monkey Room. Sure enough, there was Al himself and all the other big shots of his personal acquaintance. When I came up to their group, Bill Duffy, who was with them, asked if I knew the names of my guests.

"We don't pass anyone who isn't all right," I said.

"At least we're not Federals," Capone smiled.

I quickly noted that only nonalcoholic drinks were being served, so in a spirit of fun I sent a bill for a thousand dollars to the table. Not only was it promptly paid, but the waiter received a hundred-dollar tip.

"Doing a fine business, eh, Belle?" observed Owney Madden with his usual twinkle when he dropped in later. "You're okay!"

There were problems that night to us in the know, as the beau monde unknowingly rubbed elbows with the underworld. In the course of the evening, Mrs. George Washington Kavenaugh and Mrs. S. Stanwood Menken flashed in, wearing their magnificent diamonds. Mrs. Kavenaugh was never any revenue to my club because she did not drink. On that night she actually cost me money because I had to telephone immediately to the Seventeenth Division for plain-clothes men. Important guests were better taken care of in those dark, clandestine days than now in the light, open, law-abiding days.

But though the wad of bills my secretary handed me at the end of that spectacular evening was enormous, it meant less to me than the enormous roll of applause I received from my delighted guests and later from the press. The *Evening World* went so far as to query: "Can it be that Belle is going to push Texas out of her spotlight?" It was unanimously conceded that I was original in creating a playground for the children of the night who wanted a snappy show, swift dance music, and "no curfew," as Stanley Walker put it in *The Night Club Era.* This figure of speech was further pointed up by T. E. Powers, the famous cartoonist, when he swung me across the city, hanging valiantly to the clapper of a bell, to keep Manhattan fun alive.

All in a whirl of flushed exultation, I laid my tired head on my new bank roll that night and dreamed the world was still an amusing place. Coming down the next morning, I found life hard reality once more.

Only a few hours before, my staff had filed by me, bowing their obsequious good-nights. Now this same staff, who should have been bustling about their appointed duties, were staging the original sit-down strike. Outraged, I asked the meaning of such behavior and learned that my envious menials, gauging my success of the night before by the steady flow of champagne, had decided to chisel in. Abandon the ticket system, I was told, or they would refuse to work.

There was nothing I could do but submit. Either I accepted their conditions or I could not operate again that night. It was to my sorrow that I gave in, for after the ticket system was abolished the gold dust my staff handed me was in rolls of hundreds rather than thousands. One of my assistants was a virtuoso who knew his bank notes as well as any Ponzi. The melodies he played on my till became a concerto most disconcerting, and the thin remains I received each night after closing was proof of his tuneful improvising.

With my men up on their feet and back at their posts, I thought everything would be clear sailing. But that very night my secretary announced the arrival of two police inspectors.

"Good evening, Belle, just thought we'd drop around and see your show. Hot stuff, eh?"

The "uncensored dances of the jungles of Africa" apparently had landed on the censor's desk! The inspectors were both merry-looking chaps, if you can describe a police officer as merry until he has transacted his business.

Quickly I said to my waiter in French: "Serve these gentlemen a cold bottle, and send a bucket of strong tea and a pot of glue up to my room."

Then, turning to my visitors: "If you will excuse me, I will see if the show is ready."

Slowly and calmly I went up the stairs. But as soon as I

was out of sight, I fairly flew into my room. There, tearing off all the lace I could find on my undies and evening dresses, I quickly dipped it in the tea and then, armed with the pot of glue, flew into the girls' dressing room. "Hold still, girls!" I cried, and I quickly glued strips of lace on their nude upper torsos. Tight-fitting lace jackets and straw skirts are a trifle incongruous; but the law was bent on morals, not aesthetics. Anyway, the combination of the lace and the cold bottle was apparently a happy one because the show passed inspection.

There were other worries too: for example, the night when some sophomores from Yale smuggled slimy, oozy eels into the club and turned them loose in the brook that ran through my miniature golf course. But the eels sought a wider range and, quitting the water, went eeling all over the entire putting green, to the accompaniment of screams from every woman present.

Yet, whatever the emergency—and we were never without one—every night I had to show a smiling, carefree face.

Not a day passed in which some man didn't inform me that I needed him to run my business. Some of the more daring ones moved in, their entire luggage consisting of evil intentions. One man went so far as to bring carpenters and tools and start the erection of a second service bar. Bootleggers, too, were always muscling in.

"But I didn't order any champagne," I would remonstrate.

"I know you didn't, sister, but you'll take it—get me?"

These boys might have stopped short of loosing black widows, but they would not have hesitated to loose a band of hoodlums.

It was in my Country Club that I learned the immense revenue in hat-checking. On this little game nearly every night club in New York was decorated and furnished. In my club I permitted no vending of dolls, fuzzy dogs, or gadgets, because I believed that hats and cigarettes were enough on which to make a profit. Even on these, the operation used to gross three thousand a week.

Give a dog a bad name and they hang him; give a woman a bad name and she makes the columns. The publicity I attracted during these parlous days netted clippings from all over the world. Some writers quoted Everett Harré's windy rhetoric in the invitations to my opening—even French journalists in translation; *Time* and *The New Yorker* ran stories. Naturally the club was jammed every night. But I was unmade as well as made by the publicity, for out went Uncle Sam and bought white ties and tails for his agents, as well as Fraschinis and Rolls-Royces. I was raided with pomp and circumstance in those days, and so often that one columnist wrote:

> Count that day lost whose low descending sun
> Sees no dry forces pursue Belle Livingstone.

For a night or so after a raid the place would be as bare as a fan dancer, but thirst springs eternal in the human throat and soon my guests would be back again, laughing, swaying, swinging, paying. As for myself, I was always so happy at their return that I did not see the handwriting on the wall, and no one took the trouble to point it out to me. A merry party was always to be found around my table. Glasses were constantly being raised to a newly-wed or engaged couple; to an expectant father; to a divorcée just back from Reno; to a new star; to someone whose birthday called for forgetfulness rather than reminder. Any excuse would do for more champagne. I lived, as Nina Wilcox Putnam put it, "distinguishedly, luxuriously, extravagantly, but not posthumously." Optimist—or should I now say fool?—that I was, there I sat, my heart glowing with pride because of the constant procession of distinguished persons who honored my club with their visits.

I remember one night when perhaps the most important

banker in America was in the club with his son and an elderly aunt. The son, knowing a little better about such matters than his father, asked me to tell him honestly if there was any danger of a raid. As we had just had a friendly raid that evening (one in which the police took a bottle and an employee as a matter of routine), I was able to say honestly that the raids were over for the evening. I omitted, however, telling him how impressed the police had been when I had pointed out his distinguished father.

While I never arranged for out-of-town evenings, it was extraordinary how often a crowd of the smart set from Washington, Boston, or Pittsburgh would arrive and monopolize the entire place. One evening a few Biddles blew in from Philly and wanted the royal box. When I explained that the *loge royale* had been engaged weeks in advance for a party that evening following the Yale game, they laughingly rejoined that they would leave when the party came in. Every time I glanced at their box, another Biddle had arrived or was arriving. The whole Biddle clan must have been there when the others finally showed up. But in the glorious haze of a good dinner, they apparently forgot they had made a reservation and the Biddles were spared from being dispossessed.

Nearly every night Tex Guinan used to drop in with her press agent to look over the crowds. She never ceased to marvel at my full house of celebrities.

"My God," she used to say. "Look at all these big shots. It's just like the court balls you read about."

Texas' frequent visits to my club finally aroused vague suspicions in my mind. Could Tex be a dashing spy in the enemy's camp? I knew that she must be aware of all the attention I was getting in the press, and I wondered if these laudations for me had lighted smoldering coals of resentment that would eventually burst into flames. By this time I had learned more of her career, and I knew that she was associated in business with men who soberly kept their wits about them and their lips padlocked. I recalled an evening when Texas, Fanny Ward, and I were guests of Rajah Raboid, who bent his glowing eyes upon a crystal ball to see what the future portended. Texas, looking into the ball, insisted she saw me receiving a pair of new bracelets—bracelets and a chain between them. I remembered then that I had no Swiss Guards.

There was no reason for rivalry. Texas had the masses while I had the classes. There was room enough for both of us in New York. I loved the Irish mind of Texas, with its frolicsome, unpredictable wit, and I wanted to show the world that we had a united front.

It may be wondered how such gilded traps as Texas' clubs and mine could have flourished in the face of all the financial anxiety of those depression days. My own belief has always been that, for many of our customers, it was a form of escapism—that for a few hours' respite from their fears of worse disasters to come they were willing to pay while they still had it. They knew their fun was overpriced, but the future was uncertain—so why not?

About this time I received a letter from a Mr. Wright of Chicago. The letter, written on Chicago Athletic Club paper, asked for a card to my club, and for reference the writer submitted the names of Joe Leiter and Senator Lewis.

I was not so promiscuous as to have cards. Anyway, after a visit to my club you didn't need a card to remind you of the address; the memory of an expensive evening sufficed. However, although I had no card to send, I replied cordially to Mr. Wright, for with such sponsors as he had named I had not the slightest suspicion that he could be Mr. Wrong.

A few nights later, as I came downstairs, I found my doorman and my secretary in a huddle.

"What's up?" I asked.

"Jack has just sent away a man who had a letter from you. He said he was from Chicago."

"He and his friends didn't look okay to me," interrupted Jack.

I had a flash of memory. "Joe Leiter's friends! Run, Jack, and see if you can catch them!" I ordered.

Jack had the bad luck to overtake the car on the next stoplight. When he returned with the "Chicagoans," I apologized profusely and told my headwaiter to show them into my box while I explained to my staff the new buzzer system.

This system had been made necessary by mysterious phone calls I had been receiving, which purported to be friendly warnings but actually might have been sadistic assaults on my peace of mind. Friends, too, not realizing that my wire was being tapped, were constantly bombarding me with questions which, had I answered truthfully, would have given immense satisfaction to the tappers-in: "How many customers at your bar last night?" "How much champagne did you sell?" "Did you drink your place dry?" Some of these queries could not have been more damaging had they been offered with malice prepense. Texas used to call every night to tell me what her receipts had been; and, no matter how fabulous the sum, I always made it a point to top her claim by two or three thousand dollars. All this chatter was later used against me.

One of my Chicago guests stayed with me that evening and showed no little interest in the precautions I had taken, especially the signal system designed to announce any approaching danger.

Imagine my surprise when I returned to the ballroom to find Mr. Wright on stage, with my band leader's megaphone in his hand, and hear him bellow: "Ladies and gentlemen! The next feature on this program is a specialty by Uncle Sam, commonly known as a raid!"

Pandemonium!

How fast the waiters scuttled! Some had musical instruments under their arms; some had grabbed gardenias and pulled their handkerchiefs up in view in their dress coat pockets; some had even begged the protection of women guests to permit them to impersonate escorts.

As I was taken into custody once more, I could not avoid realizing that the path of a purveyor of liquor was becoming increasingly hard and that if I continued in the night club business, I would have to endure more and more indignities in order to procure for my guests their pleasant, privileged evenings.

I have often been asked: "On the level, Belle, what kind of liquor did you serve in your speakeasies?"

I served the best to those customers who I knew had palates to appreciate the best. My real stuff came from abroad. None of the American ships ever brought me anything, but I knew most of the captains on the boats from Le Havre and Cherbourg, and it was undoubtedly because these captains were all blind in one eye that I was often able to get twenty cases at a time, sometimes unaddressed, set down at my door in the chill, gray morning hours by French or British seamen. Discretion forbids my mentioning names, but three famous French firms kept me well supplied with vintage wines and brandy undiluted, and the director of an old English house sent whiskies.

One day a young deb came to me almost in tears. An uncle who had just returned from Europe had brought her as a present nothing but a silly bottle of white wine. I looked at the label and offered to make everything right by exchanging a bottle of synthetic champagne for it. She left, wreathed in smiles. Next day Viscount de Vauchie, Louis Bouché, Ernest Boyd, Lewis Gallantière, and I gathered

around a table and gave thanks to be able again to delight
our palates with anything as delectable as Château Yquem.

But I never cast pearls before swine. For those who lacked
the rudiments of gustatory education I unhesitatingly set
out my choicest swill. I really had little power of selection
of the domestic poison that came into my hands. I knew
bootleggers were buying up old whisky barrels for as high
as $150 apiece, shaving the insides, and stewing the shav-
ings in alcohol that had been used on corpses in the hospitals. This witches' brew was nevertheless drained off by
some customers without complaint.

Christmas 1930 was in the air and, recalling the magnificent work done by the Salvation Army in France in 1917, I
determined on a Christmas offering to help their good
cause. I hung the walls of my club with Salvation Army
flags and streamed dark red and blue, the Army's colors,
from the crowns over the boxes instead of the gaudy gold
that usually adorned them. The talented Madame Lenora,
who put on my ballets for me, costumed one in the style
made famous by the *Belle of New York*. To make it es-
sentially a Salvation night, the guests as well as the dancers
were given tambourines to thump and rattle. Mrs. S. Stanwood Menken, circulating among the guests, singled out
the most affluent, presented them with her fountain pen
and her most gracious smile, and asked them to remember
the Salvation Army with a little check trimmed in purple
ink.

The next fête was a welcome to the New Year of 1931 in
which, aware as I was that the American businessman
never really separates himself from his business, I brought
a reminder of the market to him in the form of a ticker-tape
ballet. Madame Lenora's twenty-four young girls, wrapped,
mummy-like, in gold ticker tape, whirled around and

around until they had unwound—enough; then vanished in
a blackout. I charged twenty-five dollars per plate and the
club was jammed. No one else had dared ask that much.

The morning after New Year's when I came downstairs
I was surprised (or astounded, as the purist corrected his
wife when she came upon him kissing the maid: "You are
astounded, my dear, I am surprised!") to find that my barmen, the cashier, and the doorman had all taken a run-out
powder, leaving neither word nor reason for their departure.
I could not allow their desertion, however, to affect the
continuance of my business, so that night I opened my own
door, my own wine, my own cash register, and through the
latter operation I found more money than I had seen for
some time. To help me out, some of the most exclusive guests
who ever served behind a New York bar mixed the alimen-
tary depth bombs.

Thank heaven, I again had paid help the next evening,
when the gentlemen from Washington appeared, or the
police station would have been crowded with society barmen. On that night I had one of the richest and folksiest of
crowds. While mature ladies of the social register were walking out of the best fashion pages, the younger ones were
dancing their shoes thin. Bankers were fraternizing with
literary lions. The Federals reached new heights in organization that night. Their entire company picked up cues with
no prompting; there was not a single hitch in any of the key
positions from which the raid was operated. With the electric switchboard manned by their men, the cases of liquor
carried out by their porters, the police vans arriving on the
moment—everything was timed to perfection.

Nor could any colorist have executed a better color
scheme. The red-carnation badges of identification, worn by
the agents, exactly matched the red satin pajamas I was
wearing when the buzzer surprised me up in my room. Also
I must have seen red as I recalled my many past rides in

prison vans and the distasteful hours I had spent locked in cells with the scum of femininity, while I waited for some dilatory bondman to release me.

Before I knew what I was doing, I had jumped out onto a housetop and, like a mountain goat, was leaping from roof to roof with a couple of carnation-decorated Federals in close pursuit. "No use, Belle!" one shouted. "We've got you!"

"Not yet!" I retorted, though I knew they were gaining on me.

Atalanta never ran with greater will, but where she stopped for the golden apples I had to stop to pick up my breath. Then I felt the hand of the law on my shoulder and heard again those hideous words: "Belle Livingstone, you are under arrest!"

Ignominiously brought back to the club, I donned the somber tailored outfit which I kept for my rides in the pie-wagon. Later, as I stood waiting under guard, I watched the detectives search the house for my liquor hideaway. It was a stiff test of self-control, not to allow a muscle of my face to betray me when they were getting warm.

If I had had anyone to make a bet with, I would have put my money on the little German carpenter who had devised the false wall in one of my upper chambers, and I would have won. This wall was truly one of the most perfect fakes that could ever have been imagined. It swung as a complete unit, leaving room to enter, at either side, into the hiding space behind it. The mechanism was worked by an electric switch, one button hidden in my room and one in the hall. As a rule I am very poor at keeping secrets, but this one I had guarded absolutely. I never allowed anyone but myself to push those buttons. My bootleggers used to deliver their stuff as early as six in the morning, which was bedtime in Country Club days. Alone in the big house, except for the porters down below cleaning up the debris of another exuberant night, I used to take the bottles out of their straw jackets, stash them away behind the fake wall, then push the furniture back in position against the wall. Then I would take the tell-tale straw covers down to the basement and burn them and sweep up the last wisp of evidence.

Finally the Federals gave up the search, defeated, and it was time for us to leave.

As we started, one of the officers said to me: "We always thought you were smart, Belle. Will you tell me why you defied that injunction that was served on you last week?"

"What injunction?" I gasped.

"Why, to shut up shop."

Suddenly I remembered an incomprehensible legal paper still lying untranslated on my desk. I had meant to show it to my attorney, but the emergency of finding myself staffless had driven it out of my mind. I had been so obsessed with the determination to outwit my barmen, who I felt were trying to force me to close, that, in defying them by carrying on, I had unwittingly defied Uncle Sam!

Throughout my life a thread of comedy has always been interwoven with tragedy. Tonight was no exception. As the van started, I gave a Lot's-wife glance back over my shoulder. A man was nailing a large white placard on my front door, and from the lights of the photographers' flash bulbs I could read the inscription: BELLE OUT OF ORDER.

6 _The Bat Sinister_

My heraldic markings should have been bars, so often have bars appeared on my life's road; but a bar of justice had never marked the route until January, 1931, when I stood in court before Federal Judge Caffey.

"The United States against Belle Livingstone!" called out the bailiff in stentorian tones.

On the wall behind the bench hung the Stars and Stripes symbolizing the States that were against me, and never again shall I see our flag without recalling the fine head of Judge Caffey outlined against it.

Mine was rightly called a "dry" case because so little liquor had been found in my Country Club. The Federals, strangely enough, had not succeeded in discovering my hideaway. But as Jack Dean, the witty husband of Fanny Ward, said: "Out of the few bottles they did find they made a case." And with the judge calling me to order every time I tried to get gay, the case got drier and drier.

Assistant United States Attorney Charles Finkelstein, who acted as prosecutor, tied me in every kind of knot except the nuptial. When he asked me my profession, I replied: "Author. And this should make a good chapter." At this I was properly put in my place by Judge Caffey: "Madam, madam, madam! No levity!"

When Attorney Finkelstein became insistent that I name the person, lost from my background, who had been backing my club, I, not wanting him to know that the only backer was on the witness stand in front of him, and remembering a famous gentleman who was thoroughly lost, quipped irreverently: "Judge Crater!" This remark brought forth another volley of "Madams" and a rapping of the gavel to call the courtroom audience and myself to order.

Finally it was all over, and then came the hush which preceded the judge's summing up of the case. Judge Caffey first praised the prosecutor for his handling of so flagrant an offender, and next complimented my lawyer for his able defense. He then turned to me and, in a very serious discourse, described the obligations and responsibilities of his office and the power vested in him and explained how long or how short a sentence he could legally impose on me. From the maximum to the minimum he descended, then took a breath and ascended from the minimum to the maximum. When he paused for another breath, I was prepared to be sent away for life, grateful if I were allowed even to live.

"However," finishing his peroration, he cleared his throat and paused dramatically, "however, because of your age and your ignorance I shall give you only thirty days."

The morning papers stated that when I heard the sentence my face "went white beneath its coating of rouge." Wrong, my dear reporters, for I have never used rouge. Suffused with blushes of champagne my face has often been, but never rouged. I admit, however, I may have registered shock. The sentence itself was bad enough, without being called old and ignorant into the bargain. I began to feel a trifle faint.

United States Deputy Marshal Runge took me in charge and conducted me to Marshal Mulligan.

"Where can I get some brandy?" I whispered.

The idea that a woman sentenced for her association with brandy should make such a request, even after receiving the shock of a jail sentence, astounded the marshal, and he sternly reminded me that I was a prisoner for *just that sort of thing!*

Marshal Runge touched my arm and hustled me off. To elude the waiting crowd of reporters, we left my car at one exit and made our getaway by another. The non-sightseeing bus provided by Uncle Sam was at hand, but the marshal called a taxi and we started off at a mad pace.

"Why the rush?" I inquired.

"It will count for a day against your sentence if you are in jail before four o'clock," he replied. "We have only a few minutes to make it."

We were headed for 126th Street and the old Harlem Jail, which was being used while the new one connected with Jefferson Market was being built. When we arrived, a crowd was waiting, even the reporters whom we thought we had eluded.

"Want to make a statement, Belle?" somebody called.

I started to explain to the boys that if I had only been on the inside of the Prohibition racket all this would not have happened to me, but before I could finish, some quick wit said: "Never mind—you'll be on the inside now!"

The jailer, Edward Glennon, who I was to learn was called "St. Peter" because of his keys, came forward to greet me and said with what I am sure was complete unconsciousness of the parody: "Miss Livingstone, I presume?"

The matron then hurried forth to receive me from the custody of the marshal, and in her care, amid the flashing of cameras and cheery good-bys from the press, I disappeared from the world behind the great clanging iron doors, with all their complements of bolts and bars.

Down iron steps she took me and opened more iron doors. The jangling of her heavy keys was my introduction to the music I was to hear for thirty days. I got up to the jangling of keys, and the last thing I heard at night was the jangling of keys. The matron, who, instead of calling me by my first name, as is the custom with prisoners, still addressed me as "Miss Livingstone," said that Major Brewster, the warden, had told her to put me in the prostitutes' ward because he thought I would be more comfortable there. This news handed me my first smile.

I was given Cell Five. Here my thirty days' instruction in unicellular existence commenced with walls—walls—and more walls. I was down between walls; a few steps forward and I came against a wall; a few steps backward and I backed into a wall. The cell had stone floors, an open toilet in the corner, and an iron bed furnished with a heavy gray blanket and a hard little pillow stuffed with corn husks. To find myself back on a corn-husk pillow—the same kind I had slept on when I was a child in Kansas—seemed to complete a circle in my life pattern.

Canned salmon with raw onions was the *pièce de résistance* on my first supper menu. I heard from the prisoners later that they had all been curious to see whether I would snub my prison fare. As it happens, I like both salmon and onions and, being hungry, I surprised everyone by eating with a relish. Furthermore, denied the luxury of a knife and fork, I quickly went back a few hundred years and used my fingers.

This jail menu was a far cry from my supper twenty-four hours earlier at La Maison Lafitte at which Monsieur Borgo, great restaurateur of the old school, had officiated like a priest conducting a service. With an imperious glance he signaled his acolytes to remove the covers of the dishes and display the contents for my delectation. The coffee served, he brought a bottle of precious brandy and himself poured it into the large crystal goblet as if it were a libation. Now it was tin plates and serve yourself. Afterward wash the tinware.

A motley crew of prostitutes and shoplifters slumped over the tables, poor half-creatures yearning for something, they knew not what. All wayward women, and all wanting, as far as I could see, to stay wayward. And the stupidity of them! They couldn't have stayed out of jail if they had tried. During the first evening in their company I felt, like Baudelaire, "the wind of idiocy pass over me." Listening to their conversation, as I was forced to do, I learned that these women had no aversion for the oldest profession in the world and no intention of reforming; their one desire was to serve their sentence and return to making easy money. With them it was "good-by" today and "hello" tomorrow, for most of them were constantly in and out of custody.

I sensed at once the hostile barrier these prostitutes had erected against me and, as I had to spend thirty days among them, I wanted to pull it down. So, sauntering into the conversation that first evening, I said: "Well, girls, we are all guilty of selling *some*thing. If we had given it away, we wouldn't be here, would we?"

This silly pleasantry seemed to delight them. I was at once admitted to their uncharmed circle and from then on became their confidante.

Locking-in time, when keys play their horrible part and when behind the heavy bars of a cell one is left for the night like a trapped animal, was to me the worst of my jail experiences, and the helplessness of being locked in was just as terrible the last night as the first.

On my iron bed, under my short blanket, I listened to the hourly call of "All's well in the Tombs!" answered by "All's well in the Market!" A light sleeper derives a certain comfort when, on a big liner steaming through unseen dangers, he hears "All's well!" sung out by the watches. He knows the ocean ways are guarded. But the cry in jail, where all is anything but well, brings just another shudder of revolt.

That night, as I lay wondering if fortune had gone stale for me, the throaty, deep whistle of such a departing boat started a sequence of remembrances. I recalled Oscar Wilde's cynicism: "Life is just a *mauvais quart d'heure* with a few exquisite moments." How I wished I could have a few of my moments back! I had had my gold and squandered it in luxury; I had had my villas on the Mediterranean and gambled them away, and my dahabeah on the Nile was now but a memory.

A single light, shining down through tiers of cells above me, created deep shadows in my own cell. Looking into the shadows through half-closed eyes, I seemed to see walls hung in rich brocade. Lifting a hand, I touched the rich lace that fell in cascades from the canopy on my bed and caressed the satin, sable-trimmed coverlet over me. A touch of rough blanket quickly brought me back from dreams of glories past to the harsh and gloomy present. With the sickening realization that my next new day would not peep caressingly in at me through a foam of billowy ruffles at my windows—that in fact there would be nothing caressing about any new day in jail—I turned my face to the wall and finally slept.

Plop—a raw electric bulb flashed on in my face at the unchristian hour of five next morning. The cold gray walls on which I opened my eyes were sufficient reminder of where I was, without a female Cerberus snarling through the bars: "Come on, you're in jail now. Get out and eat your breakfast!"

This old matron, who wore a shield over a hole where there had once been a heart, was known as one of the departmental burdens. She loved to terrorize the new prisoners.

When the slamming of doors and dishes began, I recalled that the "girls" had called the jail the House of Slams. That name was certainly descriptive of the clatter. Steel doors slammed, iron doors slammed, keys slammed, pails slammed on stone floors, tin plates slammed; each slam an expression of someone's bitterness against life. Even the matrons were not free from this noisy demonstration of nerves.

It was a relief when those who were due in court had been herded away. After the clamorous, clanging departure of the police wagon, with its load of prisoners, there was a brief calm. Dustless tables were dusted; mops were swished over spotless floors.

I was taken upstairs to be fingerprinted, and as the matron held each inky finger and rolled it into the records, I shuddered. The act itself was nothing, yet everything. It branded my mind with the thought that I was now officially associated with crime. Next I was clothed in prison garb, a none-too-well-fitting blue-and-white striped gingham. The stripes, insignia of servitude, tended to rip to shreds whatever morale I had left. On going back to my cell, I received a routine visit from one of the commissioners, who informed me that I must expect no privileges. However, the official had no sooner left than I had the inestimable privilege of receiving my first hamper of mail. Letters benevolent, letters malevolent; letters of sympathy, of rebuke, of bad verse; fan mail, crank mail.

"God, I wish somebody'd write me!" I heard one of the inmates complain to the matron who delivered the hamper.

"Who'd write you? The cops?" snapped Cerberus.

The girl sighed. That she might have the thrill of opening some letters, I pushed a stack of my mail toward her, together with a hairpin as makeshift paper-cutter. In jail, I had already learned, attempts at suicide are averted as far as possible by the exclusion of knives, scissors, nail files, mirrors, and paper-cutters.

Bill Moore sent me a thesaurus for my crossword puzzles, and Tommy Smith some books. I wanted to share the books, but my offers met with no interest. Some of the "girls" had more important matters on their minds than reading. The shop-lifting members of our sorority had to keep their light fingers in practice.

My first day seemed endless. Over and over, in the cell next to mine, a young girl kept humming "Melancholy Baby." On the other side a Polish woman moaned a dirge in her native tongue. Cerberus on guard took in everything that happened in our division and barked orders right and left. Her first bark to me had a certain whimsy in it.

"Hey, ain't you the Jane that run over the housetops? All right, take this mop and run over these floors now!"

The one big diversion of the jail day was the arrival of the patrol wagon at four o'clock each afternoon, with its consignment of new boarders. Then the shuffling of cards in the never-ending games of solitaire ceased, listless faces came to life, and everyone involuntarily moved to the iron grill in curious interest over the new arrivals. The guard changed then, too. The next matron, with her clean, soap-scrubbed, happy Irish face and her rough-and-ready sense of humor, was a welcome relief from Cerberus.

The new "prossies" would breeze in like girls home from school for the holidays, find their corner, and start buzzing. Jail had no power to dampen their high spirits. One of them recognized my face—it had been in print almost as often as Lydia Pinkham's—and sang out: "Hello, Belle! No champagne in this cooler, eh? And no radio! What a dump!"

Mattie Washington, a witty colored girl, heard this and

called back from her cell: "Yo'-all's de-tained here—not entertained."

When the matron handed the newcomer a blanket and told her to make her bed, she yelled: "What! We even have to make our own beds!"

"Sorry," cracked the matron. "It's our maid's night off."

Even after we were all locked in our cells for the night and the lights were out, the girl's querulous comments came seeping through the bars.

"My God! This cell is no bigger than a snooper's heart, and the bed's as hard!"

It may amaze some to know that lines of social demarcation are drawn as strictly in jail as in the outside world. One of the girls from another division said to me one day: "It's rotten you should be down here with the prostitutes. You ought to kick and make them put you up with the gun molls. That's your privilege as a Federal prisoner."

The first question put to each new arrival was always: "What are you in for?"

"They said I murdered a guy," one said loftily in answer to this stock inquiry.

After the speaker had left, one of the "prossies," class-conscious over being considered in the lowest stratum of jail society, spit out: "Them murder dames ritz us plenty, don't they?"

In Europe a workman is pardoned for bad language, his betters reasoning that since the poor fellow is uneducated he must be excused the profanity and foul language he uses as a substitute for richer expression. But in this country I have noted among the better classes a growing appetite for four-letter words, both in print and in speech. For such unsophisticates I would only wish a pair of good ears and thirty days in the prostitutes' ward in Harlem Jail. The coarse jokes, the repetitious obscenities, and the foul profanity with which the "prossies" stimulate themselves are suggestive of some of today's best sellers.

One day I asked one of the worst offenders where she had learned so much bad language and shuddered at her quick reply: "I never learned it. It's a gift."

The girls in the colored division used less profanity and were cleaner in body and clothing than their white sister offenders. As the song says, "All God's chillun got wings," and here all God's chillun had winged feet that shuffled and danced as they mopped and broomed the floors. At night they lifted up their winged spirits in laughing, lilting songs. They bore their bad luck uncomplainingly. It was all part of life's puzzle which they left to the Big Judge to solve. One Southern colored girl, her white teeth gleaming in a wide, good-natured grin, said when she heard she was going to court: "All Ah kin say is, like de man dat met de bear: 'Lawd, if yo' don' help me, please Lawd, don' yo' help dat bear!'"

The suffocating sense of helplessness I experienced when bolted in a cell made me wish that those who condemn paroles could have some firsthand knowledge of what they condemn. Anyone who has ever spent even one day in prison would want his fellow prisoners to be given one more chance. But even when a prisoner is paroled, he sometimes gets scant help from those whose only experience in life has been in safe, transgression-tight hothouses. Most offenders who try to limp back into life after soul-destroying days in jail will meet rows and rows of turned backs. Happily for these shunned creatures, the strange camaraderie generated from jail associations endures after the incarceration is over. It was through being in jail that I learned of the silent army of former cell mates, who, without the cold formality of any organization, constitute a body of sympathetic helpers. The outcast finds doors left ajar, food on tables, money slipped into empty pockets.

The officers of the jail were as patient and indulgent as their shields permitted and in most cases treated the prisoners as decently as they were allowed. I asked a matron one day if she didn't feel sorry for some of the unfortunates.

"We can't afford to show any sympathy—we'd crack up," she confided.

She was right.

However, I was sorry for the poor vapid creatures, all like myself victims of some weakness for pleasure or some silly vanity. Unfortunately a stay in jail didn't seem to straighten things out. Hearts remained ablaze with sin. The whole place ached and throbbed with bitterness. It was never quiet. The constant pulsation never ceased. Justice must live, and this beat was its pulse.

One can never know how immoral New York is until he has looked upon the host of creatures scraped off the streets every day. I was told that at Easter and at Christmas the round-up of shoplifters fills the jails; at other times, failing the ladies with longings for pretty things, and the "frails," the police do general city cleaning by wiping outcasts off the park benches.

The old, decayed, broken bodies, forbiddingly repulsive, are thrown into the jails to be cleaned up. No soldiers carted out of the trenches in France ever had more cooties on them than have these derelicts. But instead of being glad of a bath and fresh, clean garments, they rave wildly and clutch with a grip like *rigor mortis* their old, filthy rags. Lady Godiva herself came riding in one afternoon in the pie-wagon instead of on her legendary horse. She had not a stitch to cover her except an overcoat which a policeman had sacrificed in the name of decency.

Odoriferous jail smells still linger in my memory. Whenever the clean-up brigade descended upon us and put their Flit guns into action, spraying everything that crawled, including the prisoners, with more horrible malodor, I used to paraphrase Barbara Frietchie: " 'Shoot if you must this old gray head, but keep the Flit away!' she said." Even the patchouli the prostitutes brought in on their clothes was a welcome relief to my nostrils. I used to hide my face in my handkerchief, hoping there might still linger a vestige of Guerlain. I wrote my maid to pour a whole bottle of *Après l'ondée* over my coming-out dress, before she sent it in to me.

But if the worst official ordeal was to me the smell of Flit, the worst to the "prossies" seemed to be the well-meaning social worker. Bright and early one morning one of these, with a professional smile on her face, was admitted to our cell block. A new crop of perfumed streetwalkers had been carted in the day before, so the lady seemed to have a fruitful field for her endeavors. But the seed she sought to sow fell on stony ground. Streams of jeering, vile insults spurted from the cells as she made her rounds. The "prossies" made it apparent to her that they were more concerned with freedom for their bodies than with improvement of their morals.

The Salvation Army worker, a very decent sort, gave out calendars on which were scriptural passages condemning crime. Her gift helped me to mark off my days and now occupies a page in my press book.

Each Saturday in the prison chapel there was a Jewish service, and each Sunday there were Catholic, Protestant, Christian Science, and Salvation Army services. I don't know how uplifting these were, but I do know they must have been diverting because all the girls went and stayed through, in much the same manner they would have sat, I am sure, through four showings of a movie.

I must question those splendid lines of Lovelace: "Stone walls do not a prison make, nor iron bars a cage." Don't they now? Ask some of the poor creatures whose sighs I shall always hear whenever I think about the prison. True, one can make the best of a wretched prison as of a wretched home. It is only a question of adaptability. Fortunately I have a chameleon nature and can make myself at home anywhere. As Elinor Clarage once wrote in the Cleveland *Plain Dealer*: "Belle Livingstone can sit down on a bench and talk to the raggedest tramp, then go to tea with a duchess. Belle believes in exploring every stratum of life, in meeting every type of person."

I know of no place where a sense of humor is so vitally necessary as in jail. All my life I had worked to acquire pleasing behavior, spent years in smoothing out rough places in my turbulent disposition and in fighting down the bad temper with which I was born; and it was only through my sense of the ridiculous that Harlem Jail did not destroy completely everything I had gained.

The fact that I smiled through my tears did not mean that I was blind to the repellent surroundings. As I touched every phase of life within those walls, I saw the foulness of sin stirring in all those souls, like maggots in a dead rat. To this day the smell of disinfectant calls to mind those cells crawling with ill-meaning, sniggering women. For years the fetid atmosphere, moral as well as physical, which I bore away from Harlem Jail almost suffocated me.

A prisoner there may see only members of her own immediate family and her attorney; so, when the matron came to my cell one day and announced a lady to see me, I could not imagine who my caller might be. When I went downstairs, there stood beautiful Carol McIlwain. Somehow she had succeeded in passing the guards. How she laughed at my gingham uniform! The three weeks of shine on my powderless nose reminded her of the present she had for me, and, completely ignorant of jail discipline, she handed me a magnificent vanity case. Later, of course, I had to turn it over to the jailer until I was freed because it contained the tabooed mirror. Among my vast New York acquaintance, Carol was the only woman who tried to get in to see me.

Every Saturday night Earl Carroll came in person and left a basket of flowers for me. Regulations forbade flowers or delicacies of any nature because of the possibility that dope might be smuggled in thereby. Anyone who has seen the tortured, writhing drug addicts lined up, awaiting impatiently the daily visit of the doctor, will realize the wisdom of this precaution. Earl's flowers, therefore, were placed on the chapel altar to gladden everybody's hearts on Sunday. One day the girls asked who sent them.

"A great judge," I said.

"Judge!" they screamed.

"Yes, a judge—a great judge of beauty."

Finally the day came when I had paid my debt to society. The last of my thirty days was marked off on the Salvation Army calendar, and my fan mail was packed in my little bundle of belongings. My maid had sent my coming-out gown so drenched with perfume that it actually dispelled the prison odors. My invitations for a coming-out party, written from Cell Five on Harlem Jail stationery, had been posted.

In leaving Harlem I was taking nothing with me but my new-found knowledge of scrubbing. I was leaving behind me the Flit brigade, the blasphemy of prisoners, the rustle of shuffling cards, the one tantalizing light that shone all night and by which one could neither sleep nor read, the eyes of the matron peering hourly through the bars. Leaving all these behind, or so I thought. Little did I realize they would be recurring memories throughout the rest of my life.

As the last minutes ticked off, my last jail picture appeared. It was no prettier than the others. The "prossie" who was tattooed from her finger tips to her shoulders was going wild with joy at being freed. She threw her arms high in the air and yelled: "I'll be throwing these picture arms around the neck of a handsome sailor before night!"

"Be sure the sailor ain't a flick, dressed up for the Janes that follow the fleet!" screamed a voice.

"To hell with you, you dirty streetwalker!" she bawled, and with a walloping kick sent her stool across the bull pen.

The matron called for order but got a stream of vituperation that gushed forth like the bursting of a sewer pipe. "You matrons would be looking for jobs if we didn't go wrong—so what the hell!"

A sudden silence announced the arrival of St. Peter with the keys. "Your friends are waiting for you, Belle."

I took my package and waved good-by to the girls. The white girls shouted their farewells; the colored ones broke into "Home Sweet Home." At the exit St. Peter shook my hand, then opened the massive door—to freedom!

A crowd was there to greet me, among them Cary Grant. Arthur Menken, son of Mr. and Mrs. S. Stanwood Menken, who was in charge of the Pathé Film photographers, asked me to say something in French to my friends in France. I looked up at the jail, where at every barred window I pictured helpless hands waving blindly—tortured hands such as Doré drew when he illustrated Dante's *Inferno*. The vision of those hands made me step to the mike and fairly scream: *"À bas toutes les bastilles!"*

7 By Repeal's Early Light

I have had the good luck to be on hand in strategic points when two important events in history took place. I was in Paris when peace was declared after World War I, and in New York when John Barleycorn was exhumed.

The months that intervened between my stay in Harlem Jail and the end of the Volsteadian era I employed variously, hectically, and, without exception, unprofitably. I ranged the United States from east to west and from north to south, and finally, like a homing pigeon, found my way back to the familiar and well-loved haunts of Manhattan.

During those mad Country Club nights I had made first and last nearly a quarter of a million dollars. And it had been well-hidden, in safe-deposit boxes in many different banks, under many different names. I used my mother's

name, and both my grandmothers', and some deceased
aunts' and cousins'—dragged them all through the dirt. It
would hardly have been safe in those days to make written
memoranda of these matters, and I smile now to think what
a dickens of a time I used to have trying to remember who
I was. I used to walk up and down in front of a bank, saying
to myself: "For heaven's sake, who am I here? My mother?
My aunt? My grandmother?"

After my release from prison, with what I had left over of
these ill-gotten gains, plus my considerable liquor reserves—
smuggled out of the club with my personal belongings—I
felt reasonably well-heeled for a new start. But where? The
injunction I had so blandly disregarded, which had ruled
me finally and forever off the Manhattan gin tracks, had left
me no choice but to accept some hinterland.

Reno, everybody said, was the obvious place for me; Reno
was the widest-open town in America, where enforcement
was a farce; in Reno the Truckee River sometimes ran dry,
but never Old Man River Booze. Besides, there was always
the legal gambling!

After all the years I had lived on the Continent, I should
have remembered that in any gambling town there is
always an underworld that runs everything—a clique that
calls the shots in every racket, decides who may and who
may not operate and under what terms, even elects public
officials. This was as true in the Reno of the Thirties as anywhere else, except that in Reno the underworld was at the
same time the uppercrust. A little confusing until you got the
idea.

At the time I was there, it was reputed that a certain
financier, owner of seventeen banks in Nevada, was the real
ruler of the little city, though Mayor Roberts sat in the chair;
that the said financier and three partners formed a four-
headed Octopus which strangled every business that didn't

pay money into their till; that no one could possibly operate without their sanction, and that to them every form of vice —from the dirty, painted girls in the red-light district to the flourishing hophouses—made obeisance.

The Octopus, moreover, had its own way of dealing with outsiders who tried to become insiders. This was the silence treatment, which might result in anything from a few days in the hospital to a few appropriate remarks to the mourners. Yet there was I, an elderly dowager, naïvely believing that if the mayor was for me, who should be against me? It is hard now to credit myself with having been such a nitwit.

Taking my memories of Reno out of the lumber room of discarded years and sorting them over, I can see that I should have been able from the first to detect a certain uneasiness among my friends. Bob Scripps, booming out on a visit, asked me first thing how I was fixed. I thought he meant financially, and said "Fine." Ex-Governor Schrugan from time to time inquired cautiously if I was all right. I thought his references were to my health, so again and again I said "Fine." Jack Dempsey used to drop hints, very guarded ones.

But I opened—yes, I opened—in what had once been a cowshed on the Old Carson Highway, Augean stables that I had personally helped to clean. Finally it was ready, gilded to a fare-ye-well, with a bar forty feet long, a gambling room equipped with roulette, crap, twenty-one, and baccarat, and a snappy colored revue where the girls wore one bangle apiece—all under a giant neon sign rearing into the night sky and bearing the words BELLE LIVINGSTONE.

Next day there were rave reviews in the press:

> Belle Livingstone had a great opening. I tell you she puts on the niftiest show west of Broadway. . . . Her cowshed is jammed; she's taken away all the business from the Willows, Silver Slipper, and Deauville. Took in one thousand seven hundred people last Saturday night at eight bits a cover.

Fatal raves! The Octopus promptly threw out its tentacles for the "Empress of the Barnyard," as I was dubbed by one UP correspondent. In spite of the fact that the governor had given me Nevada and the mayor had given me Reno, the underworld now gave me the works. In the weeks that followed they installed in my place a man to provide my liquor, another to watch my cash register, others to stand back of my crap table and my roulette wheel. They carried out a campaign of psychological terrorism to the point where I felt obliged to hire a guard to watch my cottage while I slept.

Finally came a complete blockade on my liquor, and what night club can exist without liquor?

After the Reno fiasco and a few more equally depressing attempts—in Dallas, San Francisco, and Phoenix to brighten the Prohibition landscape in the tradition of the Great Open Spaces—I confess the *salon* idea never once had the temerity to show its face west of the Mississippi—I was persuaded to come back East to open a night spot on Long Island, and there in Easthampton, in the summer of 1933, I embarked on what was to be my last attempt at defiance of the Eighteenth Amendment.

Here I tried once more to return to the Continental atmosphere, dreaming of a transplanted Deauville, and here once more the dream turned into a nightmare. This time it was thanks to three ex-hijackers who coolly muscled in, installed their own crooked gambling paraphernalia, administered paralyzing drugs to my partner and Mickey Finns to me when we protested, and at the end of the summer backed up a truck one night and carted away the whole establishment—decorations, furnishings, everything.

This performance was truly a piece of unmitigated knavery, but could the pot call the kettle black? Not when the kettle carries a gun. Those who operate outside the law of the land find themselves perforce under the law of the jungle, where the strong prey on the weak and the fittest survive. The idea was finally being borne in upon me that perhaps I was not one of the fittest.

Furthermore, at that point I was fed up with hinterland. I had given it a thorough trial, from one ocean to another, and more than ever had become convinced that you turn your back on cake when you turn it on the great city. I was homesick for Manhattan and, stand or fall, I decided I would henceforth make it my battleground.

Thus it was that when repeal came peering in the window that morning of December 5, 1933, it discovered me back in New York, living in one of those hotels filled with old ladies that are the last stop before Potters' Field. During the dry era the old girls used to totter around the lobby, weighed down by the time of day, returning to their rooms just in time to be lowered into their armchairs for "Amos 'n' Andy." But with the opening of legal bars, these knob-twiddlers took a new lease on life. After their first cocktails, they perked up and looked twenty years younger. Chipper as spring robins, they hopped in and out of the elevator.

Besides the changes that repeal had made in my hotel, I began noting changes in the streets. Fancy colored awnings, reminding me of gay dragons, were being stretched across pavements before portals which even I had never suspected of concealing speakeasies. From behind unhealthy kitchen doors were emerging a whole new generation of restaurateurs. It seemed as if every waiter, bus boy, and dishwasher, lured by the thought of easy money, were rushing into business. Emblazoned on the new canopies were the names of the ambitious Henris, Jeans, Armands, Guidos, Marios, and Alfredos from the Prohibition catacombs. How gratified their owners must have been to see at last the bright lights shining on the names they had had to deny, over and over again, during the underground days.

The flood of repeal bars that spread over all Manhattan threatened to swamp as well as soak the public, but still more sons of the sink poured from still more kitchens, ordering still more mirrors, fountains, draperies, and carpets. Many of these ex-waiters were far from ideal restaurateurs, ignorant and inexperienced in the nuances of fine living. Others were egotistic and opinionated. Speakeasy days had spoiled the waiter by giving him a delusion of grandeur. When repeal came in, it was hard for him to realize that the days of royal favor for one who could produce a drink were over. No more of those plushy yachting trips to Palm Beach as pal of a wealthy customer who always carried a favorite bootlegger aboard.

Everywhere was evident the lawlessness and the violence introduced by the gangster. If you had gone with me on a pub crawl shortly after repeal you would have found a wild, gay-colored patchwork covering the East Side of New York, from Forty-second to Sixtieth Street. Wild and gay if you looked at the top side at night, but if you were still on your feet by daylight and able to look at the reverse side, you might have seen some very crude stitches. Paris hot spots were like Sunday schools compared to some of these places. You could go plenty gutterish east of Fifth, and on a *ronde de nuit* in the mink-and-sable district you would often see the best people acting the worst after midnight. It didn't do to resist the bill in one of these sucker joints either, because a leftover gorilla, who would pick your eye out and eat it for a grape, was always on hand to bounce out resisters.

It would not be correct to assume that repeal hung a garland of success around the neck of every catacomb operator who emerged into the open and stretched out a canopy. Oddly enough, I found that some who used to wear a worried look watching the door for Federals were now wearing it as they watched for customers. Some whose underground places had gone over big found themselves unaccountably deserted by patrons when they came up into daylight.

In one place, feeling conspicuous because I was the only customer, I asked if I might order a cocktail without the place falling apart. The owner at once went into his act. He begged me to feel the seat of the next chair.

"People, people, all day people. You see, Madame, the seats are still warm from the people. Miss Peggy Joyce and her party just left."

The waiter, not a loyal accomplice, whispered as he served the cocktail that there were people, people, all right, but all going past the door.

The proprietor of another flop was a good-looking Irishman who had drained plenty of purses in his gold-blown speakeasy. With repeal, an ambitious decorator did over and overdid everything in his place, and after the small document permitting him to dispense liquor legally was framed and hung over his gaudy bar and an uproarious dragon canopy bridged his sidewalk, he sat down to listen to a quick, snapping tune from his cash register. But alas, the contraption was mute.

"I'm kayoed, Belle," the owner moaned to me. "I've tried everything. Nothing works. This place just has the kiss of death on it."

The kiss of death, I fear, was on a good many in those parlous reconstruction days.

After the advent of repeal, my friends assumed that, being now freed of legal obstacles, I would, of course, return to night-club life. But there were obstacles other than legal: I was broke. The Reno debacle had left me not two nickels to rub together. I did take a brief flyer in Boston, where on Lem Prior's bankroll I livened up that staid old city with The Blue Train, named for the crack European express that used to take the smart world from London to the Mediterranean. But when Lem died unexpectedly, after only a few months, both train and I went off the tracks. I was not really sorry to close. The chilly social climate of the bean and the cod would soon have sent me shivering back anyway.

I never opened again in New York. My *salon*-saloon days had ended in that insane footrace over the rooftops in which the red pajamas lost to the red carnations.

For the country at large it was the repeal legislation in Washington that marked the end of the mad, orgiastic Prohibition era, but for me it was the funeral of Tex Guinan.

Poor Tex! Exiled from her beloved Broadway! She had offended Dutch Schultz, who swore that she should never operate in New York again while he lived. She never did. From New York she had transferred to Chicago, later to the West Coast to play in *Broadway Through a Keyhole,* and then went on tour in Canada. There she had died and had been brought back to New York to be buried.

In spite of the fact that Tex had always been a devout believer in the Church and a liberal donor to it, there was first a great to-do to find a priest who would bury her. Then a second emergency arose, in which I was sent for. Texas, determined to keep her chin up to the end, had several times had it lifted. The process of embalming had put everything in reverse and now Tex's chins were beginning to unroll. What to do? I sent out for tulle and swathed her decently and artistically. More chins let go; I flew for more tulle.

I think Texas had just such a funeral as she would have liked. Orchids covered her bier. Crowds lined the streets and surrounded her cortege. Some of the biggest gangsters ran the risk of following the hearse in their armored cars, though of course they did take the precaution of keeping themselves covered by cars of their bodyguards cutting in and out of the solemn procession.

Texas and I were two women who passed vigorously
rather than happily through Prohibition. Although temporary figures, we were clearly visible. The world is prone to
say glibly that there is no one who cannot be replaced. But
Texas' throne still remains draped in crape, and I must confess I don't see anyone on my dais either.

Epilogue

The Melody Lingers On

Above my bed, in the one-room basement apartment in the East Fifties that I now call home, hangs a copy of Van Gogh's *Sunflower*, given me by a friend who wanted me to be always reminded of my beloved Kansas beginnings. Of course, it reminds me of other things too—notably my own lifetime philosophy of following the sun. Wherever the warmth of good living and good times was to be found, there I have always turned my face.

One day when Fanny Ward and I were lunching, she gave me quite a shock by asking: "When are you going to write your memoirs, Belle?"

To me the writing of memoirs has always seemed almost as final as the writing of a will—something you do just before. That particular day I was feeling far from final; in fact, very healthy, and I said as much. Nevertheless, the idea took root, and eventually I gave Fanny my story to read. Her comment was horrified:

"But, Belle, this book will never sell!"

"Why not?" I wanted to know.

"There's no sex in it!"

"No sex!" I snorted.

"Well, you know what I mean—no details——"

"Listen," I said, "I'm writing for sophisticates. Do they need blueprints?"

"It'll never sell," she repeated. "Today all the public wants is sex, and lots of it. You have to play it up big—everybody says so. But this—why, this is more like a social history. People won't expect this sort of thing from you. From you they'll want dirt."

"I can't help it," I said stubbornly. "For better or worse, this is it."

Later I wondered if I should not have followed the advice I once received in a letter from Richard King, one of England's fine writers: "You should really do a book of philosophy, Belle. There are plenty and to spare of those books turned out by bulgy-foreheaded old gentlemen from the easy chair of their studies, but too few drawn from the experiences of life itself. With your downright hang-the-genteel-susceptibilities outlook, you should do this very well. How refreshing it would be!"

See life steadily and see it whole, is the classic formula. Well, at times I may have seen life a trifle unsteadily, but I have seen nearly all of it. Furthermore, I am one of the few who have dared to live their own philosophy. It is a truism that most people take their adventures vicariously. When they feel the urge for thrills, they go to a play or a movie and let high-salaried actors project the desired experiences for them. When they crave excitement, they read novels. I instead, have always provided my own thrills.

In my first existence I lived by thumbing my way, throwing caution to the winds. In my second I lived even more individually, more recklessly, more violently, more Rabelaisianly than in my youth. Although I was fifty-two years old that September day in 1927 when I landed in New York to begin my second existence, it was as though someone had handed me back my teething ring and commanded me to start all over again.

And now, in my seventies (on January 20, 1950, I celebrated my three-quarter-century mark), I am apparently in a third existence, thereby proving what Caesar said—that "all gall" is divided in three parts. Here I am still preferring forbidden fruit, still daring to pick it. Certainly I shall never throw around my shoulders the smug and musty mantle of prudence. Even my recent stay as a cardiac patient in a New York hospital—the first time I have been the guest of the city since Harlem Jail days—has not dimmed my ardor for living.

The best part of this third existence is that I am no longer disturbed by memories of indignities and I can laugh at those who reproach me for my purposely careless life. Credulous immigrants used to come to New York looking for a pot of gold at the foot of the rainbow. I found my pot of gold and walked away with the rainbow. I spent the gold; now I'm living off the rainbow.

Security hounds, who believe in acquiring rather than enjoying, should have listened in one day when an old friend from those golden years in Paris came to call on me in my basement hovel. This friend of the acquiring kind had managed to hang on to everything she had ever owned except her hearing.

She pulled her chair close to mine and, adjusting her hearing aid, shouted into my perfectly good ears: "Belle, you poor darling, it's heartbreaking to see you in such surroundings as these! My dear, when you had all that money, why didn't you save enough to buy yourself into one of those nice old ladies' homes?"

The very thought of thus going to seed made me shudder. I was reminded of a remark the beautiful Langtry once made to me in Monte Carlo. When her husband, Sir Hugo de Bathe, bought a chicken farm near the Riviera, Langtry said in her softly modulated voice: "Imagine, Belle, spending one's last days in chicken dirt!"

The truth of the French maxim *Tout lasse, tout casse, tout passe* bears in on me whenever I see, filling the windows of a secondhand shop, mute, dust-covered trivia, once objects of the tender devotion of someone who has now laid them aside forever. Once I was a slave to furnishings, which I thought I possessed but which in reality were possessing me. Now, knowing how enduring *bibelots* are and how brief life is, I am willing that the dust may gather on anything but me. My back is still as straight as an Indian's; my skin firmer than any beauty specialist would have dared to promise; my walk alert, like the walk of all who enjoy living precariously.

Tay Pay O'Connor warned me years ago never to let myself be buried until I was dead, and I shall follow his advice. No one will ever see me sitting around listening for the rustling wings of Death. Let Death do a little rustling to catch up with me.

Perhaps the most fitting place in this country for the repose of my ashes would be the great sarcophagus which once blossomed with flowers in front of my Fifty-eighth Street Country Club, but that has been long since removed. However, there is a still more fitting resting place waiting for me in that little Barbizon cemetery in the Forest of Fontainebleau, where years ago I had erected for myself a monument according to my own tastes.

No one is going to sit on me there. I've seen to that. Before

I left France, I planted at the foot of the monument a spiny American cactus. If the reader of graveyard literature will take the trouble to peer above this sprawl of prickly verdancy at the inscription chiseled in the marble, he will read:

THIS IS THE ONLY STONE I HAVE LEFT UNTURNED